THE DEVELOPING CHILD

Bringing together and illuminating the remarkable recent research on development from infancy to adolescence, for students of developmental psychology, policy makers, parents, and all others concerned with the future of the next generation.

Series Editors

Jerome Bruner
New York University

Michael Cole
University of California, San Diego

Annette Karmiloff-Smith
Neurocognitive Development Unit,
Institute of Child Health, London

THE INFANT'S WORLD

Philippe Rochat

HARVARD UNIVERSITY PRESS

Cambridge, Massachusetts, and London, England / 2001

FOR RANA

Copyright © 2001 by Philippe Rochat

Printed in the United States of America

Library of Congress Cataloging-in-Publication Data

Rochat, Philippe, 1950–
    The infant's world / Philippe Rochat.
        p.   cm.—(The developing child)
Includes bibliographical references and index.
ISBN 0-674-00322-5 (alk. paper)
1. Infant psychology.   2. Infants—Development.   I. Title.   II. Series.
    BF719.R63   2001
    155.42′2—dc21   00-054268

CONTENTS

This book provides an overview of what researchers like myself have recently found in experimentally probing the infant world. My main goal is to communicate enthusiasm for infancy research and share with readers what I view as important, meaningful findings regarding the life of babies.

The reader is advised that this work is not yet another infancy textbook attempting to exhaust issues, empirical facts, and theoretical conceptions on infant behavior. The following pages reflect a particular conception, shaped by intuitions, theoretical affinities, as well as fifteen years of my own research and collaboration with other infancy researchers. I offer one possible account of infant psychology, and I do not pretend that this book contains the lasting truth about infants and their development. To balance this presentation, in many places readers are provided with some pointers toward alternative theories and interpretations. Readers should also refer to the original publications listed in the reference list. Nothing replaces one's own scrutiny of original sources.

Like other stories on the topic, my story of the infant world will be successful if it stimulates the reader's curiosity and sense of wonder about infants. As secret keepers of our origins, infants are the most basic expression of what it means to be alive as humans in this world—alive with the potential for the formidable mental growth that leads infants between birth and the second year toward sophisticated self-awareness, enculturation, and discernment of a consensual world that can be talked about and thus shared symbolically with others.

There are so many things that we take for granted as grown-ups: from maintaining balance, reaching, grabbing, communicating, and perceiving emotions, to making sense of events involving physical objects or people. Developing infants show us how much is at stake and how much it takes to be functioning adults in a meaningful environment.

The psychological world of infants is treated here in relation to what infants learn and know about their own bodies, physical objects, and other people. The book is organized around the idea that the psychological world of infants is best captured when considered in relation to the three ontological categories of the self, objects, and people. From birth and probably even prior to birth, these categories correspond to fundamentally different psychological experiences. The self, objects, and people form different contexts or basic domains from which infants develop particular skills and general abilities. I believe that this distinction is useful in trying to clarify and organize infant psychology at the origin of development. The assumption that the self, objects, and people form basic domains of development does not mean that the three domains are strictly compartmentalized. What develops in one must certainly interact with what develops in the other two. It will become apparent to readers that much work is needed to specify such interaction: infancy researchers typically study the self, physical (objects), and social (people) domains in isolation.

The first chapter of this book presents basic facts regarding human infancy. These facts provide some historical, biological, and evolutionary insights as a backdrop to experimental research on infants and their development.

The next three chapters describe research and theories regarding infant behavior and development in relation to the self (Chapter 2), the object world (Chapter 3), and the social world (Chapter 4).

The last two chapters of the book deal more specifically with the issue of infant development. Chapter 5 presents putative key psychological transitions in infancy that cut across and originate from developmental progress in infants' understanding of the self, objects, and people. Finally, Chapter 6 provides a review and discussion of the various developmental mechanisms that are too often presented as single causes of infant behavior and development. The idea behind this chapter is to convey the sense of the difficulty in describing with too simple causal terms how and why infants develop the way they do.

Infancy researchers aim at a moving target. There is great variation among infants in their developmental trajectories, a variability determined by a rich network of multiple causes and circumstances. Yet all infants develop the same mental abilities to become increasingly encultured and aware of the world that surrounds them. Capturing general features of infant psychological development while not sacrificing the complexity of individual developmental trajectories and circumstances is a huge challenge—one not meant for the fainthearted.

I would like to acknowledge the generous help of Tricia Striano, a former student and invaluable research collaborator: she pitched in at absolutely every stage and at all levels of this book project. My wholehearted, warm thanks to you, Tricia! My gratitude to Elizabeth Knoll for her strong and encouraging support during the entire review process, as well as to Julie Carlson for her talented and insightful copy editing. Finally, but not least, thank you to all the babies and parents who support infancy research by volunteering in hundreds of basic experiments taking place every day at research centers and universities around the world. Without their willingness to participate, there would be no such book.

Our understanding of the infant world is rapidly emerging from prolonged darkness. After centuries of oversight and neglect in the study of modern psychology, infants are finally being considered a major source of scientific enlightenment regarding the origins of the human mind. Infants are now systematically scrutinized for the way they develop, perceive, act, think, feel, and know. But this is only a recent fact.

The Long Neglect of Infancy

When modern psychology emerged in the late nineteenth century as a specialized discipline in which the scientific method was used to study how the mind works, pioneer psychologists did not consider children, particularly infants, as deserving much scientific attention.

Wilhelm Wundt (1832–1920), who established the first experimental psychology laboratory in Leipzig, Germany, considered that infants could not help in the understanding of the adult mind because of the unpredictable, erratic nature of their behavior. In his 1897 *Outlines of Psychology* he wrote, "The results of experiments which have been tried on very young children must be regarded as purely chance results, wholly untrustworthy on account of the great number of sources of error. For this reason, it is an error to hold, as is sometimes held, that the mental life of adults can never be fully understood except through the analysis of the child's mind" (Eng. trans. 1907, cited by Kessen 1965).

Experimental psychologists like Wundt believed infant study to be irrelevant because the experimental method that they used (systematic introspection) could not work with young children, who cannot report and reflect on their own experiences. It took decades for developmental psychology and in particular infancy research to gain recognition in mainstream experimental psychology. As a case in point, the first specialized scientific journal on the subject, *Infant Behavior and Development,* was founded by Lewis P. Lipsitt in 1979, less than thirty years ago.

Aside from methodological considerations, the denial of any scientific worthiness or even any particular intellectual attachment to infants has much deeper roots. Until recently infants have been viewed as frail, both physically and psychologically, easily damaged, and therefore unstable and difficult to investigate. It is important to remember that only a few decades ago, infant mortality was very high. In the early 1900s, for example, it is estimated that 26 percent of all deaths in New York City were of infants in their first year. Not that long ago, then, the chances that infants would survive their first year were slim. Such a reality did not favor strong early attachment to infants, nor did it favor a view of infancy as an important formative phase of the individual.

In an interesting book on human birth from an evolutionary perspective, anthropologist Wenda Trevathan (1987) notes that in many non-Western cultures with high infant mortality, birthing rituals and perinatal care are focused primarily on the mother, not the newborn child. For the first hours after birth, the attendants make every effort to bring the mother back to health after delivery and typically ignore the infant. In these cultures, mothers are valued for their potential to give birth again in the near future. From the point of view of group adaptation, such a practice makes sense. Newborns will eventually become successful progenitors but only in years to come, and only to the extent that they beat their dismal odds of surviving infancy and childhood. In contrast, the mother can bear another child in just months.

To walk in some Western maternity wards today, by contrast, is to walk into a space-age control room dedicated to neonates. In newborn intensive care units, it is now common to see infants born three months prematurely, weighing less than two pounds. Externalized fetuses, they are kept alive only by being hooked up to the latest beeping and flashing technology. These infants beat survival odds that were inconceivable only ten or fifteen years ago. Medical progress in support of both premature and term infants definitely changed the view of infancy as the fragile beginning period of child development. Infants became more permanent, predictable, and controllable in their health. They also became more stable and reliable objects of scientific inquiry.

The long denial of any scientific worth to infants has deep historical roots. The intellectual neglect of the infant world is already evident in ancient works of art intended to depict infants. From the Middle Ages and well into the seventeenth century, infants were typically portrayed as small adults. As pointed out by the historian Philippe Ariès (1962), until the French Revolution paintings and sculptures representing children, and in particular the religious depictions of Madonna and Child, reflect an apparent denial of any specificity to childhood. Infants are often painted as miniature versions of adults, not as young individuals with age-specific postures, attitudes, or activities. This Zeitgeist finally began to change around the turn of the seventeenth century and the end of French monarchy or "ancien régime." In the context of the European history of ideas, this change corresponds also to the first publication by philosophers of treaties on education that started to consider infancy as a potentially important formative period, one worthy of intellectual and scientific scrutiny.

Early Educational Preoccupations

The first thorough intellectual forays into the infant world were by philosophers who tried to shed new light on the education of children. Writings and reflections pertaining to infancy and early experience from poets, physicians, and philosophers are sprinkled throughout Western literature from antiquity on. For example, the Greek historian Plutarch (ca. 45–125 A.D.) writes about the merit of breastfeeding by the biological mother, condemning the use of the wet nurse whose love for the infant is corrupted by the material need to be hired for money. By the time of Renaissance, the French poet, anatomist, and humanist François Rabelais (ca. 1483–1553) was writing satirical and humorous essays, fantasizing about the education of a fictitious and grotesque character (Gargantua). Such reflections on infancy are rather indirect, anecdotal, and nonsystematic, used to put forth a political or stylistic agenda. But during the eighteenth century, namely the century of the Enlightenment that inspired innovation by educational doctrines, things changed markedly. More direct and thorough reflections on early development appear in the philosophical and essay literature.

British empiricist John Locke (1632–1704) and French romantic philosopher Jean-Jacques Rousseau (1712–1778) provide the first clear and comprehensive statements on the education of children, including reflections on infancy as a formative period of development. The comments of Locke and Rousseau on education contain important ideas that continue to have some relevance for today's research in infancy. The original aim of both authors was to dispense advice on how to educate children, and by doing so they introduced the revolutionary idea that such considerations should apply to all stages of child development, including infancy. In their treatises the child appears for the first time as explicitly worthy of systematic study. With these works, Locke and Rousseau laid the groundwork for modern developmental psychology, including infancy research.

Following the request of a friend who wondered how to handle his new baby, John Locke (in *Some Thoughts Concerning Education*, first published in 1693) reflected on what might be an optimum system of nurturance. Such reflection was pragmatic at the outset, but ended up with a particular theory on development and the child. Consistent with his empiricist view, which emphasizes the role of experience, Locke construes the environment of the child as the main determinant of behavior. In his letters on education, we find ideas and principles that are precursors of modern behaviorism, including the importance of positive reinforcement and a controlled environment.

In contrast to Locke, Rousseau speculates that children have a limited need for control and that educators should become noninterventionists who nurture children's natural curiosity, adventure-some nature, and individual pace of learning. Rousseau bases his view on the romantic assumption that infants are born fundamentally good and are only corrupted when during puberty they access the adult, "civilized" world. Rousseau pioneered child-centered principles of education whose underlying notions continue to be debated in contemporary developmental theories. These notions include the orderly succession of developmental stages and the functional specificity of child behavior at each of these stages.

Compared to Locke, Rousseau reverses the notion that children need to be educated. This strong position on education also forced a new focus on children who begged to be *understood* rather than controlled and admonished.

Rousseau had strong opinions regarding infancy, the starting state of psychology in development. For example, he conjectures that although infants have an innate ability to learn, their mind is at the outset a cognitive wasteland. In "L'Emile," (1762) he wrote, "We are born capable of learning, knowing nothing, perceiving nothing. Suppose a child born with the size and strength of manhood, entering upon life full grown like Pallas from the brain of Jupiter, such a child-man would be a perfect idiot, an automaton, a statue without motion and almost without feeling; he would see and hear nothing, he would recognize no one, he could not turn his eyes towards what he wanted to see." (quoted in Kessen 1965, pp. 76–77)

What follows in this book will hopefully convince you that Rousseau's depiction of the newborn as an idiot automaton is far from true, that infants have great learning abilities from birth and even before. But Rousseau's conceptualizing effort had the great merit of encouraging interest in infancy and in the origins of development that are now testable beyond mere philosophical speculations.

The Enlightening Infant

Infants eventually started to be considered as an invaluable source of information regarding not only education, but also the foundational aspects of the human mind: how it evolved and the basic principles that guide its working. From the educated infant of the eighteenth century, then, comes the scientifically *enlightening infant* of the nineteenth century.

The enlightening infant was born in the midst of blossoming evolutionary theories on the origins of species. The Darwinian revolution and other evolutionary views in biology initiated the scientific inquiry of infant psychology and continue to influence modern research in this area. In particular, the idea of a possible recapitulation of species' evolution (phylogeny) in the development of the individual (ontogeny) is an intrinsic part of the debate on the origins of species. The recapitulation idea presumes that what occurred over millions of years in the evolution of species, from fish to primates, might be repeated (that is, recapitulated) by the members of each species over the months, weeks, or even days of his or her individual development. Infant development started to be viewed as possibly duplicating, at a much accelerated scale, human evolution. Testing the recapitulation hypothesis entailed comparing the ontogenies of different species, including humans from the outset. In light of the recapitulation idea, infants gained in scientific status and became objects of basic research in evolutionary biology.

When the recapitulation idea began to circulate, systematic studies on the development of human infants were almost nonexistent. The first careful accounts and tentatively controlled longitudinal observations on infant development were baby biographies, which began to be undertaken around this time. The physiologist and psychobiologist Wilhelm Preyer (1841–1897), for example, studied both pre- and postnatal development in many different species, and as part of this project, collected systematic observations of his own child. Although essentially descriptive, Preyer's observations constitute one of the first systematic records of infant behavioral development.

It may surprise some readers to learn that Charles Darwin (1809–1882) is not only the father of the most influential account of biological evolution, but is also viewed as a pioneer of infancy research. Darwin kept a detailed diary of his son's first two years of behavioral development. Based on these observations, he published a seminal essay on the expression of emotions in animals and man (Darwin [1872] 1965). What intrigues Darwin and drives him in the careful observation of his infant son is the account of a natural history of behavior, across species and in ontogeny. The relation between developmental principles at work in phylogeny and ontogeny is a central concern.

The twentieth century marked a new era in the study of infant psychology. Infants started to be considered for their own sake, beyond theoretical concerns regarding biology and evolution. This change was certainly not estranged from the diffusion by the turn of the twentieth century of Freud's theory on the infantile origins of adults' neuroses. His theory reinforced the general idea that understanding infants and their experience with the world may reveal the building blocks of the adult's mind. Although Freud reconstructs infantile experience based on adult material, others, like Piaget, started to document the embryogenesis of the adult mind by observing and experimenting on infants directly.

Jean Piaget (1896–1980) contributed decisively to establishing infancy research as a worthwhile endeavor, both theoretically and scientifically. He systematically observed his own three children between birth and eighteen months and compiled his findings in two seminal books first published in the 1930s, *The Origins of Intelligence in Children* and *The Construction of Reality in the Child*. These books continue to be an important source of inspiration for contemporary infancy research.

Piaget's intention in studying infants is primarily to provide the foundation for an explanation of cognition in general and the origins of knowledge in particular (cognitive development). In his attempt, he contributes decisively to the wave of current basic research in infancy. This research is inspired not only by educational or evolutionary concerns, but also, primarily, by developmental questions regarding the ontogeny of the human mind. His focus became the foundational aspects of adult psychology as revealed by infants. In Piaget's works, the infant is finally considered to be one who can enlighten our study of psychological origins.

From the age of long intellectual neglect across the centuries and the denial of any scientific worth in the recent history of modern psychology, this new status of the infant has come a long way.

Getting into the Mind of Infants

The word "infant" refers literally to "one who is unable to speak." The fact that infants are yet unable to express themselves within the conventions of any symbolic or referential systems is a major challenge for those interested in trying to decipher the infant's mind. Unlike other psychological investigations, infancy research cannot rest on convenient questionnaires and other tests based on verbal instructions. It calls for special techniques, not unlike those that animal and comparative psychologists invent in order to document the behavior of other nonverbal creatures.

In trying to decipher the infant world, infancy students are left with two options. One is to observe babies and experiment on them directly. The other is to adopt the reconstructive technique pioneered a century ago by Sigmund Freud (1856–1939), who recorded and systematically interpreted what adults remember and reconstruct of their past infancy via dreams and free associations. Freud's approach is in essence adult oriented. It informs the adult's subjective view of his or her own infancy, and has little to say about the infant world itself.

Many current and popular therapy techniques perpetuate Freud's reconstructive approach to infancy. Claims are made, for example, that adults benefit from reenacting their own birth and behavior as infants. Even researchers with combined clinical and experimental inclinations sometimes argue that the physical reenactment of infant behavior (their posture and action) might help us understand infants' subjective world. But aside from possible therapeutic benefits, such techniques provide nothing objective about infants and the way they relate to the world.

The only way to approach the infant world as an object of study for its own sake is to observe babies directly in an environment where systematic experimentation and validated recording, controlled as much as possible for the interference of the adults' own

experience or subjectivity, can occur. To a large extent, direct observation is what parents engage in when they try to figure out their infant, whether in emergency care situations or in more casual play, as
the parent, for example, anticipates a potential fall or tries to make
the baby smile. In the midst of their intimate relationship, parents
monitor their infant's behavior closely, trying to foresee and remedy
the infant's needs. Intuitive parenting is a remarkable phenomenon
that cuts across cultures and social strata. Parents, of course, are bi-
ased toward perceiving certain things rather than others in their
own children: how cute and smart they are, how much they are in
pain or in bliss. But parental intuition is based on hundreds of hours
of direct behavioral observations from which fine behavioral patterns are detected and interpreted.

In fact, infancy researchers like myself are often guided by casual
reports from parents about supposed reasons for a particular behavior they observed in their infant. Aside from being inspiring, such
parental theories are more often than not confirmed in highly controlled laboratory experiments using large samples of infants. This
testifies to the validity of such reports and to the fact that, beyond
their role of bringing infant participants to the laboratory, parents
are invaluable collaborators in infancy research.

To observe infants directly is to pay attention to the unfolding
of their behavior in relation to particular circumstances, some of
which are more controlled than others. In less controlled circumstances, infants are freely observed and their behavior documented
as they respond to their natural environment and daily activities.
Such natural observations are not unlike the diaries some parents
keep of their own infants, or the baby biographies that flourished in
the nineteenth century. Natural observations might include some
tentative validity control; for example, the researcher may attempt to
replicate observed behavioral phenomena at other times and in similar situations with other infants. Such efforts, however, cannot replace laboratory experiments that control systematically the circumstances of the behavioral observations.

In recent years, clever experimental methods have been devised to
conduct systematic and reliable infant studies. They provide rep-

licable data and allow the induction of testable theories on infant psychology. These methods, or experimental paradigms, typically tap into abilities that are part of the infant behavioral repertoire from birth, such as crying, sucking, tracking objects visually, kicking, or orienting the head. These abilities might also include physiological responses such as heart rate or electrical brain activities recorded via surface electrodes. These methods provide systematic controls of the circumstances in which the behavior may or may not occur, as well as a reliable means of quantifying the magnitude of behavioral occurrences.

The systematic measurement of behavior and the control of the circumstances surrounding the behavior are the only ways around infants' lack of explicit expression. It is by induction from systematic measurements of behavioral responses that we get reliable access to what might happen in babies' heads: what they might feel, perceive, or think. Among all of the clever experimental stratagems that infancy researchers have devised to figure out what happens in the infant's mind, the habituation paradigm has been probably the most productive in deciphering what infants can perceive, discriminate, and even conceptualize. It is the prototype of induction from systematic measurements.

The habituation paradigm is based on a behavioral phenomenon that is pervasive in animals and that human infants manifest early in life: a decrease of the behavioral response over time as a stimulus is repeated. When a stimulus is presented over and over again, infants will first reduce their original level of response and eventually not respond at all. Habituation is simple, reliable, and easy to measure. It also allows for the assessment of the circumstances that might reverse it—in other words, what might cause a "dishabituation."

Suppose that you are interested in knowing whether infants perceive colors, and in particular whether they can differentiate between primary colors such as yellow and red. You can figure that out by presenting infants with one of the two color cards over and over again. You will time infants' gazing at the card, and when you notice that they pay no more attention, you will flash the other color card. If the infants recover their visual attention, this suggests that they discriminate between the two colors. With this simple experiment, you have gained an answer to your question and now can come up with new, more specific questions and answers that will help refine your theory about infants' perception of a colored world.

The habituation/dishabituation method is applicable to almost any psychological content, whether it is recognition of the mother's face, the detection of emotion, speech perception, or object categorization. This is a very reliable way to figure babies out, and much of our progress in understanding infants is based on the habituation/dishabituation paradigm. Other methods of direct experimental observation have also proven very fruitful in the domain of infancy research. I will describe many of them in subsequent chapters as I present research and findings.

The recent boom in infancy research is unquestionably linked to progress in available behavioral recording techniques. Probably the most important has been the availability of video technology allowing the real-time storage of infant behavior that can be replayed and observed frame-by-frame. Such technological progress has had a tremendous effect on the field, opening opportunities for fine-grain analyses of infant behavior, allowing for more reliable scoring, and making research accessible to a larger number of infancy students. Yet although technology is indeed important, it is only a means to an end. It needs to be harnessed by sound methodology, good questions, and meaningful theories that give basic reasons for studying infants.

The Unique Characteristics of Human Infancy

In the quest to understand the infant world and in trying to figure out the developmental origins of the human mind, it is crucial not to lose track of what is specific to human infancy in comparison to early developmental stages of other species. Human infancy has unique features that help make us what we are: symbolic and culturally oriented individuals.

Compared to other mammals, humans have a long gestation time and a comparatively slower development. We live longer and mature more slowly than other mammals of comparable body size (for more details see the thorough discussion in Gould 1977, pp. 366 to the end). Prenatal development, in particular the emergence of anatomical features that are analogous across mammal species, unfolds in the same orderly fashion—but within markedly different time frames. In comparison to mouse embryos, for example, human embryos develop the same anatomical features much more slowly. Furthermore, compared to the mouse embryo, the developmental rate of the human embryo slows as a function of prenatal development. At the beginning of gestation, a mouse day of development represents about four human days. By the end of gestation, a mouse day of prenatal development represents fourteen days of human development (Adolph 1977, cited by Gould 1977). This progressive retardation stretches the time frame of human gestation and determines the physiological and behavioral state of the infant at birth.

In comparison to other primates, and in particular to our closer evolutionary relatives (orangutans, gorillas, and chimpanzees), humans have a comparable gestational timeframe. Human gestation is forty weeks, whereas those of our close primate relatives range between thirty-four and thirty-nine weeks. Once again, however, what is particular to humans is the marked retardation in pre- and postnatal development. For example, the overall growing period for humans spans about twenty years. In chimpanzees it spans only eleven years. Interestingly, the chimpanzees' life expectancy is also reduced by half compared to humans, as if nature compensates slower and stretched out development with longer lives.

In mammalian evolution, there is also a general trend from large litters of altricial (fast growing and underdeveloped) young to small litters of precocial (slow growing and overdeveloped) young. In this general evolutionary trend, humans represent a noticeable exception: their litter is small and their young are most definitely altricial—helpless and underdeveloped at birth. Why do humans represent such a noticeable exception in mammalian evolution?

In comparison to other primates, human infants are born too soon. According to some estimates, for humans to have the growth level at birth of other great ape species, their gestation time should more than double (from nine months to approximately twenty-one months). So why this precocious birth in humans? One theory is that the rich stimulation of the extrauterine environment is necessary for the human brain to develop. This stimulation would determine the higher learning and unique psychological functioning developed by humans. Accordingly, the development of intellectual power would depend on a supportive and stimulating environment. This is not a far-fetched idea, considering recent data provided by developmental neuroscientists demonstrating the great plasticity of the human brain beyond birth (discussed more fully later).

Another contributing factor, one linked also to the particular demands of human brain growth, might simply arise from the amount of food required to support human physiological growth. Beyond forty weeks of gestation, it is feasible that the fast development of the fetal brain can no longer be supported by maternal energy reserves and supply. This would contribute to the premature birth of human infants. Outside of the womb, via breastfeeding and other forms of external nourishment, infants would get access to richer sources of energy to support their highly demanding growth.

Yet another intriguing explanation for why humans are born early focuses on the evolution of vertical posture and bipedal locomotion in humans. The emergence of bipedal locomotion in primate evolution is associated with a change in the configuration of the pelvis bone and has had the dramatic effect of narrowing the birth canal in humans (Trevathan 1987). In evolution, the narrow pelvis associated with bipedal locomotion would have limited the maximum cranial growth of the human fetus and thus determined the accelerated time of human birth and the continuing gestation outside, instead of inside, the womb (sometimes referred to as "exterogestation," Montagu 1961).

For over fifty years, anthropologists and evolutionary biologists have accumulated evidence suggesting that the emergence of bipedalism in human evolution probably had dramatic effects on brain size and behavior. The freeing of the upper limbs that accompanies bipedal posture is probably linked with dramatic changes in the capacity to manipulate objects and eventually tool manufacture (Vauclair and Bard 1983). This view is seductively simple, but we should keep in mind that it is based on only a correlation between certain evolutionary phenomena (for example, the emergence of bipedal locomotion, brain size changes, pelvis changes in human evolution), and not on evidence of any causal links. To my knowledge, there is no direct evidence that any one of these variables caused others. What is fairly certain, however, is that these variables must have interacted over evolutionary time to produce modern humans and to determine the length of gestation of babies.

The premature birth of humans might have had cascading consequences at all levels of child rearing and have ultimately contributed to make us the modern humans we are. As for any other species, the survival of humans depends on the optimal (hence safe) rearing of the young: children are the living warranty of our genetic perpetuation. It is easy to consider that we humans have evolved particular ways of organizing ourselves to reproduce and raise our young in the most successful ways. These ways are constrained by the slow and protracted development of the altricial human infant. In turn, these parental ways might have had dramatic consequences in the evolution of the specific characteristics of human adults. As I will suggest in the next section, there are potentially great developmental consequences attached to prolonged immaturity. The specific timing of human birth and the comparatively slow development of human infants most probably have had cascading effects on the evolution of human psychology.

Consequences of Prolonged Immaturity

With immaturity comes social dependence and supervision. The prolonged immaturity characterizing human infancy is associated with richer parenting compared to other primate species. Psychological scaffolding from parents is pervasive from birth, fostering infancy as a period of play, teaching, exploration, and experimentation. This scaffolding is particularly pronounced in humans and is an important expression of how unique we are in primate evolution.

Human parenting entails a degree of empathy that is not equated in other primate species. Even when tending to infants' basic physiological needs such as feeding or washing, parents engage spontane-

ously in helping their infants develop psychologically. They participate in infants' experience, mirror their expressions, and talk to
them with particular intonation and voice contours (Fernald 1989;
Kaye 1982; Gergely and Watson 1999). During feeding, for example,
mothers are often compelled to maintain eye contact and caress
their infants. They demonstrate affective attunement by frequently
commenting on their babies' action, whether it is a smile or the expression of gas after a feeding. They typically manifest joy when the
infant shows signs of contentment and sound subdued when the infant frowns or cries (Stern 1985).

From birth, mothers tend to place their infants in an "en face"
posture to capture their attention and engage in social exchanges.
They are often inclined to present their face in full view of the infant
to encourage eye-to-eye contact. Face presentation and eye-to-eye
contact in playful social exchanges are marked features of human
mother-infant interaction in general, and unquestionably cardinal
features among Western middle-class parents.

In comparison to that of other primate species, and because it
is more protracted and enculturated, human infancy is a period
of greater opportunity for observation and learning. Infants spend
months observing and experiencing the world around them while
being intensively monitored and taken care of. Infants are continually helped or scolded in their attempts to do something, and taught
and encouraged to perform new actions. They are provided with
stimulating, playful objects that are appropriate to the range of their
behavioral repertoire: rattles to shake, pacifiers to suck, faces to
track. This corresponds to what Russian psychologist Lev Vygotsky
(1896–1934) describes as the "zone of proximal development" or the
knowledge and skills that children gain with the assistance of more
advanced social partners (Vygotsky 1978). Infants do not develop in
isolation, and from an early age caretakers operate as reliable teachers in addition to basic care providers. Infants are supported and
guided by experienced people as they learn new skills in a kind of
apprenticeship (Rogoff 1990).

Aside from being fed and kept clean, and central to their early
sociocultural apprenticeship, human infants tend to be compulsively

entertained by caretakers. Sleeping quarters of infants, at least in an American middle-class family, are a good example. Infants' rooms are typically overflowing with toys specially designed for entertaining the baby and stimulating natural play. The toys are manufactured and offered to the infant, from the earliest age, on the basis of the adult's theory, expectations, and ideology: black and white mobiles for the crib, safe graspable rattles, pink teethers for a baby girl. All of these things are expressions of a parenting culture that is unique to humans.

Over months, the main duties of infants are to play and observe. Fed, washed, and their health monitored, they are given the opportunity to entertain themselves. Infants' progress is typically nurtured with new appropriate challenges: for example, when learning to walk they are first encouraged to stand on their feet and walk while holding both hands of a grown-up, then to hang on to the adult with only one hand, and eventually to walk with no support toward an adult kneeling in front of them with both arms spread out to receive them. Each successful attempt is acknowledged with positive facial expressions and verbal comments. In this example, courage and perseverance is rewarded and loudly shared. This is part of the intuitive parenting that accompanies infants throughout their development. It is a trademark of human infancy and the primary entry of infants into the culture of their parents.

The importance and function of infancy as a protracted play period protected and fostered by caretakers is eloquently discussed by Jerome Bruner, another pioneer of child study. Reflecting on the nature and use of immaturity in humans, Bruner (1972) proposes that the prolonged immaturity of human infants creates a critical opportunity for them to learn by observation, and in particular to learn about tool use, which is an important index of primate evolution. Bruner suggests that a main function of play is to test the limits of one's own actions in an environment that is made safe and enticing by caretakers. Parental protection and monitoring allow infants to take limited risks in experimenting novel acts, such as negotiating obstacles in the environment like stairs, or tasting foliage that could be poisonous. Under constant parental supervision, play provides infants with the license to try out an almost risk-free environment. It is a unique learning opportunity that is the trademark of the human infant world.

Because it is relatively inconsequential thanks to the caretakers' prevention, play also invites infants to try new combinations of behavior. In other words, play fosters creativity—the exploration of new means to achieve particular effects, attain particular goals, and discover new objectives. Suppose for example that a mobile is attached above the crib of an infant as a stimulating visual tool. The infant might discover by accident that she can touch the mobile with her feet and set it in motion. She will repeat the action and by doing so might realize that by simply kicking her legs abruptly without touching the mobile, a similar effect is produced. The mobile is solidly attached to the crib, which moves when the infant's legs pound the mattress. In this succession of playful activities, the infant discovers different means to an end and fosters a sense of herself as an active participant in the world. Gratuitous play activity and curiosity contribute much to infant development. The infant's propensity for such play and curiosity, in turn, is culturally assisted and directly encouraged by the parents who tied the mobile above the crib.

Growth in Infancy

Aside from being a protracted, highly supported period of play, infancy is also a period of marked changes in size and motor skills. Growth is particularly pronounced in human infants, who are born sooner and develop at a slower pace compared to youngsters of any other primate or mammalian species.

Babies start off clumsy, displaying very little postural control and spending most of their time sleeping. Anatomically, the brain continues to develop over the months following birth and the rest of the body gets more muscular, gaining weight and reversing its disproportion relative to the head. As with any biological system, the growth occurring in infancy is both structural and functional: it pertains to changes regarding both the anatomy and the behavior of the infant.

Infancy can be conveniently defined from a functional perspective as the period of development from birth to the onset of independent walking. There is some merit to this definition because walking is a clear landmark in postural and motor development. When infants learn to walk, they can explore independently larger portions of their environment without having to touch the ground with their hands. Aside from postural and motor development, the onset of walking by approximately the end of the first year corresponds to when infants start to be verbal beyond babbling. It is around this time that infants usually start uttering their first conventional words. Note that there are significant differences among individuals in the timing of such landmarks and that the point here is not to suggest that one landmark might cause the other. They just appear to be correlated in developmental time. Both bring the infant psychologically closer to adults and older children, if not in size, at least in posture and communicative ability.

Prior to the onset of walking and first words, other milestones are passed, including manual reaching, independent sitting, and crawling. Once again, despite important interindividual variations, there are some obvious regularities across infants in the timing and sequence of behaviorial changes that accompany physical growth in infancy. The emergence of independent walking is correlated with the development of new action systems, all of which are linked to the progressive freeing of the upper limbs from the encumbrance of maintaining balance while sitting or standing upright (Rochat and Senders 1991).

Interestingly, this progression also characterizes human evolution: the hands of humans became freer as erect posture and bipedal locomotion developed. As I mentioned earlier, based on comparative bone measurements it is now well established that the emergence of erect posture in primate evolution was accompanied by changes in the configuration of the skull and brain. At a behavioral level, the development of an erect posture is linked in human evolution to the emergence of tool use and tool manufacture. In the same way, the development of erect posture in infancy correlates with the progressive enhancement of perceptual and motor functioning of the hands. Stable sitting and erect locomotion are inseparable from the emergence of more sophisticated ways of mastering objects and acting in the world. This kind of analogy explains why early evolutionary biologists in the nineteenth century might have been tempted by recapitulation ideas.

Tool use and tool manufacture represent major steps in primate evolution. By analogy, the emergence of manual reaching and object manipulation is an index of major changes in infant cognitive development. We will see in the next two chapters that the development of tool use in infancy is linked to the cognitive association between means and ends, and hence the emergence of planning and anticipation. At a broad functional level, infant postural and action development over the first eighteen months of life mimics important aspects of postural and action development that developed over approximately 6 million years in human evolution.

The sequence of landmark motor development was first documented in the systematic observations of Arnold Gesell (1880–1961). Filming individual infants in repeated sessions at regular and close intervals over the first months of life, Gesell documented the normalized emergence of landmark postural and motor development. In the footsteps of baby biographers such as Preyer and as a medical doctor interested in the welfare and education of young children, Gesell's main aim was to provide a thorough documentation of the embryology of normal behavior in infancy by using available film techniques and a large population of infants. The apparent predictability of the sequence and timing of this development led Gesell to conceive of it mainly as the product of programmed physical growth and brain maturation.

When biological maturation is invoked to account for developmental changes such as postural and motor development, it is unfortunately tempting to minimize the role of experience (nurture). Considering nature and nurture as mutually exclusive is a fundamental error. There is predictable physical growth in infancy, but the question is how this growth determines infants' relation to the environment and hence influences their experience of it. A healthy infant will reach successfully for objects at around four months, sit independently at around five months, stand with support at around eight months, and walk at around twelve months. This regularity exists despite some noticeable differences among individual infants. From a psychological perspective, the question is how does reaching for objects, sitting independently, standing, or locomoting affect infants' experience of the environment? How does progress in these areas influence the way that infants understand themselves, objects, and people around them? Infant psychology is fundamentally and unquestionably the product of an interaction between nature and nurture, functional and structural growth.

Research in infancy provides overwhelming evidence of the link between structural and functional growth. Newborns, for example, have poor independent head-neck support. They progressively develop the muscles and muscle control to hold their head steady. Researchers have shown that such development, which can be accounted for in terms of mere muscular maturation, has significant repercussions in the way infants engage with a social partner in face-to-face, playful interactions. Progress in head-neck control correlates with increased smiling and prolonged eye-to-eye contacts (Van Wulfften Palthe and Hopkins 1993).

When physical maturation takes place, it is associated with major psychological consequences. Other researchers have shown, for example, that the emergence of independent locomotion (crawling and walking) is positively correlated with progress in spatial cognition, in particular the emergence of the notion that objects continue to exist when out of sight, or so-called object permanence (Kermoian and Campos 1988). The development of independent locomotion appears also to be linked to the emergence of social referencing, by which infants consider their mother's happy or fearful facial expression before trying something potentially dangerous like crawling toward a swimming pool or approaching a hot stove (see the review of such research in Bertenthal and Campos 1990). Some researchers have even demonstrated that nonlocomoting infants, placed in walkers that support them and allow them to scoot around, begin self-propelled exploration of the environment within minutes. This exploration is more wide-ranging and advanced than any exploratory activities they might have undertaken beforehand (Gustafson 1984).

Research on brain development in infancy demonstrates further the indissociability of structural and functional growth. At birth, the brain has all of its building blocks, namely neurons or nerve cells, that will be used in the baby's lifetime. From birth on, there is a tendency toward progressive attrition in the number of neurons, a process called neuronal loss or programmed cell death. Cell death in postnatal brain development has been documented in many neural systems or regions of the brain, although the pace and magnitude of this process vary across brain regions. Research with chicks, for example, demonstrates that there is a stable number of neurons in the visual cortex across the lifespan. In contrast, programmed cell death accounts for the loss of half of the motoneurons (subcortical nerve cells responsible for motor control) in the spinal cord during postnatal (posthatching) development (Hamburger 1975).

In general, there is a large excess of brain cells at birth that are selectively eliminated during development based on whether they are activated and whether they find a target area to innervate. In certain brain regions, like the visual cortex, most neurons find some connection with other neurons because they are densely packed. Cell density limits the process of cell death in this particular region. In other regions, like the spinal cord, selective cell death is more pronounced because targets for neurons are more limited. These facts demonstrate that even at the level of brain growth, the enormously complex network of neurons forming the nervous system is actually *sculpted* in the course of ontogeny, mainly by selective attrition from experience. The remarkable plasticity of the brain in development points once again toward the mutual relationship between nature and nurture in infant development.

The most striking evidence of brain plasticity in development and the role of experience in shaping the infant nervous system is provided by studies regarding changes in the number of connections between neurons, or development of synaptic connections (synaptogenesis). Synapses are the gaps between the ending of one nerve cell and the receptive end (dendrite) of another nerve cell. Pre- and postsynaptic cells communicate via chemicals or neurotransmitters. The capacity of the nervous system to support the processing of information depends on the connectivity among brain cells, and the degree of connectivity is indexed by synaptic density.

Synaptogenesis in the human cerebral cortex begins by the second trimester of pregnancy—after most of the billions of neurons forming the fetus's nervous system have already found their targets—but it occurs mainly after birth. For example, the number of synaptic connections in the human visual cortex at birth is only about one-sixth of that found in adults. Interestingly, synaptic connections there show a ten-fold increase between birth and six months, with a sharp decrease starting at twelve months of age, and from two years on, a slower decrease. In other words, at least for the area of the visual cortex, there seems to be a dramatic rise and beginning of a fall in synaptic density during infancy. In fact, there are markedly more synapses in a six-month-old infant than in an adult. Why? Probably the early overproduction of synaptic connections allows for the pruning or selective elimination of functionally unspecified nervous connections as a function of the baby's experience with the environment (not at random).

In fact, the brain shows remarkable plasticity across the lifespan. Adults who have suffered a stroke can show documented brain repair that is enhanced by a strict regimen of physical therapy and other exercises. Paralyzed patients can sometimes recover movements following a stroke that has damaged motor areas. Such phenomena are possible because new neural networks develop, bypassing and taking over the damaged brain tissues.

Research in developmental neuroscience points to the fact that synaptic connections are eliminated if they are not activated. The neural pathways of the human brain undergo major changes in response to environmental stimulation and as a consequence of active encounters with the environment. This developmental process is particularly pronounced during infancy, and to a lesser extent during childhood and adulthood. The impressive brain growth occurring in early development is not merely reducible to a preestablished genetic program because it depends on the infant's interaction and experience with the environment. This basic process has inspired new brain-based models of development labeled as connectionism or connectionist modeling (Elman et al. 1996; see also Chapter 6).

In summary, a major aspect of brain growth in infancy is the ontogenetic "sculpting" of neural connections in relation to experience, a process that is particularly active during this early period of development. Note, however, that synaptogenesis in infancy does not appear to take place at the same rate in different regions of the cerebral cortex. For example, synapse elimination in the visual cortex (back of the brain) is much faster compared to that in the frontal cortex (front of the brain). This is particularly interesting considering that the corticofrontal region of the brain is involved in advanced executive functions, such as searching for a hidden object, recognition over time of the place where an attractive object has been hidden, or detouring around an obstacle to reach for a desired object. We will see in Chapter 3 that complex action planning, including manual search for hidden objects, does indeed develop weeks after infants demonstrate almost adultlike visual capacities. Once again, this example illustrates the inseparability of structure (physical changes in the brain) and function (behavioral development in relation to specific tasks).

Because neural networks in infancy do not develop independently from experience, the structure-function relation is not simple. It is mediated by the experience of the infant as perceiver and actor in a meaningful environment. But what is meaningful to infants? I will argue next that infants develop in relation to three basic categories of infantile experience: the self (that is, one's own body), physical objects, and people. These categories are inseparable pillars that support and hold the infant world together.

Deciphering the Infant World

Figuring out what is meaningful for infants entails supposing what might be the formative elements of their mental life. It requires considering what might be the building blocks of their psychology and what is relevant to their development. Not unlike in other areas of science, such ideas guide research and ultimately determine how infants are theoretically accounted for. If, for example, researchers assume that the social aspect of infant behavior is all important, then a social infant is accounted for. In contrast, if they assume that infants are primarily oriented toward the exploration of physical objects, then a more rational infant physicist will be brought forth. Infancy research, not unlike any other scientific enterprise, is always guided by fundamental assumptions and ideological choices, a "theoretical carving."

It is intriguing to think about the reasons for particular theoretical carving and why researchers are inclined to focus on one particular aspect of infant psychology rather than another. In other words, what determines researchers' own take on the infant world? There is only limited serendipity underlying scientists' choice of issues and priorities in research. Instead it reflects a Zeitgeist, an intellectual and political climate: the particular aesthetic of an era, what is fashionable and mainstream. This is particularly evident when considering the historical reasons for studying infants.

Current infancy research is part of a tradition that is deeply rooted in Western philosophy, in particular the tradition of dividing mental life into separate arenas such as cognition, perception, motivation, attention, social behavior, emotions, or personality. The resulting representation of mental life is a sort of juxtaposition of separate "psychologies" that function as distinct units. Such parsing does not foster what is particularly apparent in infancy: the great interdependence of all of those arenas.

Since antiquity, deciphering the mind has been a major exercise among philosophers who thought about the nature and origins of mental life. Aristotle (384–322 B.C.) distinguished discrete categories of emotions, sense perceptions, and intellects. René Descartes (1596–1650) introduced the distinction between primary and secondary qualities of sensation to account for the origins of perception within a mechanist framework. The German philosopher Immanuel Kant (1724–1804) considered that knowledge and the functioning of the mind can be reduced to thinking in relation to a limited number of basic a priori (ontological) categories such as time, space, and causality. Such categorizing of mental phenomena has had lasting influences.

The philosophical tradition of parsing mental phenomena influenced the modern scientific approach to the mental life of infants. For example, the pioneer work of Jean Piaget on infant cognition is based on the Kantian parsing of a priori categories (space, time, causality, and objects). Following Kant's framework, Piaget assumed that these categories reflect the world as it is known by the infant, a world essentially dominated by midsize physical objects. Following Kantian parsing, Piaget approached children as little physicists experimenting primarily with objects and theorizing about them.

To a large extent, the Kantian categories adopted by Piaget in his study of infant cognitive development pertain to the nature of knowledge in an abstract, formal sense. Piaget's approach to infant cognition is more epistemological (pertaining to formal knowledge) than psychological. Take the category of space, for example. As reasoned by Piaget, it might be a specific domain of cognition for which particular principles apply: that objects are permanent even if they perceptually come and go, that objects cannot be two places at the same time, and that they move continuously through space (they do not pop out of nowhere when entering the perceptual field). But such a view of spatial cognition does not account for other, more psychological ways that infants apprehend space. For infants, space is more than an object of formal reasoning. It is primarily the environmental context in which they develop perception and action. Space is where infants take their first steps, learn to explore, and locomote in new ways. Space is a place for boldness and independence in avoiding obstacles and dangers. It is where one gets lost and eventually reunited. Space might be an abstraction of basic principles, but for infants it is primarily a very real, concrete location for perception and action.

One way to account for infant psychology is to start with the possible range of basic experiences that infants have in their environment. Such an approach begins with a description of the infants' environment, not with speculations about what might be in their heads. It is an approach that tries to avoid any kind of separation or dualism between infants and the environment they experience. Within this approach, infant psychology is fundamentally inseparable from a description of the environment and what infants might be capable of experiencing when interacting with it. The idea is to consider first the ecological niche of infants, and from there to figure out how their minds work in relation to it.

We share the same world with infants, but not their environment. We breathe the same air and witness the same objects and events that are controlled by the same physical laws. We share with babies the same body structure and are equipped with the same sensory systems. But we do not engage in the same kind of activities, nor do we have the same needs and motivations.

The ecological niche of infants is specific and comes with particular kinds of experience. Imagine an infant in her crib, just fed and diapered, awake and happily looking around. She might bring one of her hands to her mouth and suck one of her fingers. Or she might explore the colorful lining of the crib. She might also make eye contact with a talking face leaning over her with a smile. Each instance captures one of three primary categories of experience that are the foundations of the infant world: the experience of the self, objects, and people. These three very basic categories of experience are contrasted and invariant from the moment infants are born, and each corresponds to specific perceptual and action phenomena that babies are equipped to experience and learn from.

When infants bring their hands to their mouths, touch any other parts of their own bodies, move a limb across their fields of view, or cry, these actions are accompanied by perceptions that uniquely specify the infant's own body (that is, the *self*). When an object touches the baby or the baby hears someone else's voice, the perception is of things in the environment that are different from the self (that is, *objects*). Aside from self and physical things, *people* are a distinct feature of the infant environment. Babies experience them differently than either their own bodies or other physical objects. We will see that infants from birth are particularly attuned to people, preferring for example to look at facelike displays over any other non-facelike visual stimuli. Aside from possible prewired attunement, people have the special feature of reciprocating and engaging in prolonged face-to-face interactions: games with high-pitched vocal interventions, particular facial expressions, and of course, the predominantly human sustained eye-to-eye contact. These three fundamentally distinct and contrasted classes of experience—the self, objects, and people—are differentiated from birth and even possibly in the womb. They are, I propose, the constitutive elements of the infant world and the basic contexts of the development of infants' mental life.

In the next chapter, I review the first aspect of this three-sided presentation of the infant world: the self in infancy.

2

THE SELF IN INFANCY

Great psychological phenomena such as love, hate, or jealousy are not only the most meaningful experiences in our lives; they are also particular sets of neurochemical reactions occurring in certain ways and involving specific regions of the brain. Current neuroscience research using brain imaging and electrical activity recording techniques provides abundant demonstrations of the *embodiment* of psychological phenomena. Clearly thoughts, ideas, and emotions are not ethereal systems that exist above and beyond the way the body functions and is organized. Mental life is indeed grounded in the physical body.

From a less mechanical point of view, the embodiment of psychology is also evident when considering babies' early inclination to investigate their own bodies and to learn systematically about them. The body is a privileged object of exploration in infancy, and as we will see, much of infants' behavior is oriented toward their own bodies and how the body relates to the environment. The direct perceptual experience of the body is *permanent*, unlike that of other physical objects and people in the environment. People and objects come and go; the body does not. From birth, one's own body is the companion of all psychological experiences.

By perceiving and acting, infants discover the invariant structure of their own bodies and what they can do in relation to the environment. They also learn about the body as a locus of pain, pleasure, and fluctuating moods. My goal here is to suggest that the early inclination of infants to explore their own bodies forms the cradle of self-perception and the developmental origin of self-knowledge. For infants, the body is a major feature of the world.

The Origins of Self-Knowledge

The problem of the origins and development of the self is arguably the most fundamental problem of psychology. What do we know about ourselves as sentient and active entities in the world? How do we acquire and what is the nature of such knowledge? Dealing with these questions in terms of both species evolution (phylogeny) and individual development (ontogeny), biologists and child psychologists have devised ingenious experimental paradigms to track emerging signs of self-knowledge.

In classic experiments, individuals of different species and young children of various ages were presented with their own image reflected in a mirror. Their behavioral reactions were systematically recorded to detect any signs of self-recognition. The question underlying the mirror technique was whether individuals saw themselves or saw someone else in the specular image. This question has been considered as a sort of litmus test of self-recognition and the capacity for self-knowledge.

In a clever manipulation, a dab of rouge was applied surreptitiously to the individual's face prior to his or her being placed in front of the mirror (Figure 2.1, top). Some apes (some individual chimpanzees and orangutans in particular) and children, starting at approximately eighteen months of age, touched their faces at the location of the rouge, providing evidence of self-recognition (Lewis and Brooks-Gunn 1979; Gallup 1971; Povinelli 1995; Tomasello and Call 1997). Following the rationale of this experimental paradigm, the self-referencing behavior of touching the face could only be explained by the individual's identifying the perceived mirror image as the embodied self.

The question of course is whether the rouge task truly identifies self-knowledge and whether children younger than eighteen months, because they do not pass the rouge test, have no sense of themselves as differentiated entities in the world. Indeed, recent progress in infancy research suggests that prior to mirror self-recog-

Figure 2.1   By the middle of the second year, infants begin to recognize themselves in mirrors. They show self-consciousness and self-referencing when discovering that they have a spot of rouge on their face (top). They also start displaying withdrawal and embarrassment in front of their specular image
(bottom). By the end of infancy, children become progressively aware of themselves for themselves, but also for a virtual audience judging them in relation to
social standards. (Photos by L. R. Pascale)

nition, infants demonstrate some sense of their own bodies as differentiated entities that are organized, are situated in the environment, and have agency. This early sense of self has been called the infant's ecological self. The sense of the ecological self does not imply self-recognition per se, but certainly some self-knowledge, and in particular an awareness of the body.

People involved in the conception and engineering of robots designed to perceive and act know how fundamental is the ability to discriminate oneself from other entities in the environment. Without such an ability, no goal-oriented action would be possible. Imagine that you have to build a robot able to search for blocks scattered in a room in order to stack them. Even this simple task would entail that your machine be able to discriminate between stimulation that originates from its own machinery and stimulation that originates from the blocks in the environment. Suppose that you endow your robot with an artificial eye and an artificial limb to detect, grasp, and stack the blocks. To be successful, your machine will have to have some built-in system enabling it to discriminate between the detection of a block and the detection of its own limb. If not, the robot might endlessly chase itself rather than the blocks. Your robot would engage in circular, self-centered acts that would drive it away from the target or external goal. Regarding infants, an inability to discriminate between self and non-self stimulation would also result in a fundamental confusion.

Developmental theorists have typically presented young infants as being in such an initial state of confusion: the famous blooming, buzzing confusion described over a century ago by William James (1842–1910). According to James, infants at birth show no signs of being able to discriminate between self- and nonself-stimulation because of a fusion or undifferentiation between infants and their environment. Within the psychoanalytical tradition fathered by Sigmund Freud (1856–1939), infants, rather than confused, are initially unrelated to the world around; they are geared toward immediate pleasure gratification with no apparent flexibility to compromise with the environment. Following Freud's view, infants behave as if oblivious to the surrounding world. Self-centered and autistic, they manifest the biological impulses of an Id or "that" rather than of an Ego ("Me"). Within the Freudian tradition, some infancy theorists, in particular Margaret Mahler and her colleagues, present the initial stage of psychological development as "normal autism," whereby infants behave as if they are independent of the environment, somehow shut off from it (Mahler, Pine, and Bergman 1975). This description of the young infant is based on the impression that during the first two months after birth, babies' behavior appears rather shut off from environmental stimulation. If not sleeping, feeding, or crying, young infants seem to spend most of their time slipping in and out of consciousness, dominated by physiological rather than psychological processes.

In the Freudian account, it is as if there is a barrier between young infants and their environment. To describe this initial state, Freud draws an analogy with the bird egg, which allows the young to develop "autistically," or in relative independence of any exchanges with the environment outside the shell, and which limits the mother's role to providing warmth.

Note that all of these theoretical propositions regarding the initial state of confusion, unrelatedness, undifferentiation, or fusion of the infant in regard to the environment are highly speculative; none of them (to my knowledge) are based on experimental data. They are essentially based on inferences from either casual observations of infants or, as in the case of Freud, the material provided by adult patients' reconstruction of their early childhood. But hard experimental data from recent infancy research literature suggests that infants from birth are not totally confused or autistic in their behavior. They actually show capabilities of perception and action that allow them to develop a sense of their own bodies as differentiated entities situated in and interacting with the environment (the ecological self).

My own research confirms that probably from birth infants have the core ability to differentiate between self- and nonself-stimulation. From this ability, infants can develop an early sense of self. Rather than being absolutely separate from their environment or confused about it, infants are attuned to it from the outset. This finding makes intuitive sense as well. For otherwise how could infants develop a sense of themselves?

Intermodal Perception and the Self

Aside from perceiving ourselves in mirrors and other reflecting surfaces, we gain perceptual awareness of our own bodies by listening to our heartbeat and our breath, feeling pain, listening to our own voice, and more importantly, moving around. The same is true for babies from birth. As Daniel Stern (1985) suggests, young infants perceive themselves primarily by experiencing fluctuations in their own bodies: stillness and movement, silence and self-produced noises, surging and fading feelings of satiety, comfort, joy, hunger, or pain. Infants experience their own vitality as perceivers and actors in the environment, and they do so on the basis of multimodal perceptions specifying their own bodies.

It has been suggested in former theories on infant development that intermodal perception was slow to emerge. Piaget (1952), for example, suggested that the sense modalities, in particular vision, audition, and touch, function as independent systems early in life. He postulated that only over time do these modalities get organized or coordinated to provide a unified perception of the world. This achievement occurs through reciprocal assimilation of the things perceived in each modality. According to Piaget, it is only when infants start to reach for visible objects at around four months of age that they begin to equate what they see with what they touch. Prior to the eye-hand coordination expressed in reaching, Piaget assumed that the touched and seen worlds of the infant are just juxtaposed and not yet unified. Similarly, he assumed that prior to the coordination of vision and audition in head-turning behavior toward a sound, the heard and seen worlds are not yet experienced by young infants as one organized whole.

If, as Piaget suggested, the initial perceptual world of infants is a juxtaposition of unrelated, disjointed impressions from the various sensory systems, then it would probably be right to talk about an initial blooming, buzzing confusion—and unreasonable to talk about self-perception by young infants. How could infants build any sense of their own bodies as differentiated from other objects in the environment if what they hear, touch, see, or feel is unrelated? There would be no way for them to pick up information that specifies themselves, in particular their own bodies, as differentiated entities. How could they tell that it is their own hand crossing their field of view, if the limb movement they experience, the air flow they feel on their hand, and the seen hand moving in front of them are not experienced as one unified perception?

The postulate of uncoordinated perceptual modalities at the onset of development led Piaget and other infancy students to interpret an initial state of fusion or undifferentiation between infants and their environment. But new data demonstrate that the bases for such interpretation are erroneous. In recent years, numerous infant studies have provided strong evidence that the perceived world of the infant is unified, not a mosaic of fleeting and unrelated sensations. From a very early age infants are shown to perceive a world that is common to all sensory systems. Even at birth, the various sensory systems are shown to work in concert, specifying for the infant a unified world across modalities. Things seen, touched, heard, or smelled are not perceived by young babies as disconnected and unrelated. A few published empirical examples support these claims. These examples demonstrate that infants manifest sensorimotor integration involving different sensory systems (for example, vision, touch, and audition) from birth, and that early on they are capable of relating perception across modalities (such as oral touch and vision).

The first example pertains to newborns' head orientation to sounds. For a long time, newborns were not thought to have the propensity to align their face toward a sound they had heard. Based on careful experiments using strict measures of head-turning behavior, however, many studies document that newborn infants do orient systematically toward a right or left sound source (see, for example, Clifton et al. 1981). Head-turning to sound is now among the standard items of newborns' neurobehavioral assessment, and infancy researchers use it to document auditory perception in early development (Clarkson and Clifton 1991). Head-turning does show that infants detect a particular sound produced by the experimenter. It also indicates that they detect its location in space, which proves a connection between what they hear and what they intuit about the location of their own bodies in space. To be more exact, infants are capable of proprioception—the act of perceiving based on information carried by receptors in contact with muscles and at the joints, which provide an on-line tracking of the variations in tensions and torque. Proprioception is the system by which you know where each of your limbs are in relation to the rest of your body and that informs you of your own bodily movements. If you close your eyes, pinch your nose, and shut your ears, you are still in proprioceptive contact with your own body. Because it is permanent and its experience cannot be public (you are the only one to experience your own body proprioceptively), it is the modality of the self par excellence. When you lose proprioception, you lose sense of yourself, as in anesthesia. The proprioception of our own body is so ingrained that adult and even child amputees commonly perceive phantom limbs. Based on proprioception we map the structure of our body, how its different parts relate to one another, and how it maps onto other information about the environment that has been conveyed by the other sense modalities.

Proprioception is a complex process that infants appear to manifest from birth. By systematically orienting toward sounds, infants show that bodily and auditory spaces are mapped and thus integrated rather than disjointed. Auditory and bodily movement information is coordinated onto a unified space. How would the matching head-turn behavior be possible otherwise?

One might argue that plants orient to the sun and that you would not account for such automatic orientation (tropism) in terms of intermodal integration and mapping as presented here. It is indeed appropriate to explain the behavior of such a simple organism in terms of a less complex mechanism. But infant head-turning behavior is shown not to be rigid and automatic like the tropism of plants. In one experiment, for example, researchers habituated newborns with a sound always coming from one side of their head. As predicted, infants turned their head toward the sound during the first few trials and eventually did not anymore. Instead, they started to respond to the sound by orienting their head systematically to the other side, as if they were either avoiding the sound or searching for a less boring stimulation on the other side (Weiss, Zelazo, and Swain 1988). Either way, infants were not merely responding automatically like a plant does. Rather, their head orientation was part of an active exploration by which infants from birth tend to align their nose, ears, and eyes toward novel events in the environment. By doing so, infants maximize their potential multimodal detection of events. This in turn entails an integration between proprioception, audition, and the other modalities.

Another example of early organized perception across modalities is the research demonstrating that infants as young as one month can transfer information from touch to vision. In a remarkable experiment (Meltzoff and Borton 1979), infants were introduced for ninety seconds to a non-nutritive pacifier inserted in their mouth for oral touch and exploration. For some infants the pacifier was shaped like a small sphere; for others it was shaped like a small sphere with knobs on it. So in one case the pacifier experienced by the infant was round and smooth, in another it was round but bumpy. Following the oral inspection period, the pacifier was removed and infants were presented with two slides projected on a screen side by side, each representing a two-dimensional sketch of either the smooth or bumpy pacifier. Recording visual fixations on either slide by the infant, researchers found that infants looked significantly longer at the visual equivalent of what they had experienced one or two minutes ago with their mouth only. Note that prior to the visual preference test, the babies did not have any visual experience with the pacifier. This remarkable finding has been confirmed with four-month-old infants, who matched a rigid or soft pacifier with an action demonstrating the compressed (squeezed) or rigid (rotated) qualities of a solid object presented on two films side by side. Again, infants looked longer at the visual event that matched the qualities of the pacifier they had experienced with their mouth only (Gibson and Walker 1984).

These demonstrations support the contention that infants perceive a unified world across modalities, tracking events in the environment and matching the input from various perceptual systems. I could add more examples, including some reports of neonatal imitation that suggest rudiments of cross-modal matching and intermodal calibration between vision and proprioception at birth (see Meltzoff and Moore 1997). It is well established that infants are proprioceptively engaged from birth and that intermodal perception is a fact of early infancy, not a psychological capacity that originates from the progressive coordination of action during the first months, as proposed for example by Piaget (1952).

In relation to the self in infancy, the evidence of intermodal perception from birth supports the idea that early on infants have the potential perceptual means or capacity to specify their own bodies as differentiated entities in the environment, not as elements of buzzing, blooming confusion undifferentiated from other objects. From a very young age, infants also maximize their capacity for intermodal perception in regard to their own bodies. They engage in long periods of playful self-exploration that entail the multimodal experience of bodily movements and self-produced actions. By engaging in self-exploration, infants pick up information that uniquely specifies their own body in action. This activity is a primary source of learning about the embodied self.

The Body as an Object of Exploration

Very early on, infants appear to pay particular attention to their own bodies. They have a propensity to repeat actions seemingly for the sake of repeating them. They will bring their hands to their mouths, throw their arms around, kick with their legs, and open and close their hands, often with no particular expressions of pain or crankiness, but for enjoyment. These are active yet peaceful moments that can last several minutes at a time. This is the state in which you might find infants who have awakened from a nap and are entertaining themselves by moving around as if they were checking themselves out, being simply content to dance on their own. These moments gain in importance rather abruptly at around the second month, when infants start to spend significantly more time in an alert and active state: with eyes open and moving around, yet demonstrating no particular signs of fussiness. By two to three months infants will bring their hands and feet into view for long periods of exploration and will start cooing, babbling, and making all kinds of repetitive sounds with their mouths. They might shake their heads vigorously from side to side, then stop suddenly and burst into a smile. They will repeat the sequence over and over again, like toddlers discovering dizziness by spinning until they fall to the ground with delight. Infants usually engage in this type of repetitive playful activity on their own, not with a partner or coach. It is private and linked to self-exploration.

The repetitive aspect of such actions led early developmental psychologist James Baldwin (1861–1934) to coin the term "circular reactions" to describe them. In his footsteps, Piaget (1952) accounted for three levels of repetitive actions displayed by infants, capturing their development from approximately one to fourteen months. In the beginning, such actions (primary circular reactions) are characterized by an orientation toward the body, as in the examples I used earlier. They eventually become more oriented toward objects (secondary circular reactions), and by the beginning of the second year, toward objects with intended goals in mind (tertiary circular reactions). At all levels, circular reactions are part of infants' exploration of their own bodies. Following Piaget's account, until the second month this exploration takes place within the limits of the body, but it eventually expands to include the exploration of how the infant can interact with the world of physical objects.

There is an inaccurate connotation of automaticity attached to the term circular reaction. "Circular action" is a more appropriate term to describe the repetitive self-exploratory activities that infants engage in early in life. "Circular" does capture the fact that these activities are self-reinforcing. But these systems are not closed or automatic. They are open to variations and to the discovery of new degrees of freedom within certain parameters, in particular the parameters of the body: its organization and its possibilities for action. More importantly, circular actions are a unique functional framework from which infants can pick up intermodal information specifying their own body as differentiated from other objects in the environment. The repetitive aspect of such actions provides an appropriate framework for infants to detect regularities in the intermodal perception of their own body, in particular the proprioception that guides all self-produced movements and the perfect orchestration of proprioception with visual, tactile, or auditory feedback.

Imagine a two-month-old infant lying in his crib, playfully waving and twisting his hands in front of him. He brings his hands from the side to join at midline, then stares at them while intertwining the fingers. After a minute or so, he suddenly moves the hands apart in a burst of excitement. After a few seconds, the sequence of action resumes. This is a typical behavior of young infants starting in the second month. What does it mean psychologically and in regard to the self in infancy? I would like to propose that these types of early body exploration determine the original core of self-knowledge. It is with this type of activity that infants specify themselves as differentiated agents in the environment, eventually developing an explicit awareness of themselves.

But what is the process by which they specify themselves? At the origins of development this process is perceptual; it does not yet involve any higher-order cognitive awareness. In our example, no one would assume that the infant is recognizing his own hands in an explicit way. It is yet far more rudimentary than self-recognition. He is working toward what we might call a perceptual awareness of his own body. This awareness rests on the perceptual discrimination of particular sensory experiences attached to self-produced body movements. It is based on the particular proprioceptive *and* visual experience of the hand crossing the visual field, as well as the particular proprioceptive, visual, *and* tactile experience of the hands joining and the fingers intertwining at midline.

Once again, infants gain such self-awareness by detecting commonalities among all means of perception. When the infant moves his hands, he feels them moving and at exactly the same time that he might see them moving in front of him or feel them touching one another. When infants coo and cry, in addition to hearing their own voice, they feel the air bursting out of their lungs toward the mouth, detect vibrations and tensions in their vocal tract, and experience a particular proprioception of facial and oral movements. This complex tactile and proprioceptive experience is coupled with a perfectly simultaneous self-produced auditory stimulation.

Self-produced action causes the infant to have overlapping experiences through his other senses. This is an important feature of what infants gain from engaging in self-exploration. This experience specifies the body as differentiated from other objects in the environment. When my hand crosses my visual field, for example, I perceive that it is my hand and not someone else's, because I see it and feel it proprioceptively moving at exactly the same time and by a commensurate amount.

The robust propensity of infants from birth, and even prenatally, to bring their hands in contact with the mouth and face comes also with a perceptual experience that specifies the body in a unique way. This experience, in addition to proprioception, entails a "double touch," a specific self experience. When an infant's hand touches her face or mouth, the tactile sensation goes both ways in reference to the own body: the hand feels the face while the face feels the hand. Again, this double touch experience uniquely specifies the own body as opposed to other objects in the environment.

In a recent study (Rochat and Hespos 1997), we tested newborn infants within twenty-four hours of birth to see whether they would manifest an ability to discriminate between double-touch stimulation specifying themselves, and external (one-way) tactile stimulation specifying non-self objects. For testing, we used the robust rooting response that all healthy infants have at birth: when the corner of the infant's mouth is touched, the infant turns her head and opens her mouth toward the stimulation. Following a simple procedure, we recorded the frequency of rooting in response to either external tactile stimulation (the experimenter stroking the infant's cheek) or tactile self-stimulation (infants' spontaneously bringing one of their hands in contact with the cheek). Newborns showed rooting responses almost three times more frequently in response to the external stimulus.

These observations suggest that even at birth, infants pick up the intermodal invariants (single touch or double touch combined with proprioception) that specify self- versus external stimulation. They seem to have an early sense of their own body, hence an early perceptually based sense of themselves.

The early sense of self developed by infants from birth does not only pertain to the physical body as a differentiated entity in the environment. It also pertains to how the physical body is animated— in other words, what characterizes the dynamic of its own *affectivity*. From birth, the body is indeed the locus and the medium of rich feelings and emotions that fluctuate among pleasure, boredom, excitement, contentment, or pain.

In general, the intermodal experience of the body is inseparable from feelings about its own vitality. Suppose that an infant explores his own hands by raising and moving them in front of his eyes. Suppose now that in a sudden burst of excitement, he claps them together. Aside from the intermodal perception of joint touch and proprioception, as well as the double-touch experience discussed earlier, the infant perceives the dynamic of his own vitality: from calm to being excited, then calm again. This dynamic is perceived both privately and publicly. It is privately experienced because the infant feels from within a state change, from being calm to being excited with specific waxing and waning of tensions. It is publicly experienced because the hands move in front of the infant's eyes. In a way, the movement of the hands is a choreography of what the infant feels from within. Self-exploratory activity thus provides infants with an opportunity to objectify the feelings of their own vitality via a perceived and self-produced action of the body.

By analogy, I like to think of music and what it means to be taken by it. Music grabs you when there is a resonance or match between the emotive intent of the externally created sound and your feelings. It is because of this relative correspondence that some music, more than others, inspires us to move and dance. Music can match and sometimes amplify or modulate the mood we feel from within. I think in particular of musicians who are so engrossed in playing that they start to behave in very contorted ways. The music they project to the outside reflects their own mood, mediated (instrumented) by the horn they blow or the drum they hit. Music is an auditory analog of the feelings perceived from the inside and choreographed by the musician in the act of playing.

A similar abandonment or emotional surrender in the experience of matching feelings to self-produced perceptual events is probably also at the origins of body-oriented actions in infancy. It probably accounts for the playful, spontaneous, systematic, and repetitive character of such actions. Otherwise why would young infants spend so much of their alert active time attending to their own body the way they do? I submit that it is for the same reasons that music is so important in our lives. Both allow the focal experience of fluctuating feelings and emotions.

Intermodal Calibration and Sense of the Body in Infancy

From early on, infants are sensitive to how the body is organized and the way each of its parts relates to one another. By at least three months, infants manifest an intermodal calibration of their own bodies. By calibration, I mean the sense of perfect contingency and invariant covariation across modalities that specifies the body as a dynamic entity with particular characteristics. This calibration is necessary not only to provide the perceptual foundations of self-knowledge, but also to equip the body to act on objects in the environment.

Some years ago, Daniel Stern (1985) reported some striking observations made with "Siamese," or physically conjoint, twins. These infants were congenitally attached on the ventral surface, facing one another. They shared no organs and were surgically separated at four months. Stern noticed that often they would suck one another's fingers. A week before separation, Stern and his colleagues conducted a series of tests to assess the extent to which these infants, despite their odd situation of forced binding, differentiated what was part of their own body from what belonged to the attached sibling. In one of the tests, they compared each infant's reactions to the gentle removal from their mouths of either their own fingers or the fingers of their sibling. They found that the twins responded differently in each case. Here is the phenomenon described by Stern:

> When twin A (Alice) was sucking on her *own* fingers, one of us placed one hand on her head and the other hand on the arm that she was sucking. We gently pulled the sucking arm away from her mouth and registered (in our own hands) whether her arm put up resistance to being moved from her mouth and/or whether her head strained forward to go after the retreating hand. In this situation, Alice's arm resisted the interruption of sucking, but she did not give evidence of straining forward with her head. The same procedure was followed when Alice was sucking on her sister Betty's fingers rather than her own. When Betty's hand was gently pulled from Alice's mouth, Alice's arms showed no resistance or movement, and Betty's arm showed no resistance, but Alice's head did strain forward. Thus, when her own hand was removed, the plan to maintain sucking was put into execution by the attempt to bring her arm back to the mouth, while when another person's hand was removed the plan to maintain sucking was put into execution with the movement of her head forward. Alice seemed, in this case, to have no confusion as to whose fingers belonged to whom and which motor plan would best reestablish sucking. (Stern 1985, pp. 78–79)

These observations corroborate our own observations with newborns that I briefly reported in the preceding section (Rochat and Hespos 1997). Remember that in our study, newborns had a different rooting response when their own hands touched their faces than when the finger of an experimenter did so. In these observations, infants show that they differentiate between two basic categories of perceptual information—one pertaining to their own bodies, the other to surrounding entities. As already mentioned, this information is intermodal and in most instances involves a proprioceptive component.

If young infants appear capable of perceiving their own bodies as differentiated entities, how exactly do they perceive their bodies? Stern's observations with the "Siamese" twins and ours with newborns are just accounts of a discrimination. They do not really explore what this discrimination entails in terms of infants' understanding of their own bodies. Beyond the account that from an early age infants perceive their own bodies as differentiated from other entities, what kind of awareness does it entail? Some of the collaborative research I performed in recent years demonstrates that infants from at least three months of age are aware of their own bodies as dynamic and complexly organized entities with particular featural characteristics.

To demonstrate that early on infants form expectations as to how their own bodies should look, we used a preferential looking procedure, another widely used experimental paradigm in infancy research. In this procedure, infants are presented with two visual displays (video screens in our case) placed side by side in front of them so they can look at either one. A camera is placed between the two displays, providing a close-up view of the infant's face. The recording of this view allows an exact measurement of the relative time that infants spend looking at each display. If infants look equally long at both displays, it suggests that they do not notice a difference between the two. If they do look longer at one of the two displays, they are thought to discriminate between them. Past research shows that, in general, if infants discriminate between displays, they tend to look longer at the display that is novel (Fantz 1964). When provided with a choice, infants tend to look preferentially at things that are novel compared to things that are familiar, probably out of curiosity. (Although there are studies showing exceptions to this rule, in general it is true and ties with the habituation/dishabituation phenomenon discussed in Chapter 1.)

In our experiments, we used the preferential looking technique to measure the response of three- to five-month-old infants to different views of their own bodies (Rochat and Morgan 1995). Facing two adjacent images on a large television screen, infants saw on each image their own bodies videotaped from the waist down (see examples illustrated in Figure 2.2). Both views were on-line, thus perfectly synchronous. When infants moved their legs, they saw them moving simultaneously on either screen. One of the views corresponded always to what we labeled an "Ego View" of the body. This was provided by one camera placed above and behind the infant. The Ego

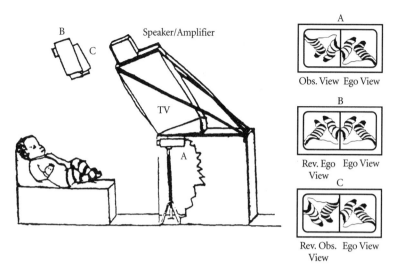

Figure 2.2 Diagram of the experimental set-up for the study of young infants'
self-exploration. Preferential looking and kicking patterns were recorded while
infants faced a large TV screen projecting two different online views of their own
legs, from various perspectives and with reconstructed spatial arrangements.
Three examples of such paired views are presented: (A) Observer View versus
Ego View, (B) Reversed Ego View versus Ego View; and (C) Reversed Observer
View versus Ego View (Rochat and Morgan 1995; Rochat 1998).

View was considered to be the familiar one, the view that infants
could experience on their own while engaging in proprioceptive visual and tactile self-exploration. This camera view corresponded to
what infants would have seen of their own legs if they looked down
at them from where they were seated. Note that this direct view was
prevented by sitting infants in a reclined seat, where they would look
up toward the TVs. At this age and in this reclined posture, infants
are not yet capable of straightening themselves up to get a direct
view of their legs. We put black-and-white striped stockings on the
baby's feet, and each time they moved their legs they caused scratch-
ing sounds that the babies simultaneously heard. The socks and auditory feedback were meant to make the visual displays interesting,
enticing infants to look at the television screens and to kick. The
more the babies moved, the more things happened on the displays
and the more interesting they were.

Within this experimental setup, we measured whether infants preferred to look at the Ego (familiar) View of their own legs over a novel view, in particular the view an observer might have when placed in front of the infant. The Observer's View originates from a nonself location and reverses the direction that the legs move in the display compared to the Ego View. Let me clarify this point. In the Ego View or looking from their own perspective directly at their legs, when the babies feel proprioceptively their legs moving to the right, they see simultaneously on the television screen their legs moving to the right of their visual field. There is a spatial congruence between proprioceptive and visual information. In contrast, if they look at their own legs from an observer's perspective, when they feel their legs moving to the right, they see their legs moving to the *left* of the visual field. This reversal creates a conflict between what is felt proprioceptively and normally seen of the own body moving. It thus violates the intermodal calibration that specifies the body from a self perspective. The question we raised in our research is whether young infants might already be sensitive to such differences. If they are, this would indicate that early on the infant forms a spatial map of his own body, expecting it to move in particular ways according to what he himself sees. This mapping of the body would be based on an intermodal calibration of bodily experience.

What we found confirmed this idea. In general, when infants were presented with an Ego View and an Observer's View of their own legs, they looked significantly more at the Observer's View. The Observer's View appeared more interesting, presumably because it is different than what infants normally experience when moving their legs around and looking at them directly. Interestingly, we also found that as infants looked at the Observer's View, they also generated more leg movements, as if they were more actively engaged in exploring the novel proprioceptive-visual relation provided by this view.

We performed many other experiments (Rochat 1998) that confirm these findings and also show that infants might be sensitive to the featural characteristics of their own legs and the way they move not only in relation to a global frame of reference (that is, left or

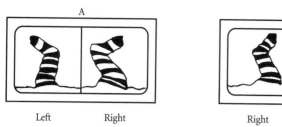
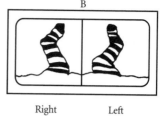

Left   Right   Right   Left

Figure 2.3 Composite and reconstructed online views of the legs presented to the infant in Morgan and Rochat (1997). One presentation (A) corresponded to a normal ego view. In another (B), the legs' location was switched, changing the way they are normally attached to the rest of the body. Infants from three months of age showed signs of differential looking between the normal and reversed composite views of their own legs.

right movements in relation to the outside environment), but also in relation to one another.

In one experiment (Morgan and Rochat 1997), we presented infants with a composite view of their own legs, with one camera filming the right leg and another filming the left. The two views were projected side by side on a TV screen in a way that reconstructed a normal Ego View. At one point in the experiment, we switched the position of the camera views so that the left leg appeared on the right of the screen and the right leg appeared on the left (see Figure 2.3). In this new view, both factors changed: the relative movement of one leg in relation to the other and the overall appearance or featural characteristics of the legs. In regard to relative movement, this new view changed the way that one leg moved in relation to the other. When for example one was felt by the infant as moving toward the other, it actually appeared on the screen as moving away from it. And in terms of featural characteristics, this new view changed the way that the legs were seemingly attached to the rest of the body. In particular, it reversed the bending of the knees from outward to inward.

We found that three- and five-month-old infants looked differentially at (hence discriminated between) the normal and reversed composite view of their own legs, when both relative movement directionality and featural characteristics (bending of the knees) were altered. In a subsequent experiment, we covered the infants' legs with bulky socks to hide changes in the bending of the knees between the normal and reversed composite views of the legs. In this condition, infants appeared to look equally at both views; they did not show any signs of discrimination. Based on this negative result and on the fact that infants did differentiate between the two views when featural characteristics were visible, we deduced that infants did pick up on these characteristics in the original experiment.

These findings help us to understand what infants perceive of their own bodies, beyond perceiving them as differentiated from other entities in the environment. In the experimental setup we used, infants were presented with different views of their own legs that were somehow "disembodied" as they were projected onto the TV screens, away and in front of the infant. There was no spatial coincidence between the proprioceptive and visual feedback experienced by the infant as she engaged in self-exploration. Despite the rather unusual context of this experimental setup, infants did reveal that they know something about their own bodies: they discriminate between what corresponds to their own bodily experience and what does not. In relation to our experiments, this discrimination is based on the intermodal calibration between proprioception and vision. But beyond that, it is based on specific expectations about what is familiar and what is novel in the appearance of the legs on the screens. From our observations, we can infer that infants expect their own legs to move and look certain ways. When they feel them moving in one direction, they expect to see them moving in the same direction. They perceive their own bodies in relation to an intermodal space. Furthermore, they expect the parts forming their own bodies to be organized and for their body parts to relate to one another in particular ways. When they feel one limb moving toward another, they expect to see it move not only in the same general direction, but also in the appropriate direction *relative* to the other limb. They refer their expectations to a perception of the body as an organized whole with particular featural characteristics, not a collection of disjointed parts.

Overall, these observations suggest that infants' awareness of their own bodies includes both their position in space and the relationship of one body part to another. But do infants recognize that they are seeing their own legs on TV? Certainly not in the same way that they will recognize themselves in front of a mirror in a few months' time. But there are some indications that infants might detect temporal information that is crucial for determining whether what they see in the mirror pertains to their own body or to someone else's. You have perhaps seen the classic comic skit where one actor dresses up exactly like another and faces him in front of a pretend mirror, mimicking every gesture the other makes. The imitator tricks his partner until his imitation lags too far behind the original and he gets caught. The perception of one's self moving in a reflecting display, whether it is a mirror or an on-line video display, depends on the perfect correspondence between proprioceptive and visual feedback. If the visual feedback is temporally off, it specifies someone else doing similar things.

Some researchers have shown that from around five months of age infants are sensitive to the temporal discrepancy between the on-line view of their own legs moving on a TV screen and the movements of another infant's legs moving on another TV screen (Bahrick and Watson 1985). In this study, both infants' legs were covered with the same socks, so both pairs looked very much the same. The only salient difference was that one pair (the infant's own legs) was perfectly synchronous with proprioception and the other pair (another infant's legs) was not. One specified the self; the other someone else. When confronted with both views, infants looked significantly more at the other child's legs—those that did not perfectly correspond with what they felt of their own. Thus they discriminated between the movements of the two pairs of legs and were attracted toward the one that specified the other person.

The results of this study do not show that five-month-olds "recognize" themselves—or what is not themselves—in either display; we know on the basis of the rouge task and other tests that this ability develops at a later stage. What can be said, though, is that by five months infants detect temporal information that specifies a nonself entity and are more engaged in attending to this information, probably because it offers more novelty. John Watson (1995), an infancy researcher (not the father of behaviorism), suggests that until approximately three months of age, infants are particularly attuned to the perfect contingency of intermodal feedback that specifies the self, and that beyond this age they appear to switch to a preference toward feedback that is not perfectly contingent. This would tie into the idea that by this age infants start to develop social interests, displacing an originally self-oriented attention toward others.

It is reasonable to think that infants need to calibrate their perceptions of their own bodies before they can start to pay attention to others. We have seen that the intermodal calibration of the body starts to be clearly observable by at least three months of age. This calibration provides infants with the necessary basis to start exploring how people relate to them. The prerequisite of social exploration is indeed the sense of self that young infants appear to develop in the intermodal exploration of their own bodies.

Self-Oriented Action: Orality

Oral goals and the propensity of young infants to stimulate their oral regions is an important, if not primary, organizing force of early development. It is probably also central to the origins of self-awareness, in particular an awareness of the body as a system with physical boundaries and specificities that can be differentiated from other objects in the environment.

In a series of studies I conducted in collaboration with Elliott Blass and other colleagues, we studied some possible determinants of newborns' propensity to bring their hands in contact with their mouths (Rochat, Blass, and Hoffmeyer 1988; Blass, Fillion, Rochat, Hoffmeyer et al. 1989). We established that a few hours after birth, neonates do not bring their hands to their mouths by accident: particular conditions control and predict this behavior. For example, after dispensing a drop of sweet solution (water with 15 percent sucrose) on their tongues with a syringe, newborns show a dramatic increase in hand transports to the mouth. In general, following the sucrose stimulation, infants seem calm and then transport relatively smoothly one or both hands to the mouth, with the fingers eventu-

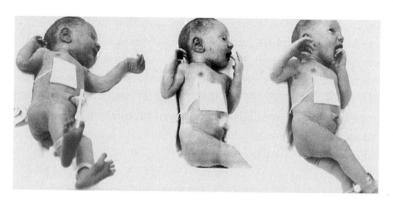

Figure 2.4 Hand-mouth coordination in a neonate. Immediately after birth, newborns capture their own hands for sucking and exploration. From left to right, here are three successive snapshots of such coordinated activity by a twenty-minute-old newborn. Note how the mouth opens in anticipation of contact with the hand. (Cleo, photos by P. Rochat)

ally pushed inside for sucking. Interestingly, if a pacifier is inserted in the baby's mouth immediately following sucrose stimulation, we found that the newborns are much less likely to follow through with a transport of the hand to the mouth. The insertion of the pacifier somehow cut short the activity, probably by fulfilling its goal.

It is interesting to note that previous developmental theories, in particular Piaget's, dismissed hand-mouth contact at birth as being organized and oriented. Rather, it was considered random and accidental in newborns and as the result of coordination between manual and oral activities only during the second month. We have now demonstrated that hand-mouth coordination is not only evident at birth, but also part of a complex system of actions that can be controlled by specific stimulation.

The goal-oriented nature of hand transport to the mouth by neonates is also proven by the fact that the mouth opens in anticipation of contact with the hand. We found many instances where one of the hands is lifted up and goes straight toward the mouth, without preliminary tactile stimulation of the face and the perioral region (see Figure 2.4). In such instances, the mouth of the infant is opened wide prior to contact, ready to receive the hand. Such observation demonstrates further that this behavior is neither accidental nor the product of a chain of simple stimulus-response links, but the expression of an organized action system oriented toward a functional goal. Infants may not be aware of this goal, but the action is organized around it. It seems, too, that this action system is engaged even prior to birth: fetuses have been observed sucking their thumbs and bringing their hands to their faces and mouths. It is not rare to see bruises on newborns' wrists or hands from their own sucking in the womb.

The problem of awareness in neonates is thorny; the idea that newborns have innate high-level motor or cognitive abilities is unsubstantiated. But it is important to stress that infants are born behaving in an organized way, not at random or under control of some haphazard electrical storms happening in their brain. They behave within the context of action systems (for example, hand transport to the mouth or sucking) regulated by particular functional goals (such as oral contact or food). This functional context constrains behavior at birth and provides infants with not only the means to ensure their survival, but also opportunities to learn about themselves and the world that surrounds them.

The mouth is highly sensitive and remarkably well equipped to function as a main point of access to the interior of the body and a main attractor, organizer, and terminal point of infant behavior. In comparison to the rest of the body surface, it has the highest concentration of tactile receptors. This fine orotactile reception, combined with the gustatory and olfactory systems that are also concentrated in the oral region, makes the mouth a powerful information-gathering tool for food selection, object exploration, and self-exploration. It is a privileged locus of learning in early infancy, and this learning goes far beyond sucking and food ingestion.

When I first started to study infants, I was interested in the oral-tactile activity of newborns. My aim was to document whether newborns showed any signs of using their mouths as an exploratory device; that is, for purposes other than sucking and food ingestion. I found that they engage not only in sucking activities but also in activities that are perceptual and exploratory (Figure 2.5). In these

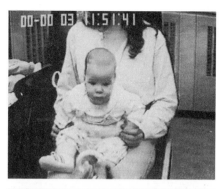

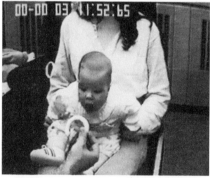

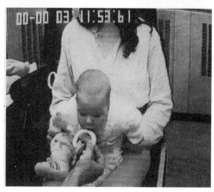

Figure 2.5 The mouth is a primary locus of object exploration. By the second month, infants actively use the mouth to inspect even inedible objects. Notice the three successive snapshots of a four-month-old infant who is leaning forward to capture an object with her mouth. Her mother was asked to hold both her hands down to her side, preventing the infant from using her hands to transport any graspable things to her mouth. The infant finds a new, creative way to fulfill her oral goal. (Photos by P. Rochat)

studies, I recorded newborns' oral activity in relation to different rubber pacifiers I put in their mouths for sucking (Rochat 1983). These pacifiers varied in shape, texture, and elasticity. I analyzed babies' oral activity by recording the pressure they applied on the pacifier with their lips, gums, and tongue. The pacifier was connected via tubing to an air pressure transducer that transformed air pressure variation in the pacifier's chamber into an electrical signal picked up by a polygraph for later analysis. In other words, I obtained a graphic analog of the pressure applied by the newborns to the pacifier.

What I found is that aside from typical sucking patterns, in which babies regularly start and stop sucking, infants also suck in random-like patterns that use nonrhythmical, disorganized movements of the tongue, lips, and jaw. Such nonrhythmical movements increase as a function of the eccentricity of the pacifier (when compared to the shape, texture, and elasticity of the biological nipple). This research shows that newborns use a different, nonfeeding pattern of oral response to learn about objects in their world.

So, aside from food, what do infants gain from their oral inquisitiveness? Freud ([1905] 1962), and in his footsteps Karl Abraham (1927), based much of their psychoanalytical view of human personality on oral eroticism and the original drive of young infants to stimulate the oral zone. For Freud, the mouth is the erotic zone that drives behavior at the onset of development, the primary locus of pleasure expression and hence of affective transactions between the infant and the outside world. Orality would be the original stage of personality development and oral stimulation a primary source of pleasure for the infant. I cannot dwell on the details of this theory, but what is important is that it reminds us that young infants' propensity for oral contacts needs to be considered first as pleasure oriented. Oral stimulation certainly seems to be a primary reinforcer of infant behavior. But beyond the erotic motivation and the pleasure associated with food, oral contacts provide infants with opportunities to learn about themselves.

We have seen that self-touch is accompanied by a unique intermodal perception that differentiates one's own body from other entities in the environment (that is, proprioception plus double touch). Aside from this information, which appears to be picked up by infants from birth, oral self-stimulation and the transport of hands to the mouth also help specify the oral cavity as an entry to the inside of the body. By moving their fingers in and out of their mouths, infants must get acquainted with the fact that there is an interior to their own bodies: that they have an inside as well as an outside, and that the inside is enveloping and wet, the outside open and dry with a different temperature and texture. As proposed by some psychoanalysts, the mouth is the cradle of perception (Spitz 1965). We might add that as the primary locus of self-oriented action, it is the cradle of self-perception.

Developing a Sense of What the Body Can Do

Do babies have a sense of their own power? This question seems far-fetched, but we will see that in light of some findings it is not. From birth, infants learn to control their environment: they figure out how to get food, attention, and comfort, and they cause interesting perceptual events to happen, such as seeing a mobile in motion, hearing mother's voice, or seeing mother's face appear on a screen.

Of course, infants do not start with explicit intentions to obtain and control resources in their environment. From birth, however, infants are capable of learning to make their own bodies instruments of cause and effect. They work hard at it and are actively engaged in exploring new links between what they do and what happens when they do it. In this engagement, infants learn something about themselves: self-efficacy and a sense of their own body effectivities.

The sense of being more or less linked to events happening in the environment is a predominant aspect of self-perception. As grown-ups, we perceive ourselves mainly in what we do and in the results of our own actions. We only spend so much time in front of a mirror or inspecting directly our own body parts. More than a static body image, we have a sense of our own agency in the world, what we are capable of achieving, what we have achieved or failed to achieve. We perceive ourselves as more or less in control of situations in the envi-

ronment that we have caused or to which we are subjected. I propose
that infants engage in a similar process but at an implicit level.

At a young age, infants certainly do not yet understand explicitly that they might be the cause of certain effects, but they probably have the means to develop a sense of their own efficacy in the
world: a sense of having the power to produce certain effects. Self-
efficacy is the sense of a link between one's own actions and some
consequences, not yet an understanding of causation (self-agency)
per se. It is probably perceived directly by young infants as they notice things happen nearby during or immediately after their action.
Again, intermodal perception is at the core of such a sense, and the
challenge for developmental psychologists is to try to figure out how
the explicit and rational sense of self-agency might emerge from an
implicit and perceptual sense of self-efficacy. I will deal more with
this question later, but first, how does self-efficacy develop originally
and what is the empirical evidence to support such an aspect of the
self in infancy?

In the 1960s, before the current wave of infancy research and
when behaviorism and learning theories were still dominant in the
field of psychology, some researchers naturally wondered when infants start to show behavioral plasticity and learning (Lipsitt 1979).
To address this question they devised clever experimental situations
that tapped into newborns' behavioral repertoire (Papousek 1992).
They tried to condition newborns, in the same way that Pavlov conditioned his dogs, by following a classical conditioning procedure:
a neutral stimulus is paired with an unconditioned response and
eventually becomes a conditioned stimulus triggering a conditioned
response. So for example, newborns were shown to learn to orient
their heads to the right or left following a particular auditory stimulation. The sound (neutral stimulus) was paired with a milk bottle
that touched the same corner of the infant's mouth, thereby normally triggering a rooting response (unconditioned response). After repeated exposures to such pairings, young infants turned their
heads in anticipation of contact with the bottle as soon as they heard
the sound. The sound started as neutral and became the conditioned

stimulus, and the head turn, initially unconditioned, became the conditioned response.

At the time, demonstration of classical conditioning by young infants was discussed in comparison to learning in nonhuman species and in relation to brain development, in particular to the development of cortical functions in infancy (Lipsitt 1979; Papousek 1992). If evidence of classical conditioning by young infants points to their behavioral plasticity and learning potential, it does not demonstrate that they are actively engaged in the learning process. In relation to the self, the infants do not have the opportunity to get acquainted with their own power in doing things in the environment. In the example above, infants are provided with the pairing between the sound and the bottle; they do not have to work at it. They can passively associate the neutral and unconditioned stimuli that are offered to them by the experimenter.

To investigate whether young infants might be actively engaged in learning, some researchers modified the classical conditioning setup. Infants were placed in a situation where the rewarding stimulation was triggered by their own responses, therefore reversing the stimulus-response sequence of classical conditioning to a response-stimulus situation, the so-called operant conditioning paradigm. In pioneer research infants were, for example, placed on a mat with their heads resting on a pressure-sensitive pillow that allowed the recording of head turns (Papousek 1992; Watson 1972). Each time the infants turned their heads, a mobile hanging above the crib was set in motion. By the age of three months, infants were shown to increase significantly the frequency of their head turns when reinforced by the activation of the mobile. This kind of observation indicated that young infants are capable of being actively involved in learning and are sensitive to the connection between what they do (head turn) and what is happening in the environment (motion of the mobile). In relation to the self, this attentional predisposition or innate curiosity allows them to start experiencing their own power in the world. This is an important process of infant psychology.

Researchers have used operant learning, sometimes combined

with habituation procedures, to study issues such as early memory and speech perception in infancy. Studies by Carolyn Rovee-Collier (1987) have captured the nature of procedural memory in infants as young as three months by using an operant procedure. In these studies, infants lie in a crib with an attractive mobile above them that they can set in motion by kicking one of their legs. One end of a ribbon is tied to one of the infant's ankle and the other end to the mobile. Infants quickly learn to activate the mobile by kicking. In various experiments, once infants had reached a learning criterion (a certain amount of kicks per minute), they were retested hours, days, or even weeks after the first training session.

In comparison to infants who did not participate in the experiment and who experienced the mobile moving independently of their own action, infants who where trained to operate the mobile relearned much faster in subsequent sessions. This means that they remembered what had happened to the mobile in this setting when they kicked. Aside from a memory of the mobile and of the game, it also means that they learned something about their own efficacy in the particular experimental situation.

To study infant learning ability and perceptual competencies at an even younger age, researchers have tapped into newborns' expertise: oral activity, including sucking. Typically, infants are given a pacifier for sucking. The pacifier is connected to an air-pressure transducer that captures variations of air pressure in the pacifier's chamber as babies suck or chew on it. The transducer transforms the captured air-pressure variation into analog electrical signals that can be read, recorded, and used by a computer. This computer, in turn, can feed back to the infant visual or auditory stimulation that corresponds to the infant's particular patterns of sucking. So, for example, infants will hear a certain sound every time they suck hard on the pacifier or suck at a certain predetermined rate. Or perhaps they will hear the sound only when they suck following a pause (no sucks) of a minimum duration.

Using this general procedure with different schedules of reinforcement, infancy researchers have been able to establish remarkable competence in very young infants. Neonates are shown to regulate their sucking on a pacifier to hear their mother's voice instead of that of a female stranger (DeCasper and Fifer 1980). When placed in a situation where sucking in one way (for example, having long pauses between bursts of sucking) is accompanied by the voice of the mother reading from a book, and sucking in another way (for example, pausing briefly between bursts in sucking activity) is accompanied by the voice of another female stranger reading from the same book, newborns tend to suck in the pattern required to hear their mother's voice. Familiarity with the mother's voice is understandable because the auditory system is well developed at birth and even during the last trimester of pregnancy.

Recently, using a similar paradigm but with contingent visual stimuli, researchers have shown that neonates will suck in certain ways to have their mother's face, rather than another female's, appear on a screen (Walton, Bower, and Bower 1992). Other, less recent experiments showed that two- to three-month-olds will suck in particular ways to maximize the brightness of a visual display, and even to bring a movie they see into focus (Siqueland and DeLucia 1969; Kalnins and Bruner 1973).

Much progress also has been made in studying the early development of speech sounds by adding habituation to this experimental strategy. Infants younger than six months are reported to learn quickly that sucks above a fixed amplitude threshold are rewarded by a certain sound. Typically, the sucking response rate of the infant increases during the first three minutes of reinforcement and then decreases as a sign of habituation. After a certain habituation criterion is reached, infants are presented with a novel sound as reinforcer. The increase in sucking rate following the auditory consequence change is used as an index of dishabituation and hence of discrimination between habituation and posthabituation sounds (Jusczyk 1985).

In recent research conducted in my lab, we tried to discover what young infants are actually attending to when placed in a situation where their sucking activity is accompanied by contingent sounds. In relation to the issue of the self, infants might show operant learning, or even perceptual discrimination and categorization as presented earlier, without any sense that they actually *cause* the event they hear or see. Accordingly, infants would simply learn by shaping the behavior (sucking in a certain way) associated with the most powerful of two reinforcements (for example, mother's voice, mother's face, or new speech sound). This learning would be based on behavioral shaping and simple associations; it would not require any sense of volition or self-efficacy on the part of the infant. Like rats pressing a lever to obtain food, this would be good old conditioning in disguise and nothing more.

In our research (Rochat and Striano 1999b), we rationalized that one way to show that infants are not merely conditioned by contingent reinforcing consequences would be to demonstrate that they are actively exploring the consequences of their own actions, in particular the way their own actions are linked to particular consequences. The basic idea was that evidence of such exploration would index a sense of self-efficacy. To test this idea, we imagined a situation where infants heard different sounds that were perfectly synchronous with their own sucking on a pacifier (Figure 2.6). It is important to stress that in all of our experimental conditions, infants were always provided with a contingent auditory event that coincided with pressure above a low threshold. So in terms of timing, infants were reinforced just as they were in the earlier example. What we changed was what they heard.

In one condition, each time the infants sucked, they heard a trill of discrete sounds with a random pitch or frequency from low to high. The trill lasted for two seconds, then stopped; it resumed with the next suck above threshold. We called this condition "random." In another condition, each time the infants sucked, they heard a continuous sound that varied in frequency (pitch) from low to high in a way that was commensurate to the low and high pressure applied by the infant on the pacifier while sucking. This we called the "analog" condition because the sound was an analog or mimicked the pressure recorded on the pacifier.

We wanted to find out whether infants would suck differentially in the "random" condition than in the "analog." Both of these condi-

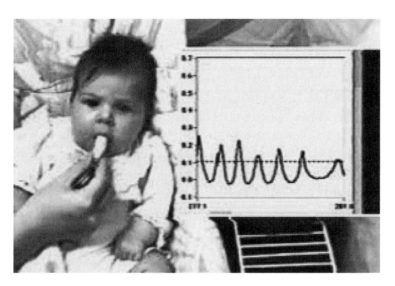

Figure 2.6 Infants from birth can learn to cause particular auditory or visual events by sucking on a dummy pacifier. Here, a two-month-old infant engaged in sucking and listening to contingent sounds. The right side of the figure shows the online computer recording of pressure variations applied on the pacifier by the infant. The horizontal, broken line represents the pressure threshold above which the infant heard a contingent sound (Rochat and Striano 1999b).

tions were equally contingent (one suck caused one simultaneous sound). But one condition also provided infants with an auditory analog of their actual proprioceptive *effort* in sucking. Again, the idea was that if infants sucked differently in each case, this would strongly suggest that they have a sense of their own power and self-efficacy, and do not simply associate any sucking activity with any perfectly contingent auditory events.

We tested first a group of two-month-old infants and found that indeed they responded differently in the random condition versus the analog. In the analog condition, infants appeared significantly more subdued in their oral response, generating more frequent pressures on the pacifier that were just at the threshold of sound production. In this analog condition, infants did appear to explore more their own abilities to produce particular auditory consequences that reflected their own proprioception. Overall, infants showed signs of greater attunement to the link between what they did and what they heard in the analog condition compared to the random.

Interestingly, we tried to replicate these findings with newborns but could not. Newborns sucked equally in both conditions, providing no behavioral signs of a sense of self-efficacy or ability to initiate explorations. The mere conditioning interpretation appears to hold for neonates. In my view, the reason for this is that an important transition occurs at around two months, and that deliberate, systematic self-exploration emerges at around this age and not before. I will return to this interpretation in Chapter 5, particularly when discussing what appears to be a "two-month revolution" in infant development.

Some researchers have collected intriguing observations of two-month-old infants. They strongly suggest that by this age, infants pay particular attention to the effect of their actions on the environment: they seem to develop expectations about what will happen and are happy to fulfill these expectations and discover new outcomes. These observations are based on the analysis of facial expressions during operant learning. In one study (Lewis, Sullivan, and Brooks-Gunn 1985) a cord was tied to a music box and attached to one of the infant's wrists. Each time the infant pulled on the cord, it triggered interesting sounds and sights from the music box. Compared to a baseline period when the cord was not attached to the box, infants learned within minutes to trigger the music box with the appropriate arm action. The frequency of arm pulls increased markedly, and infants showed their pleasure by smiling.

Even more intriguing was what happened during a second baseline period, called the extinction period, which immediately followed the learning phase. During this period, the cord was disconnected, so that arm pulls had no effect on the music box. During the extinction period, infants continued to pull the cord at even a higher rate in an apparent attempt to activate the music box. In addition, they expressed frustration in their lack of success by displaying a marked reduction in smiling and a significant increase in expressions of *anger*. It is hard to imagine a better demonstration that infants have a sense of their own power. While learning to act and to cause interesting consequences, infants build expectations regarding their own effectivity in the environment. They show pleasure when they are successful and frustration when they are not. The transition from smiling during the learning phase to the expression of anger during the extinction phase indexes the infant's sense of self-efficacy and the anticipation of particular consequences of self-produced action.

It is important to note, however, that some alternative, "leaner" (simpler) explanations of the reported phenomenon are feasible. Let me point to one as an illustration of how researchers debate issues and usually come up with accounts that are presumably less removed from the data and hence less speculative of infant behavior. It is possible that the reduction of smiling and increase in expressions of anger during the extinction phase are simply due to a change in infants' arousal. During the learning phase, infants have the opportunity to hear the music box and therefore get aroused by it and smile. During the extinction phase, they do not get aroused; therefore they smile less and show more distress (anger). In other words, what would be mainly expressed during the extinction phase is not frustration, but boredom mediated by a change in the general arousal state. This alternative interpretation calls for less volition in the infant. Whether this leaner interpretation is closer to the truth awaits future research that will be the same experimental paradigm but control for the general arousal state.

Beyond two months, infants develop new action systems allowing further experience of their own power and efficacy. As infants develop postural control such as independent sitting or locomoting, they discover new body effectivities and adjust the perception of themselves as agents in the environment (Rochat 1997). This development eventually culminates with the use of objects as tools to expand their effectivity. At this point in development, infants will demonstrate new capacities to coordinate means and ends via planning and show a more explicit understanding of their own causation

(Piaget 1952; Frye 1991). We will see in Chapter 5 that this happens at around nine months of age, close to the end of infancy if we consider its upper limit as the onset of independent locomotion.

Prior to locomotion, however, infants often express intended actions and a sense of their own body effectivities. They start to reach systematically for objects at around four months of age, with the hands eventually taking over the mouth as the dominant zone of tactile contacts (Rochat and Senders 1991). By four months, infants have become compulsive in attempting to reach and grasp objects in order to bring them to the mouth. The mouth remains a favorite terminal point of contact, even if the eyes and hands start to be well coordinated. In general, by around six months infants become mainly interested in exploring objects with the hands—banging the objects, fingering them, and transferring them from hand to hand. A lot of manual skill development occurs between two and six months (Rochat 1989). As manual skills develop, infants also develop a new sense of their own effectivity in the environment. They appear to plan actions depending on what they feel they can or cannot do, developing a sense of the limits of their own capability for action. This planning reveals a sense of their own power and efficacy (Field 1976; Rochat, Goubet, and Senders 1999).

I will present one more piece of empirical evidence in support of this contention. We tested infants ages five to six months who were proficient reachers but more or less capable of independent sitting. When infants start to reach, they typically cannot yet sit on their own without any external body support. If poorly supported and intending to reach, they are at great risk of losing balance and missing their target, if not hurting themselves by falling. So, for infants, there is often a trade-off involved in reaching for a distant object: to reach and fall, or not to reach and not fall, especially if the infant is not well supported. This trade-off issue is a very important aspect of infant psychology that we understand by providing cushions, seats, and other physical supports.

With postural development, infants increase their degrees of behavioral freedom, therefore changing their body effectivities. So for example, when infants start to sit on their own, the balance control they gain also means that they can now reach for objects farther away by coordinating arm and forward trunk movements without losing balance. We performed some experiments demonstrating that six-month-old infants, when they start to become proficient reachers, do perceive the limit of their own body effectivities. In one experiment, we placed infants that were either able or yet unable to sit on their own in an upright infant seat and analyzed their reaching for an attractive object placed at various distances in front of them (Rochat, Goubet, and Senders 1999). The nearest distance placed the object about thirty centimeters from the infant's torso, in alignment with the toes. The other three distances expanded from this referential distance by five inches. At distances 1 and 2, the object was within reach of the infant. At distance 3, it was at the limit of prehensile space: the infant could eventually touch it, but only by stretching the trunk and upper limbs forward. The question guiding the research was whether or not infants would attempt to reach for the object when placed at the farthest distances, depending on their relative sitting ability. For each thirty-second presentation of the object at a particular distance, we measured the frequency and duration of infants' gazing at the object, as well as their propensity and latency to reach. We found that infants who were not yet able to sit on their own, and hence did not have the same degrees of behavioral freedom, showed significantly fewer attempts to reach for the object at the farthest two distances, compared to the group of infants who could sit independently.

In another study (Rochat, Goubet, and Senders 1999), we attached either light (2g), or heavy (200g) bracelets to the wrists of young reachers between five and six months of age. The idea was that reaching with heavy bracelets would limit how far forward the baby could lean without losing balance. If infants were sensitive to this constraint, they should try fewer times to reach far while wearing the heavy bracelets. Note that these bracelets did not bother the infants and did not prevent them from moving their arms. Results show that infants were more likely to attempt to reach for the faraway object when wearing the light compared to the heavy bracelets. These results suggest that infants use visual and proprioceptive information to adjust their attempts to reach for a distal object based on perceived body effectivities, even if these effectivities are changed temporarily.

As for any other self-generated and goal-oriented actions, the planning of early reaching behavior is based on the perception of body effectivities. This perception integrates the infants' sense of their own body's capacity for action and their particular situation in the environment. The argument proposed here is that this perceptual ability is a primary aspect of the sense of self in infancy. It corresponds to the sense of the ecological self (Neisser 1991; Neisser 1995; Rochat 1997), which is an emergent property of any biological system that does not merely respond to stimuli but acts, explores, and invents new means to achieve functional goals. In humans, this ability is expressed at, and develops from, birth. But at least in our species, the development of self-knowledge implies much more than the progressive discovery of body effectivities. Infants do not appear, for example, to recognize themselves in a mirror or identify themselves in a picture until the very end of infancy or beyond.

The challenging developmental question is how infants eventually develop an awareness of themselves as recognizable entities from the early intermodal sense of the body and self-efficacy presented so far. This question pertains to the origins of an ability to perceive oneself not only as a differentiated entity that perceives and acts, but also as an object of reflection and recognition (the conceptual self). How does the idea and specification of "Me" as a concept emerge in development, and what are the mechanisms underlying such an *objectification* of the self?

As a species, humans, and maybe some of our very close relatives, are the only ones that appear to make this developmental leap. I will discuss next what might prepare and announce such leap, with the idea that self-recognition has its roots in infancy—it does not miraculously emerge by eighteen to twenty-four months (Kagan 1984; Lewis 1992; Lewis and Brooks-Gunn 1979).

Origins of Self-Recognition

If early on babies develop a sense of their own bodies as organized entities differentiated from other objects in the environment, when do they actually recognize themselves and how? To address this question, it is necessary to distinguish among levels of self-awareness that can be accounted for at various stages of development: from the early implicit sense of the body in the young infant discussed so far, to an explicit identification of the self that appears to be unambiguously evident only well into the second year. The next step, of course, is to try to account for what makes this development possible.

Recently, some empirical observations have been reported suggesting that infants as young as three months can discriminate somewhat between seeing themselves on a TV screen or seeing another infant of the same age and gender (Bahrick, Moss, and Fadil 1996; for similar findings with five- and eight-month-old infants see Legerstee, Anderson, and Schaffer 1998). In general, infants spend more time looking at the other child. Does that mean that they recognize themselves on the TV? Certainly not. It might simply mean that they are familiar with their own feature (facial) characteristics based on previous mirror experiences and that the feature characteristics of the other child are newer and therefore more interesting. There is no direct evidence that the three-month-old infant "knows" it is himself on the other TV screen.

Young infants placed in front of mirrors spend a lot of time exploring their reflections, staring at themselves in the eyes and moving their limbs often with smiles and cooing. They are attracted by their specular image, but this does not mean that they recognize themselves in it. They use the opportunity offered by the mirror to experience and explore the perfect and coincident contingency between proprioception and vision. This opportunity is unique and particularly attractive to infants because it offers the visual-proprioceptive experience of larger portions of the body than the infant can see directly. As adults, we also use this affordance of mirrors to work on our appearance, except that the behavior of fixing hair and applying makeup is an explicit expression that we know it is us in the mirror. Clearly, the behavior of young infants in front of mirrors does not imply the same level of awareness shown by adults applying lipstick—or by toddlers showing embarrassment and touching their faces when they discover rouge on their noses. So how do infants develop the ability to recognize and eventually identify themselves in mirrors?

First I would like to point out that, although the mirror test may tell us something about self-recognition, it might not be the best way to assess the earliest emergence of self-objectification and recognition in development. Mirrors are unusual objects in the environment and carry with them the experience of a fundamental paradox, which I call the "self-other paradox." As mentioned earlier, when you look at your own reflection in a mirror, you perceive aspects of your body that you cannot experience directly, in particular a full view of your face. In the introductory chapter, I alluded to the importance of eye contact in social exchanges, especially those between human mothers and infants. The view of a full face with eyes gazing toward you specifies what we normally experience with others, not the self. Therefore, self-recognition in a mirror requires that you suspend this normal social experience of others facing you with eye contact. In short, mirror reflection of the own body is paradoxical in the sense that it is you in the normal appearance or disguise of another person: it is you but not you. It is you because there is perfect contingency and temporal coincidence of visual-proprioceptive information. But at the same time, it is not you because you appear like other people normally appear to you, not the way you experience yourself situated in your body. To some extent, inspecting oneself in the mirror and recognizing that it is "Me" is an out-of-body experience. What mirror self-recognition and other video and picture tasks measure is the ability of individuals to suspend what they normally experience of themselves, to step back and literally reflect on the new, out-of-body aspects such experiences reveal. Mirror images are indeed physical reflections of the body on a polished surface that call for mental reflection to be literally recognized.

In this respect, it is particularly telling to read observations by anthropologists who introduce reflecting devices to adults who had presumably never experienced their own mirror reflections. Edmund Carpenter (1975) introduced mirrors to members of the Biami tribe, an isolated group living in the Papuan plateau where neither slate or metallic surfaces exist, and where rivers are murky and so do not provide clear reflections. Here is what Carpenter reports regarding the initial reaction of adults who were confronted for the first time with a large mirror reflection of themselves: "They were paralyzed: after their first startled response—covering their mouths and ducking their heads—they stood transfixed, staring at their images, only their stomach muscles betraying great tension. Like Narcissus, they were left numb, totally fascinated by their own reflections: indeed, the myth of Narcissus may refer to this phenomenon" (Carpenter 1975, pp. 452–453). I would say that Narcissus, aside from falling in love with himself, probably was fascinated with the existential experience of the "self-other" paradox that reflecting surfaces offer.

Despite the intrinsic paradox attached to mirrors, the mirror self-recognition test remains a valid instrument to assess self-knowledge at the level of recognition. It is particularly valid to assess children's ability to *objectify* themselves and eventually get over the "self-other" paradox. Two questions about this ability are of interest from a developmental perspective. The first is when do infants start to become contemplative in the exploration of themselves, so that they are not merely experiencing their embodied self via direct perception and action? The second is what might be the process enabling infants to adopt a contemplative, reflective stance when exploring themselves? These are the "how" and "why" questions regarding the origins of self-recognition. These questions are still wide open for speculation. Nevertheless, in light of the empirical facts I have reviewed so far, some interpretative suggestions can be made.

Infants appear to be born with an ability to pick up perceptual information that specifies themselves as differentiated from other entities in the environment. The development of self-knowledge does not start from an initial state of confusion. Infants are born with the perceptual means to discriminate themselves from other objects, and we have seen that they appear to use these means to sense themselves as differentiated, situated, and effective in their environment (the ecological self).

The sense of the ecological self is determined by direct perception and action, not reflection. What characterizes infants' self-exploration when they watch themselves kicking in front of a TV is the direct experience of visual-proprioceptive correspondences, not the reflection that it might be themselves live on the screen. If they prefer to look at a view displaying the legs of another baby, it is because the visual perception of these legs does not correspond to the proprioceptive perception of their own legs moving, not because they recognize that it is another child kicking. For them to recognize that it is their own legs or, on the contrary, that they are the legs of someone else, would take an additional reflective step, namely the step toward an objectification of the self.

As for mirror self-recognition, to objectify themselves infants need somehow to combine their direct perception of the embodied and situated self in the environment with the contemplation of a disembodied representation of the self (the "Me" reflected in the mirror). Again, one is experienced directly and the other indirectly as the product of a mental reflection. But do children have to grow into toddlers to manifest such a combination of perception and representation? The mirror recognition test tells us yes, with the caveat discussed earlier regarding the paradox of mirrors.

It appears that already by two months, infants start to manifest rudiments of a contemplative stance about themselves, in addition to the direct intermodal experiences specifying their own body. They start to attend and to explore with greater discrimination the consequences of their own actions. They suck differentially when a contingent auditory feedback is congruent or noncongruent with their proprioceptive effort. They seem pleased when they are able to successfully cause particular effects, such as setting off a music box by pulling a cord, and discouraged or angry when they are suddenly unsuccessful at it.

By the second month, if infants have become inquisitive and

playful with others as indexed by the emergence of smiling and eye contact (see Chapters 4 and 5), they also become playful in relation to themselves. They start to spend a lot of time entertaining themselves and exploring their own bodies by repeating visually supervised actions either on themselves or on objects. They grab hands and feet and bring them in view for long sessions of inspection. They seize any opportunity to reproduce actions that are accompanied by interesting consequences. In addition to perceiving and acting in the context of highly organized action systems (for example, sucking, rooting, tracking), two-month-olds contemplate their own effectivity as a dynamic system that can be linked to perceived events: the auditory event of self-activating the vocal system, the proprioceptive-visual events of moving a hand in the visual field or kicking a mobile. Infants repeat these new actions often and for the apparent sake of exploring both how it feels to do them and how they are linked to other perceptual consequences.

This process marks the first step toward an objectification of the self beyond direct perception and action of the body. Infants need to break away from the direct perception of the embodied self in order to represent themselves to themselves. This does not mean that the sense of the embodied ecological self specified by intermodal perception is replaced by a conceptual self. Rather, the sense of the ecological self, which is implicit and bears no traces of conscious or intentional processes, is complemented with a new stance on self-perception that allows for explicit representation, as evidenced by mirror self-recognition.

One important development, as yet largely unspecified, occurs from the time that infants seem to show the first signs of breaking away from the direct perception of the embodied self and developing explicit self-recognition. The original process that might trigger this development is the propensity of two-month-olds to pay particular attention to the result of their own playful and repetitive actions. With such attention, they start to systematically reproduce certain effects and potentially discover their selves (that is, their own bodies) as dynamic systems with the means to achieve goals. In this process, infants are awakened to a new sense of themselves as *inten-*

tional or planful, in parallel to the direct sense of the embodied self (ecological self) that they manifest from birth. What I mean by intentional (a semantically loaded term) is a sense of themselves as planning entities that can anticipate future events and relate to past ones. It is a sense of self that, in contrast to the embodied ecological self, is not linked to the immediacy (the "here and now" aspect) of direct perception and action.

Two-month-olds who systematically change their sucking activity in order to explore contingent auditory consequences are actually probing the relation between their own proprioceptive effort and what they hear. Unlike newborns, two-month-olds become explorers of themselves as agents of certain consequences. This newly emerging self-exploration heralds the onset of the contemplative stance mentioned earlier. In addition, the fact that infants are inclined to repeat their own actions is probably an important determinant of this contemplative stance. Of all perceptual events, self-produced actions are the most frequent and reliable. They afford the experience of self-control as well as the perceptual analysis of self-produced causation. The exploration of self-produced actions and its perceptual consequences entails repetition, namely the attempt to reproduce an action, or pattern of actions, that led to a particular event (for example, sucking in a particular way to hear a particular sound). In exploring their own action via repetition, infants are somehow imitating themselves. My view is that *self-imitation* is probably an important aspect of the process by which infants break away from the direct and immediate experience of the embodied or ecological self. In a sense, self-imitation could be similar to the mantras that people practicing meditation repeat over and over to themselves, claiming to achieve out-of-body experiences of the self.

The basic idea here, which by the way remains speculative and needs further empirical support, is that infants gain knowledge of themselves as agents and intentional entities in the environment by engaging in repeated actions. In this process, they have the opportunity to detect variations and relative matching between successive self-produced intermodal events. It enables them to start relating past, present, and future physical events that are controlled by their own bodies. In the meantime, this process would specify the infants' self as an entity that relates not only to the immediate perception of the body, but also to the planning of actions (the intentional self).

It is tempting to draw an analogy between the changes observed in young infants' behavior and what seems to have happened at the scale of human evolution. In comparison to other primate species, humans have evolved cultures that seem to rest on the growing ability to reflect about the past, project into the future, and engage in symbolic functioning. A case in point is the fascinating account of human evolution provided by Melvin Donald (1991). Donald equates the origins of modern humans to a transition from episodic to mimetic cultures, or the transition from lives that are bounded to the immediacy of experience to lives that are lived not only in the present but also in the simulation or representation of this experience. This is the same kind of psychological development observed in young infants.

"Mimetic" is derived from "mimesis," which means the intentional reenactment or imitation of perceived or imaginary events. In Donald's evolutionary account, the capacity for mimesis is a characteristic unique to the modern human mind; it is not found in other ape species. If mimesis distinguishes humans from other primates, this species-specific process seems to be at work early on in human ontogeny. To quote Donald: "Human children routinely re-enact the events of the day and imitate the actions of their parents and siblings. They do this very often without any apparent reason other than to reflect on their representation of the event. This element is largely absent from the behavior of apes" (Donald 1991, p. 172).

I speculate that in ontogeny, mimesis emerges by two months. From this point in development, and based on the emerging capacity to contemplate and simulate their own actions via repetition, infants develop the decoupling ability necessary for mirror self-recognition and self-concept in general. Questions remain, however, as to why infants would start to take the contemplative stance at two months but not earlier. We can assume that the perceptual analysis accompanying self-imitation is probably an emergent cognitive property of multiple developing systems, including brain maturation (that is, increasing cortical involvement), as well as postural, motor, and social development.

Are There Different Kinds of Self in Infancy?

As with all complex issues, it is difficult to conceptualize self-knowledge without breaking down the concept into more manageable parts. In his classic account, William James distinguishes two basic kinds of self, the "I" and the "Me." The "I" corresponds to the self as experimenter of the body and in the environment. It is the existential and situated self. The "Me" corresponds to the identified or conceptual self. This distinction underscores the difference between the self that is identified, recalled, and recognized and the self that is merely experienced at a physical level in transactions with the environment. In relation to the "Me," James categorizes it further into the "material self," the "social self," and the "spiritual self." If such categorization is relevant to account for self-knowledge in grownups, is it also in relation to the self in infancy, prior to unambiguous evidence of self-recognition (namely the notion of "Me" or conceptual self)?

Ulric Neisser (1991) proposes that babies start to know themselves within the context of two basic domains: physical and social. Each provides a particular form of perceptual information that makes self-knowledge possible. In the physical domain, infants gain knowledge about themselves in the exploration of their own body and objects in the environment. In the social domain, infants gain self-knowledge in their transactions with people. According to Neisser, within each of these domains, infants develop from birth two kinds of self-knowledge, the ecological (physical) and the interpersonal (social).

In the preceding sections, I focused mainly on the body as an object of exploration, calibration, and recognition and did not mention much regarding the self-awareness that infants might gain from interacting with others. The reason is that I view infants' awareness about their own bodies as primordial to any kind of developing "selves." The self is indeed primarily "embodied," and it is the embodiment of the self that infants experience and explore first. It is true that physical and social exchanges carry different types of perceptual information, and both contribute to the development of self-knowledge in infancy and to the formation of different contexts of development. But the self is first experienced via the invariance of the body, in particular the organization of its intermodal experience, whether it is revealed by self-exploration, interaction with objects, or social exchanges with people.

What needs to be categorized in relation to self-knowledge in infancy are the different contexts of development and the different levels of self-awareness emerging across these contexts, not different kinds of self. Categorizing different kinds of self in infancy gives the false idea that infants' awareness of themselves is multifaceted and disparate. There is no empirical evidence for such a suggestion. Even if older children and adults possess multifaceted representations of themselves, infants should not be assessed at that level. Rather than compartmentalized, the self in infancy is primarily unified. The physical and social contexts in which infants develop provide them with different opportunities to learn. In these contexts, they gather different information about the perceived self: the embodied self that touches, smiles, reciprocates, and is entertained by acting in the environment.

Even very young infants experience the waxing and waning of pain, hunger, and intense joy, as well as success, failure, reward, and frustration as they become effective in planning and anticipating the consequences of their own actions. All of these experiences have a primary locus: the body, which provides action and feelings (the perception of affects) as well as emotions (the communication of these feelings).

When children start to represent themselves at a conceptual level by self-identifying and referring to the self through language and in social interactions, they reach new levels of self-knowledge. They become not only an object of thought to themselves but also, and essentially, an object of thoughts in reference to others, as proposed eloquently years ago by George Herbert Mead (1934). Such new levels of self-knowledge are typically indexed by the emergence in the second year of "secondary" or self-conscious emotions, such as embarrassment and shame (Kagan 1984; Lewis 1992). Beyond infancy, children begin to construe and contemplate themselves in reference to the perspective of others. This leads to different kinds of self-knowledge, and the self then needs to be considered as multifaceted and hence in essence of different kinds (Kagan 1998a).

But prior to language, the symbolic gateway that marks the end of infancy, the role of others in determining self-awareness is not as clear. We will see in Chapter 4 that prior to two months, infants are very limited in their repertoire of social responses and their social interactions lack reciprocity. By nine months infants start to demonstrate a marked change in their awareness of others: for example, they start to manifest anxiety when meeting strangers or they show a new inclination to include others in their exploration of physical objects.

Prior to the end of the first year, infants, although highly perceptive and responsive to others, spend a great deal of time entertaining themselves, exploring their own bodies, and acting on physical objects. Within this context, infants develop first a sense of their own body as a differentiated entity in the environment, one endowed with vitality, affects, and effectivities. In my opinion, infants do not develop different kinds of self per se, but rather two basic levels of self-awareness: the direct sense of the embodied self and the sense of an intentional self. The sense of the embodied self develops from birth, and probably even in the womb. The intentional self complements the embodied self around the second month. Both continue to develop in infancy within the specific perceptual contexts and knowledge domains that characterize transactions with physical objects and what is certainly the most obvious determinant of self-awareness: people.

The Self and Others

People are undoubtedly the main source of feedback by which we objectify ourselves. This is evident from the outset. Children's first words are usually oriented toward attracting the attention of others to themselves as well as to objects. Very early on, children objectify themselves in others, searching for social approval and learning about themselves as differentiated, unique entities.

Children and adults alike use people as mirrors to reveal who they are. Much of how we perceive ourselves is indeed measured against how we think others perceive us. Self-perception is inseparable from our perception of others as onlookers of us. This is what being "self-conscious" means, and it is close to impossible to escape the so-called audience effect. When children keep calling parents to watch them do what the children view as challenging feats, such as jumping off a diving board or riding a bicycle with no training wheels, aside from attempting to impress an audience, they are seeking confirmation of who they think they are: courageous, outrageous, funny, or smart. The perception of themselves becomes essentially social. They project and recognize themselves in others. In this process, there is coperception and cocognition, with self and social knowledge being inseparable.

But what about infants? Is there evidence that infants coperceive themselves and others? We will see in Chapter 4 that some researchers propose that infants, from an early age and even from birth, might identify themselves with others when imitating the facial gesture of an adult (such as when the adult repeatedly sticks out her tongue or makes a sad face). Yet although newborns are shown to imitate, it would be a big theoretical leap to assume that neonatal imitation demonstrates an identification with others (sometimes called the "like me stance"). What is certain, however, is that from the infant's birth, caregivers focus on nurturing social interactions and making the baby feel in tune with his world. This attunement is probably a source of coperception.

The most common way that parents interact with their young babies is by reciprocating and *mirroring* their emotions (Gergely and Watson 1996; 1999). Parents often imitate their young infant in face-to-face interactions. In this process the emotions displayed by infants are fed back to them, amplified and clearly demarcated with exaggerated gestures and intonations. This emotional mirroring is certainly a source of self-knowledge for infants because it gives them a way of seeing and objectifying their own affects: what they feel from within is projected to the outside (externalized) and then reflected back to them by the social partner. In this process, infants are exposed to an explicit, analyzable form of what they feel privately.

As adults, we are compelled to empathize with babies. When for example they start to show signs of distress and begin to cry, we typically comfort them by moving close, stroking their backs, while adopting a sad voice with furrowed eyebrows and a frown. In doing so, we actually provide infants with an emotional *simulation* of what they are supposed to feel, a simulation of their subjective life.

When infants monitor people's faces and begin to reciprocate in face-to-face interactions, they learn about people and form basic social expectations. By four to six months, we will see that infants show distress if the social partner suddenly adopts a still face or demonstrates a lack of affective attunement.

In short, progress in the understanding of others is inseparable from progress in the understanding of the self in infancy. Let us turn now to physical objects and the link that probably exists between what infants perceive and do about them, and what they perceive and are capable of doing themselves. As with the link between the development of self-awareness and social understanding, there is also an inseparability between the development of self-awareness and physical understanding.

Coperception and Cocognition

In his ecological approach to perception, James J. Gibson (1979) makes the astute point that perceiving the environment is coperceiving oneself. From the earliest stage, self-perception is inseparable from the perception of objects. When young infants, resting on their cribs, track an object crossing their field of view, they experience both the movement of the object and the proprioceptive sense of their eyes moving in their sockets. Infants pick up information specifying both the object moving in the environment and themselves tracking the object.

When sitting on a train or in a car, we all have been tricked by the illusion of self-motion: although we think we are moving because we see a car next to us move, we are in fact stationary. The view of the neighboring car specifies, wrongly in this case, our own motion. The movement of this object tells us something about our state in the environment. Infants are also constantly specifying themselves while attending to entities other than their own body. Any perception entails a point of view, namely that of a perceiver. As in the example of illusory self-movement, objects are perceived always in relation to the particular state and location of the perceiver.

Object perception does entail self-perception, and when infants start to attend to objects they also start to attend to themselves, in particular to the way objects and the body relate to each other. In development, progress in self-perception accompanies progress in object perception and action. As infants discover what they can do with objects (for example, reach for, chew, sound, or break), they also detect and learn the potential effectivities and power of their own bodies.

The same is true for cognition: knowing about something is inseparable from knowing about the self. When infants learn about objects, they also learn about themselves. When, for example, infants come to understand the notion of permanent objects—that objects continue to exist when they momentarily disappear from view—this understanding is inseparable from the developing sense of the infants' own permanence in the environment. The notion that objects are permanent is possible only to the extent that infants start to consider themselves as situated, omnipresent perceivers of objects that can be either in or out of sight, that can come and go. If infants expect an object to reappear at a particular location, they do so because of what they know about the object *and* themselves: the two processes are inseparable.

By tracking and exploring objects, infants learn to situate themselves not only as spectators but also as *actors* in the environment. When they start to search for hidden objects by going around obstacles and planning systematic moves to retrieve them, infants express a new sense of themselves as active planners in relation to anticipated goals. As they develop self-efficacy in ever more demanding tasks, infants must experience themselves as improved strategists.

Infants' sense of an intentional self does indeed develop in interaction with their progressive control over the object world. In planning what they will do with an object, infants project themselves as future actors and anticipate their own future situations in the physical environment. By developing self-efficacy and the sense of an intentional self in relation to objects, infants augment the primary sense of an immediate, directly perceived, and embodied self.

But if the interaction between the infant and the object world is a source of knowledge about the self, what do infants learn and know about physical objects as entities independent of the self? That is, what is the nature and development of infants' *physical objectivity?* I address this question next.

3

THE OBJECT WORLD
IN INFANCY

From birth, infants encounter physical objects. Objects they see, touch, hear, taste, and smell. Food, nipples, crib linings, mobiles, rubber pacifiers, trees, animals, and printed wallpaper. A world of things that do not reciprocate like people and behave independently of the self when the body is not acting on it. So what do babies perceive of these things and how do they make sense of them?

By the second month, infants start to spend a significant amount of time in an awake and alert state. Between feedings and naps, they look around and become captivated by the static and dynamic physical events that surround them and that usually happen independently of their own actions. After a nap, if they open their eyes and see the shadow of curtains dancing on the ceiling, they will typically become enthralled and give this event long periods of intense attention. In fact, by two months, when infants are not sleeping, hungry, tired, or showing any kind of discomfort, their main activity is to explore and scrutinize their environment, in particular the physical objects that furnish it.

Much research in infancy has been devoted to figuring out what infants are actually processing and experiencing when attending to physical objects. Using preferential looking and habituation paradigms, new experiments have emerged in the past twenty years suggesting that very early on, infants process and experience the physical world in rather sophisticated and rational ways. This research goes against earlier theories that considered infants as lacking knowledge about objects—as being born in a state of cognitive confusion regarding the physical world.

Early Perception of the Physical Environment

Remember from Chapter 1 Rousseau's claim that newborns are capable of learning, but of perceiving and knowing nothing? Well, this claim is far from supported by current research. It is true that infants are born with a visual system that is not yet functioning at its fullest potential. But infants from birth do perceive some of the basic features of the physical world such as depth, movement, and shapes. It is from such perception that infants eventually construe the object world.

In Chapter 2, I presented research on perception and action in newborns in the context of the self. Hand-mouth coordination, response to sucrose stimulation, head orientation to sounds, instrumental sucking: all of these behaviors indicate that from birth infants are highly sensitive to a wide range of stimulation across sensory modalities. By the third and last trimester of pregnancy, the auditory system of fetuses is highly functional. This has been established using ultrasound imaging techniques that allow the recording of the fetus's eye blinks, heart rate, and leg movements in response to pulses of noise transmitted from the surface of the mother's abdomen. These responses are reported to be reliable from twenty-nine weeks gestational age, hence eleven weeks prior to normal term birth (DeCasper and Spence 1991).

The womb is a rich acoustic environment, and by the end of pregnancy fetuses appear to learn familiar sounds, in particular their mother's voice, which is toned down and filtered by the amniotic fluid but conveys the same rhythms and relative pitches as it does outside the womb. Fetuses exposed to short rhymes read aloud each day by their mother during the thirty-third and thirty-seventh weeks of their gestation are shown to discriminate eventually between these rhymes and a novel control rhyme. After daily exposure to the maternal rhymes, recording of the fetus's heart rate shows significant deceleration when these rhymes are played back. No deceleration is recorded when the control, a novel rhyme, is played for the fetus (DeCasper et al. 1994). Exposure to specific speech sounds appears to affect subsequent reactions to those same sounds. Evidence of this remarkable auditory learning in fetuses suggests that infants can learn in utero the familiar temporal patterning of their mother's voice. The womb is indeed a noisy environment. In addition to their mother's voice, fetuses hear the heartbeat and physiological noises, digestive and others, of their mother's body. The rhythmicity of the maternal heartbeat that fetuses are exposed to probably explains in part the effectiveness of rhythmic soothing techniques for young infants. Notice how caregivers spontaneously try repetitive and rhythmic actions to calm infants or to stimulate breast- or bottle feeding. Infants are typically rocked while caregivers, in time with the rocking, say repetitive sounds, cluck their tongues (which also encourages sucking), and touch the baby.

Newborns not only hear; they also have highly functional senses of taste and smell. Neonates are shown to modify dramatically their sucking pattern when they obtain sweet water from a nipple compared to plain water. When tasting sugar, they slow down their sucking and appear to savor it. This is a very robust and reliable phenomenon that researchers describe as indexing an innate hedonic response in the child (Lipsitt 1979).

Regarding smell, newborns manifest clearly differentiated reactions when different odors of impregnated cotton swabs are passed under their nostrils (Soussignan et al. 1997). Within forty-eight hours of their birth, neonates' heartbeats, breathing, and body movements are different when they are offered vinegary (acetic acid) compared to sweet (anise) scents. They display differentiated facial expressions in response to bitter (quinine sulfate), sour (citric acid), or sweet (sucrose) smells. In response to the sweet smell, neonates smiled, sucked, and licked. In response to the sour scent, the infants pursed their lips, wrinkled their noses, and blinked. To the bitter smell, they showed distinct depressed mouth corners and an elevated upper lip; some infants even spit (Soussignan et al. 1997). Thus, infants from birth appear to discriminate among novel odors by responding in specific ways.

Olfaction in neonates cannot be reduced only to reflexes. Infants from birth and prenatally appear to make basic discriminations on the basis of olfaction. Hours after birth, neonates are shown to discriminate the smells of their own mother's body, milk, and even amniotic fluid from those of a female stranger (Marlier, Schaal, and Soussignan 1998). The experiment was done by placing swabs impregnated with maternal or nonmaternal odors to the left and right sides of neonates in their cribs. Recording of their head orientation indicated that they orient preferentially to maternal scents a few hours after birth. Such discrimination is learned on the basis of a highly sensitive olfactory system at birth.

If audition, olfaction, and gustation appear to be well developed at birth, vision is less mature and continues to develop in marked ways postnatally. Developmental psychobiologists have shown that across avian (bird) and mammalian species, the sensory systems become functional in an invariant sequence: tactile, vestibular (sense of balance), chemical (olfaction and gustatory), auditory, and finally visual (Gottlieb 1971). In mammals, including humans, the delay in visual development is due both to the complexity of the system and the lack, if not the total absence, of visual stimulation in the womb. Research on the development of vision from a neuroscience perspective using animal models points to the importance of light stimulation for the visual system to develop and become calibrated. Such a hypothesis is supported experimentally by, for example, the classic work of Torsten Nils Wiesel and David Hubel (1965) in which monocular deprivation in young kittens results in abnormal ocular dominance. Depending on the amount of light experienced, each eye will share more or less of the visual cortex area.

To develop normally, vision requires ambient light stimulation. The same is probably true for the other sensory systems, which in contrast to the visual system, get plenty of prenatal stimulation: the amniotic fluid is tasted and smelled via fetal sucking and swallowing, and rich and varied sounds are heard from sources both inside and outside the mother's body.

Prior to birth, some dim light may penetrate inside the womb, but the intrauterine environment is essentially dark. Despite this darkness, ultrasonic imaging shows that by twenty-three weeks gestational age fetuses have slow and rapid eye movements (de Vries, Visser, and Prechtl 1984). Ocular activity is thus functional long before birth, but there is no evidence that this activity is correlated to light stimulation projecting inside the womb. So what do infants sense immediately after birth, when they open their eyes and are suddenly bombarded by massive amounts of light, particularly in delivery rooms still frequently equipped with powerful surgical lighting fixtures? Neonates are not born blind. They appear to be immediately highly sensitive to light stimulation: they open and close their eyes, blinking and showing discomfort when approached by a flashlight aimed at their eyes for routine postnatal optical examination. But aside from being visually sensitive and responding to various light sources, how do they process what this light specifies about the environment, the world of physical objects in particular?

What we perceive visually as mature individuals is not light stimulation per se. In addition to being sensitive to light, we are objective perceivers. We perceive layouts: surfaces made of objects and things cluttering the environment. These things are sometimes static, sometimes dynamic. We manage to make sense of the visual environment by capturing the light bouncing in specific ways on things and their layout. The shading of an object, namely the differential bouncing of light on it, tells us about its depth, its shape, and its orientation in relation to the rest of the environment. The way this object relates to other objects, for example—its surface of support and its texture gradient, how it becomes denser in certain areas—informs us how far this object is in relation to other objects.

Picking up information in the light bouncing off the environment is an important part of perception. This is the way James Gibson accounts for perception in his ecological approach to vision, as well as all the other perceptual systems. Gibson (1979) bases his approach on the fact that the light picked up by our eyes is not random and disorganized but reflects how the physical environment is structured. It bounces on objects in invariant ways, depending on their physical characteristics and situation in the layout, and according to Gibson, we perceive the object world primarily by detecting this invariant information. Note that Gibson's ecological theory provides one particular view of perception. Many other theories exist, all trying in one way or another to account for the process by which we manage, beyond mere sensitivity, to make sense of the physical world via our various perceptual systems.

The majority of research on early perception has been performed in the area of vision, and in this area there is now good evidence that infants, even neonates, are objective perceivers. Aside from being sensitive to physical stimulation, they are *perceptive* of the object world, making some basic sense of it despite their marked visual immaturity during their first postnatal months.

Newborns' visual acuity, or their ability to detect variations in fine detail, is approximately twenty times poorer compared to adults with healthy vision. It is only by the end of the first year that infant visual acuity approaches the adult level (Slater and Butterworth 1997). The same is true for contrast sensitivity (the least luminance required to detect a visual target) and chromatic (color) discrimination, which are much less functional in the first weeks of life (Banks and Shannon 1993; Banks and Dannemiller 1987; Teller and Bornstein 1987). Researchers established such facts by measuring, for example, newborns' preference for seeing black and white stripes of uneven size and spacing over seeing solid gray. If infants look longer at the striped stimulus, this means that they perceive its details. In successive trials and by changing systematically the spatial frequency of the stripes, researchers can reliably assess infants' sensitivity to details (their visual acuity). Analogous techniques combined with habituation procedures can be used to assess infants' contrast and chromatic sensitivity.

There is also a marked development during the first months in the use of stereopsis—binocular depth cues or cues that specify the relative distance of objects. Binocular depth cues are obtained from the combination of the different views of an object conveyed by each individual eye (so-called parallax). Only after approximately six months of age do infants pick up such depth cues. This developmental trend has been elegantly demonstrated by exploiting the fact that when infants start to reach (at around four months), they tend to reach for the closer of two objects (Yonas and Granrud 1985). Young reachers were presented with a pair of identical three-dimensional objects for reaching. These objects were placed side by side in front of them, but at different distances. In some conditions, the farthest object's size was increased to match the apparent (retinal) size of the closest object. In these conditions, if infants based their perception of depth on the apparent size of the object (retinal size or size projected onto the retina), both objects would look as if they were at equal distance from the infant—assuming that infants process the fact that the farther an object is, the smaller it looks. Based on apparent size, they should reach equally for either object. But if they use binocular depth cues to perceive distance, they should perceive the differential distance between the two objects despite their equal apparent (retinal) size and continue to reach more for the objectively closest object. This is what is found with infants six months old and older (Yonas and Granrud 1985).

Aside from binocular depth cues, other types of information support the perception of objects in depth, such as apparent size, texture gradient, occlusion, or the kinetic cue of motion parallax (a depth cue obtained by changing points of view on the object—when, for example, the baby moves her head). At least some of this information appears to be picked up by newborns. Alan Slater and colleagues, for example, found that neonates look significantly more at a three-dimensional object compared to its photograph, even when one eye was covered (Slater, Rose, and Morison 1984). In the latter case, newborns had to use the kinetic cue of motion parallax to show any kind of discrimination. These findings suggest that from birth infants are probably sensitive to depth cues that are not binocular, despite their poor visual acuity.

Note that experiments demonstrating newborns' and young infants' perception of objects in three dimensions and situated in a three-dimensional space are performed by presenting objects or images close to the infant, at the optimum acuity range of about thirty centimeters or one foot away. This proximal zone is the main spatial area covered by infants' visual exploration and corresponds roughly to the distance within which an object has to be for the baby to reach for it. In fact, infants also attend to objects and dynamic events that are more distant, such as moving trees, passing cars, or people far away. Given their poor visual acuity, however, it is not clear what young infants discriminate of these events.

One intriguing question that some infancy researchers have raised is whether the poor vision of neonates might constrain them to infer and represent some invariant principles to figure out the physical world. Like astrophysicists theorizing about invisible worlds by inferring from the poor visual information provided by telescopes, infants would likewise be constrained to infer from the poor perceptual information they are able to gather. This is purely speculative and cannot be tested. But the question is stimulating to the extent that it invites researchers to try to figure out what infants make of the object world based on their limited and developing visual abilities.

In brief, if infants are born "legally blind" by adult standards, they are not born incapable of perceiving. The study of visual perception by neonates demonstrates that newborns discriminate between various outlined shapes, sometimes even those that vary in rather subtle and complex ways. They discriminate among identical patterns that are either static or in motion, and between shapes that vary in orientation only. They discriminate even between shapes forming obtuse or acute angles, and they have a tendency to look longer at high-contrast patterns (see Slater 1997 for a review). All of these findings point to the fact that despite their poor visual acuity, contrast sensitivity, and chromatic discrimination abilities, infants are born perceiving and discriminating an "objectified" world: a world made of rich layouts and surfaces, furnished with physical objects and events that can be differentiated and specified.

However immature and in need of further development, the perceptual abilities displayed by newborns provide an essential foundation for the elaboration and expression of early physical knowledge. These abilities all reinforce that from birth infants perceive—they do not merely sense and react.

Object Exploration in Infancy

From birth, infants combine perception and action, orienting to sounds they hear, tracking objects they see, and mouthing in particular ways novel objects. In addition to being objective perceivers, infants are also born active explorers of their environment. This active exploration by infants becomes particularly evident when they start touching objects with their hands to experience them multimodally. At this stage, infants manifest a new level of initiative in orchestrating their own exploratory activities toward objects. From being active spectators attending to sounds and sights, they become increasingly active *transformers* of the object world, with hands-on action and exploration that are self-initiated rather than merely responsive to external stimulation. This development, like others we have seen, accompanies an important transition around the second month.

Prior to the emergence of object manipulation, self-initiated exploratory activities appear to be primarily oriented toward the body, not objects. It seems that an interest for objects grows out of exploratory activities that are first body oriented. I would like to illustrate this point with some observations I collected years ago when I was involved in establishing the determinants of hand-mouth coordination by young infants (see Chapter 2).

In a simple experiment, I considered when infants start to be systematically inclined to bring a grasped object to the mouth for oral exploration. While babies were lying in their crib, I placed an object in one of their hands for grasping. The object was a rubber teether that had various textures and was easily graspable even for neonates. The main finding was that not until two months of age do infants start transporting the object to the mouth. Prior to two months of age, infants tend simply to hold the object in their hand without trying to transport it either to the mouth or into the field of view. Needless to say, at this early age infants also did not yet show any particular propensity to manipulate the object or involve the other hand in tactually exploring it. From birth, however, infants are systematically inclined to bring their empty hand to the mouth for oral contact and exploration. Thus early hand-mouth coordination is first body oriented and becomes object oriented only after the second month of life (Rochat 1993).

In subsequent experiments, I documented the spontaneous exploration of grasped objects by infants between the ages of two and five months (Rochat 1989). These experiments were simple. I placed a textured, soft, colorful, graspable, and novel object in the right or left hand of the infant for grasping. The infant was sitting on an infant chair facing a video camera while I stood behind the infant—out of view—and introduced the object. I placed the object in the infant's hand and recorded the infant's inclination to bring the object to the mouth or into the field of view for visual and orotactile exploration. I also systematically analyzed infants' manual exploration of the object while they were either looking at it or mouthing it.

The results of this experiment showed that between two and five months infants follow general trends in how they begin to explore an object. Starting at two months of age, when infants first bring the object to the mouth, they progressively tend to alternate between oral and visual inspection of the object: they bring it into the field of view as well as to the mouth. At the level of manual action, I observed some interesting trends. With age, infants tended increasingly to involve both hands in exploring the objects, transferring the objects from one hand to the other or holding the object with one hand while fingering it with the other. This latter behavior indexes a double functioning of the hands emerging at around four months of age: the instrumental function of supporting the object, and the perceptual function of exploring it. Both functions of the hands appear to become coordinated by this age, under visual control. Fingering of the object while the other hand supports it becomes prominent by five months as infants bring the object into view for simultaneous visual inspection. Fingering behavior thus appears to be essentially visually controlled and linked to the developing coordination in infancy between vision and manual action.

A similar developmental progression is observed in relation to young infants' propensity to coordinate vision and touch (eye-hand coordination). Neonates are reported engaging in so-called prereaching behavior when tracking an object in their proximal field of view (von Hofsten 1982). Devoting most of his research effort on the microanalysis of reaching behavior in infancy, Claes von Hofsten demonstrated that newborns tend to manifest significantly more frequent forward arm movements when tracking visually an object moving at a short distance in front of them, compared to a situation where there is no object. These observations show that there are rudiments of eye-hand coordination at birth. But it is only at around four months that infants become successful and systematic in reaching for objects they see—not only grasping them (von Hofsten and Lindhagen 1979; von Hofsten and Fazel-Zandy 1984), but also bringing them to the mouth and handling them for further exploration (Bruner 1969; Rochat and Senders 1991).

In all, research on early object exploration points to the fact that between birth and six months infants develop new ways to apprehend physical objects, from predominantly oral exploration by two months to a complex combination of manual, oral, and visual inspection that emerges around four months along with the onset of successful and systematic eye-hand coordination (von Hofsten and Lindhagen 1979; Rochat 1989; Rochat 1993; Rochat and Senders 1991).

Piaget and other action theorists consider that the early development of object exploration is the basic process by which infants gain physical knowledge and eventually become capable of representing and reasoning about the object world beyond the immediacy of perceptual experience (Piaget 1952; 1954). But research presented in the next sections suggests that an account of the origins of knowledge about objects based exclusively on the development of action is insufficient, if not problematic. This research suggests that some basic physical knowledge might precede and guide young infants in the development of their own, self-initiated exploration of objects.

The Origins of Physical Knowledge

In the past twenty years, Piaget's theory on early perception and the origins of physical knowledge has been assaulted on multiple fronts from infancy researchers armed with clever experimental par-

adigms. I use this military metaphor to mark the magnitude of the
new trend in the field of infancy research. These researchers have
called for major revisions of Piaget's views, which he based on observations of his own three children some seventy years ago, when
none of today's technology was available. Before I briefly introduce
some of Piaget's main ideas on the topic and sample some of the research calling for their revision, it is important to underline how
valid and inspirational Piaget's observations continue to be. What
current infancy researchers tend to demonstrate is not that Piaget's
exquisite observations of his own infants were invalid. Rather, they
put into question the theoretical interpretation he inferred from
them.

By observing his infants from birth and during the first months,
Piaget assumed that babies at birth, and up to approximately two
months of age, did not behave as objective perceivers. In the realm
of vision, he described them as sensing meaningless and fleeting stimulus compounds that he labeled "sensory pictures" (or
"tableaux" in French). Infants would experience these sensory "tableaux" as appearing and vanishing, without any order or particular
detectable forms. At a perceptual level, infants would experience the
blooming buzzing confusion proposed by James to describe neonates: a meaningless bombardment of sensations from the environment. Here is a representative quote taken from Piaget's classic book
on the origins of intelligence and his interpretation of young infants'
initial visual experience of the object world. In this passage, Piaget
reports first some observations of his five-week-old son looking at
his crib. "He is, for example, lying in his bassinet, looking at a certain place in the hood. I pull down the hood to the other end of the
bassinet so that instead of having over his head the usual material,
he finds an empty space, limited by the edge of the hood. Laurent
immediately looks at this, seeking from side to side. Thus, he follows, roughly, the line of a white fringe which edges the hood and he
finally fixes his gaze on a particularly visible point of this fringe"
(Piaget 1952, observation 32, p. 64).

For Piaget this behavior is purely dictated by the sensory circumstances surrounding the infant. There is no meaning yet to what the

infant sees; there are no perceived objects. According to Piaget, infants' looking at this early stage is guided by the mere act of seeing, not perceiving. Here is Piaget's interpretation of such observation by infants:

> How can such behavior patterns be classified? There is not involved, it goes without saying, any interest of the child in the objects themselves that he tries to watch. These sensorial images have no meaning, being coordinated neither with sucking, grasping or anything which could constitute a need for the subject. Moreover, such images have neither depth nor prominence . . . They therefore only constitute spots which appear, move, and disappear without solidity or volume. They are, in short, neither objects, independent images, nor even images charged with extrinsic meaning. (Piaget 1952, pp. 64–65)

The theoretical assumption guiding Piaget in his interpretation is that visual perception becomes objectified when infants start to coordinate it with other modalities such as audition and touch. When infants start to simultaneously hear and see—or touch and see—objects in the environment, these objects start to materialize as objective entities that have depth, substance, and are organized in a coherent space (such as the layout described by Gibson). It is thus via coordinate and multimodal sensorimotor activities that the physical world starts to be perceived by and would truly materialize for the infant. Following Piaget's assumption, the onset of visual perception (that is, the beginning of a perception of the object world) depends on the development of sensorimotor coordination.

As described in the preceding chapter, infants from birth do show organization across sensory modalities; they are capable of intermodal perception and cross-modal matching from a very early age. So, if Piaget's assumption is right, neonates should perceive objects, not merely experience random sensations. But this is not how Piaget construes infants at the origin of development. For some weeks after birth, infants are thought to be incapable of linking tactile, visual, or auditory perceptions to one object. For Piaget, unified object perception across modalities is learned, not a given at birth.

Obviously, this assumption of an initial state of uncoordination needs to be revised in light of current evidence of cross-modal matching and coordinated actions in very young infants (see Chapter 2). Furthermore, it appears that perceptual abilities in young infants often precede in development their ability to coordinate actions in a controlled and systematic way. Research shows, for example, that before infants successfully reach for the objects that they see (that is, before they have coordination between vision and prehension), they perceive substantial and coherent objects. It is thus not clear that object perception and physical knowledge originate from the progressive development of action, and in particular the progressive coordination of sense modalities. Current infancy research on early perception and the origins of physical knowledge points to the fact that Piaget underestimated both the perceptual and action capacities of young infants.

One logical argument against Piaget's assumption that object knowledge originates from a progressive coordination of action is that the development of physical knowledge requires some basic constraints. How can infants develop knowledge from a state of uncoordination and from an experience of the environment that is fundamentally incoherent (as Piaget would say, a variety of fluctuating sensory "tableaux")? Assuming that infants learn by trial and error, constructing the object world bit by bit via progressively coordinated actions, then what guides this development? What gives it coherence? How do infants know what aspects of objects are relevant, what invariants need to be detected in order to predict objects' behavior?

There is an enormous, if not infinite, complexity in what objects are and how they move. Without some constraints, it is difficult to imagine how infants would make sense enough of the object world to eventually predict, reason, and know about it the way grown-ups do. One possible explanation is that infants are born with some preestablished abilities to conceive objects and events in the environment. This nativist view is not so farfetched, considering the evidence suggesting that neonates already behave as objective perceivers. They might as well be objective *reasoners* of the physical world.

Many recent studies on infant cognition have pushed back the onset of remarkable abilities and supported the existence of some precocious (implicit) physical understanding. Based on multiple ingenious experiments on physical knowledge and reasoning in infancy, some of which I will review later, Elizabeth Spelke, Renée Baillargeon, and many other infancy researchers have for the past fifteen years provided intriguing evidence that infants from at least three months of age might possess core physical knowledge and reasoning that are based on basic physical principles. We will see that young infants, for example, might reason about objects on the principle that they occupy space, that they cannot be at two places at the same time, or that they exist continuously in space. Although this physical reasoning is demonstrated in infants three months and older, some researchers, and in particular Spelke, consider it evidence that infants are born possessing these core physical principles that would constrain their perception and understanding of the object world from the outset of development.

In brief, contrary to Piaget's constructivist view that physical knowledge is progressively constructed via the development of coordinated actions, Spelke's nativist view is that infants do not develop physical knowledge from scratch. Instead, they are highly constrained from the very beginning in the way they perceive and reason about the object world (Spelke 1991; 1998). Note that this view, which has triggered a host of creative and probably the most stimulating empirical works of the past two decades, remains hotly debated. Some prominent infancy researchers maintain very different views on early physical knowledge based on research that put into question both the nativist view and what is portrayed as a too rich interpretation of infant cognition (Haith 1998).

Some basic understanding about objects seems to be a prerequisite for action to develop. There is indeed a paradox in trying to conceive how infants would progressively construct objects from action, given that action is usually oriented toward and motivated by objects, as in the case of reaching behavior emerging at around four months. How could reaching behavior emerge in development without some preliminary notions about objects to which the reach act is oriented? These preliminary notions would include that objects are substantial and differentiated from the infants, and that they offer opportunities for reaching as well as occupy space in front of them. Next, I present research documenting physical knowledge and reasoning in infancy at ages where self-initiated instrumental and transforming actions on objects are still limited and chancy. Prior to manual activities that demonstrate physical knowledge and reasoning, such as the systematic search for hidden objects documented by Piaget in his classic observations on object permanence, infants from an early age do manifest object knowledge by systematically attending to them visually.

How Infants Conceive of Objects

Piaget proposed that it is only after nine months of age that infants start to endow objects with permanence. He came to this conclusion by noticing that when hiding an attractive object behind an opaque screen, infants younger than nine months do not attempt to search manually for that object. According to Piaget, this indicates that infants do not yet possess the notion that when out of sight, objects continue to exist. Infants, Piaget determined, cannot reason about perceptually absent objects; they are unable to conceive or represent them mentally as situated in continuous space. The recovery of the object from behind the screen would entail an *object concept* guiding infants in their manual search. One alternative interpretation is that the lack of manual search by infants younger than nine months in Piaget's task might be due to motoric rather than cognitive limitations (Baillargeon 1993). There is now good empirical evidence supporting this interpretation, and this section will present examples of such evidence. But first, let me try to clarify what is usually meant by *object concept.*

In contrast to percept, which is inseparable from the immediate sensory experience of an object, the concept of an object is the result of a mental operation that is separable from sensory experience. It is the product of thought: it is an idea or system of ideas.

Ideas about objects are typically grounded in perception but have a life of their own. For example, if you perceive an object moving behind an occluder (something that blocks your view of it), you witness an event that specifies its disappearance. Beyond this perceptual event, which corresponds to a direct and immediate sensory experience (a percept), the object continues to exist in your mind as an idea (a concept). From this idea or object concept, you can describe the now perceptually absent object, theorize about its current state and location in space, anticipate where and when it might reappear, or consider what might need to be done in order to perceive it again. The object concept is thus the mental image—or memory—of a perceptually absent object. It also includes any thoughts or theories about this object that might help, for example, to figure out its whereabouts while it is out of sight (for example, it magically vanished, it is hidden somewhere, John grabbed it). Either way, it requires an ability to represent objects in their absence.

I turn now to some recent evidence suggesting that an ability to represent objects is an early fact of life, evident long before infants look for objects behind a screen. In a somehow modified Piagetian search task, using no screen to hide objects, researchers have analyzed infants' reaching for objects in the dark, using infrared cameras that allow video recording in total darkness. Researchers have shown that when infants start to reach at around four months of age, they do so whether the object is seen in the light or heard in the dark, with no possible visual guidance for the reach act (Clifton et al. 1993). This propensity by young infants to reach for objects in both the light and the dark prompted researchers to use this behavior to study early object concept. The rationale is that by removing visual feedback, persistent reaching in the dark might imply some object concept or representation, because visual perception cannot guide the manual search. Such a paradigm has the advantage of using overall room darkness in place of a screen to hide an object momentarily—given that the screen experiment requires some detour or removal activity that might be too demanding for young infants, despite their potential ability to represent the object (Bower and Wishart 1972; Clifton, Perris, and Bullinger 1991).

Before nine months of age, most infants do not mind being suddenly plunged into total darkness. In collaboration with Rachel Clifton, we took advantage of this lack of anxiety by analyzing young infants' reaching behavior in the dark to test early object concept. In this research we established that by six months, when infants reach in the dark, they do so guided by a specific representation of the visually absent object for which they are reaching (Clifton, Rochat, Litovsky, and Perris 1991).

We presented six-month-olds with either a large (thirty centimeters in diameter) or a small (six centimeters in diameter) donut-shaped object for reaching and grasping. In alternated trials, each object was presented first out of reach and slowly moved closer to within reach in front of the infant. During the trial, each object was shaken by the experimenter to make a particular sound: either a jingle bell or a rattle. Following six presentations of the objects in the light, we then turned the lights off and presented again each object that the infant could only hear, not see. We videotaped infants in pitch darkness using an infrared camera and coded their reaching activity toward the object.

In general, we found that infants differentially reached for the large or the small object in the light trials. When reaching for the large object, they tended to reach with both hands forward, anticipating a bimanual contact with the object. In contrast, when reaching for the small object (identical to the large one except for its markedly smaller diameter), infants tended to reach systematically with one hand forward, anticipating a one-hand grasp of the object (Figure 3.1). Interestingly, in the dark condition, they continued to use either a two-handed or one-handed reach that corresponded with the object's size. This means that they *anticipated* which object they were going to contact based only on an auditory identification of their respective sounds.

We interpreted such anticipatory manual reaches in the dark as meaning that the infants used a representation of the object to guide their reaching in the dark (Clifton et al. 1991). This ability is the expression of an *object concept*, expressed at least three months earlier than what the same infants would predictably show in a Piagetian manual search task involving a screen.

Tapping into even more precocious abilities for action, some in-

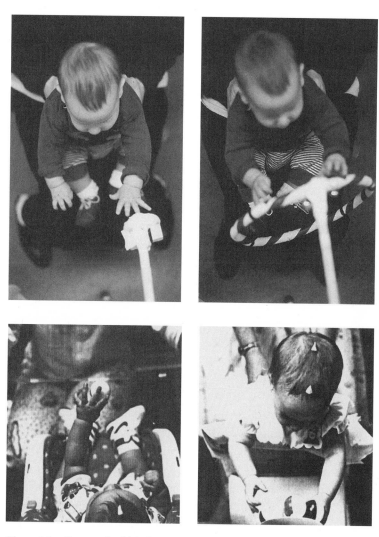

Figure 3.1 Six-month-old infants reaching with both hands when presented with a large object, and one hand when offered a similar object smaller in diameter. By this age, infants are shown to represent objects they hear sounding in the dark. They anticipate specific manual contacts, shaping their hand(s) to the size and shape of the invisible object. The white pieces of medical tape on the infant's head were used as markers for the analysis of head movements and orientation while reaching (Clifton, Rochat, Litovsky, and Perris 1991; photos by P. Rochat).

fancy researchers have devised experiments to test the object concept at even younger ages, when infants are not yet proficient reachers but pay attention to objects and physical events by being visually engaged. Framed within the so-called violation of expectation paradigm, these experiments are based on a measure of infants' visual attention to particular physical events that lead to either probable or improbable outcomes (Spelke 1985).

This paradigm is based on the simple fact that when adults, as well as infants, experience the unanticipated outcome of a physical event, we tend to scrutinize this event more and even express surprise. At a magic show, your attention is captured by the tricks because they violate the basic principles underlying your knowledge about objects: as a result, you look attentively, sometimes with raised eyebrows and dropping mouth, to figure what might have caused the illusion of the scarf becoming a rabbit or the rope vanishing into thin air.

In recent years, infancy researchers have studied with great success visual responses by young infants who witness a partly occluded event such as an object disappearing behind a screen then reappearing in ways that were either physically probable or improbable. Typically, the infant is first familiarized with repeated presentations (usually around six) of an object being occluded or moving behind a screen. Once familiarized with the event, the infant is presented again with the same event but this time, after the event, the occluder is removed and various physical outcomes are revealed to the infant. The object, for example, might be there (the probable outcome), or might have vanished (an improbable outcome). During these post-familiarization trials, researchers measure how long infants look at the revealed outcome. Following the rationale of the paradigm, if infants discriminate between the two outcomes, they should look significantly longer at the improbable compared to the probable outcome. From this discrimination, it can be inferred that infants manifest a violation of expectation when witnessing the improbable outcome. In turn, the physical knowledge underlying such an expectation can be assessed.

In a work that pioneered the violation of expectation paradigm, Renée Baillargeon and her colleagues demonstrated that
five-month-old infants looked significantly longer at the improbable outcome of an event in which a visible screen rotates through
the space occupied by a solid object (Baillargeon, Spelke, and
Wasserman 1985). In this experiment, sometimes referred to as the
"drawbridge experiment," infants were first familiarized with a
screen moving backward on a table in front of them, rotating by
180° on one of its edges. Once they had been familiarized with the
physical event, infants were tested with the same rotating screen but
this time with a solid object placed behind it that would normally
keep it from rotating all the way. In one set of trials, the screen
stopped where the object should have obstructed its motion. In
another, when the screen was perpendicular to the table and thus
hiding the object to the infant, an experimenter surreptitiously removed the object and let the screen rotate all the way back until it
was flat on the table. If the babies understand that the screen should
have stopped where the object was last seen, we would expect them
to look with renewed attention after this improbable event. This is
exactly what Baillargeon and colleagues found in this clever experiment. Infants looked significantly longer when the screen passed the
point where it should have been stopped by the object.

In subsequent experiments, the phenomenon was replicated with
infants as young as three-and-a-half months, suggesting that early
on infants are capable of reasoning about objects that are perceptually absent by representing the object mentally after it is occluded.
Based on this representation, young infants are able to anticipate
particular physical outcomes, in particular the probable or improbable movements of the visible screen (Baillargeon 1993).

Such findings further suggest that young infants possess some rudiments of an object concept that allow them to make predictions
long before they can succeed at manual search tasks. Very early on,
babies show signs of understanding that objects occupy space, are
solid, and can obstruct one another. This understanding might be
grounded in early perceptual learning and experiences, but clearly

from an early age it is separable from perception and guides infants' behavior when perceptual information about the object is temporarily absent and can only be inferred through physical reasoning.

Many other studies using a violation of expectation paradigm with partly occluded events have documented further the nature of physical reasoning and object concept in early infancy. Elizabeth Spelke and her colleagues, in multiple ingenious experiments (see for example Spelke et al. 1992) have shown that from at least four months of age, infants seem to know that objects (1) exist continuously in space and move on connected paths (continuity principle), (2) occupy space in an exclusive way, with no two objects coinciding in the exact same place (solidity principle), and (3) move independently unless they happen to be in physical contact with another object (no action at a distance principle).

So for example, Spelke, Breinlinger, Macomber, and Jacobson (1992) showed that young infants reliably look longer at outcomes in which objects appear to have passed through a solid barrier that normally should have stopped them, or passed through an aperture much too small to accommodate them. In all cases, events in which outcomes violate one or more of the three basic physical principles seem to cause significant increases in looking by the young infant.

All of these studies indicate that young infants reason and make particular inferences about events involving objects they do not see. This reasoning is based on core physical principles that infants possess from at least three to four months of age and that guide infants' understanding of how objects should behave in the environment, whether they are directly perceived or not. Once again, it is important to note that a leaner interpretation of early object knowledge exists in the literature and that the views presented here are challenged by some infancy researchers. For example, alternative theories based on perceptual learning rather than core physical knowledge are offered to account for infants' responses in the violation of expectation experiments originally devised by Baillargeon, Spelke, and their collaborators (see in particular Bogartz, Shinskey, and Speaker 1997; Haith 1998).

I would like to mention now a series of studies performed in collaboration with a former student of mine, Susan Hespos (Rochat and Hespos 1996; Hespos and Rochat 1997). With these studies, we established that if infants by four months manifest an object concept, this concept does not correspond simply to a static representation of the perceptually absent object. It corresponds also to an ability to represent objects' movements and spatial transformation when out of sight. In multiple experiments all framed within a violation of expectation paradigm, we placed groups of four- and six-month-olds in front of a puppet stage on which, for example, a colorful Y-shaped object disappeared behind an occluder. The object either fell vertically from the top of the stage behind the occluder (translation condition) or rotated behind the occluder, disappearing at four o'clock (rotation condition).

Following six familiarization trials in each condition, the infant's visual attention was measured in two pairs of trials. In these trials, after the object's disappearance the occluder was lowered, revealing the object resting at the center of the stage in either a probable or improbable orientation. The probable orientation corresponded to how the object should have looked following its partly occluded trajectory. In contrast, the improbable orientation corresponded to a 180° inversion of the object. In the improbable outcome trials, an experimenter surreptitiously inverted the object from behind the stage before revealing the outcome to the infant (Figure 3.2).

According to the rationale of the violation of expectation paradigm, infants should look longer at the improbable compared to the probable test outcome. In multiple experiments, each time with different infants and with slight variations in the display to control for any accidentally given cues specifying the movement of the object behind the occluder, we found that from four months of age, infants looked reliably longer at the improbable compared to the probable test outcome. These results are remarkably robust and point to sophisticated representational abilities by young infants.

If we admit that these results are the expression of specific expectations that call for an object concept, on what bases are these expectations formed and what do they tell us about young infants' concept of the object they see moving out of sight?

A

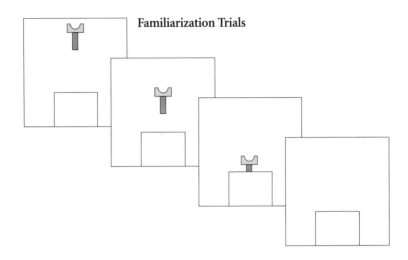

Familiarization Trials

Test Trials

Y Orientation
Probable Outcome

Inverted Y Orientation
Improbable Outcome

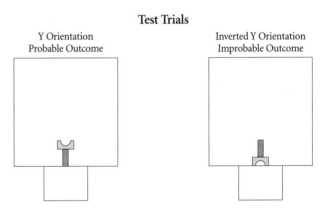

Figure 3.2   By four months of age, infants seem to represent the movements of an object while out of sight. After familiarization with an object disappearing behind an occluder, either in a vertical translation (A) or by a 180-degree rotation (B), infants tend to look significantly longer when the object reappears with an improbable compared to a probable orientation outcome (from Rochat and Hespos 1996; Hespos and Rochat 1997).

B

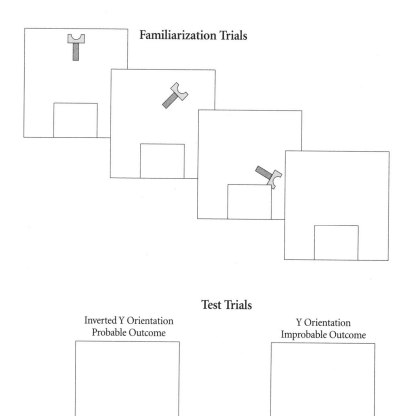

Familiarization Trials

Test Trials

Inverted Y Orientation
Probable Outcome

Y Orientation
Improbable Outcome

Based on our research, we conclude that by at least four months of age, infants are capable of generating dynamic mental imagery. This dynamic imagery or representation capability prolongs the information given by perception and allows infants to predict both visible and invisible spatial transformations. Infants demonstrate an implicit understanding that objects continue to exist when out of sight and behave in a spatially continuous way when moving behind an occluder.

In our research, infants saw the object disappear behind the occluder and managed to predict, using conceptual representation alone, the final orientation of the object. While the object was still visible, they noticed its starting orientation, motion, trajectory, and progressive occlusion. Once the object had disappeared behind the occluder, and in order to anticipate the final orientation of the transformation, infants resorted to their imaginations, in particular to some representational ability that had enabled them to track mentally the object's spatial transformations as it moved behind the occluder. It is based on this mental tracking that infants discriminated between the probable and improbable orientation outcomes.

Note that infants did consider the motion and trajectory of the object, and they looked longer at the improbable outcome not only because the object had changed orientation from the beginning to the end of the test. A control group of infants familiarized with the object only resting at the top of the stage (no motion involved) looked equally at the object in either orientation at the bottom of the stage in subsequent test trials. Furthermore, in the experimental situation, the novel (improbable) orientation outcome did match the starting orientation in the translation condition only. In the rotation condition, the improbable (novel) orientation was actually the same compared to the starting orientation. In other words, the translation and rotation conditions controlled for the possibility that infants based their response simply on a static comparison of the beginning and end orientations.

Considering that infants did not merely memorize and compare the static orientation of the object at the top and bottom of the stage, and because no perceptual cues were available to track the object as it moved behind the occluder, the anticipation of its final orientation could only be based on *mental tracking*. Again, infants showed unambiguous representational abilities, and in the rotation condition demonstrated some rudiments of mental rotation that extended the information given by perception (see Rochat and Hespos 1996; Hespos and Rochat 1997 for further details and discussion).

In summary, from at least four months of age infants are shown to possess an object concept. They can represent and reason about objects that are temporarily out of sight, showing rudiments of object permanence about five months before they can express it in the context of manual search tasks like those devised by Piaget. Furthermore, early object representations are not static mental simulations, like mental snapshots of the object. Rather, research on the mental tracking of invisible spatial transformations by young infants suggests that object representation in infancy can be mentally transformed and manipulated. From a remarkably early age object representation is dynamic, not merely static. It entails mental activities, namely physical reasoning guided by the understanding of core principles. Such reasoning allows infants to make predictions and give meaning to objects and their behavior, and in this way to enlarge their experience of the object world beyond direct perception.

Noticing Physical Causality

Infants from birth tend to be more attentive to objects that move than to stationary objects. In devising experiments, researchers know that infants are much more engaged by dynamic compared to static displays. The lack of visual acuity during the first weeks after birth might explain the particular attention that young infants devote to objects in motion. Movement provides the infant with rich information about objects as discrete, bounded, shapeful, and sizeable entities in the environment. It also might inform infants about these objects' dynamic features: what set them in motion and what kind of vitality characterizes their movements (continuous, accelerating, smooth, rhythmical, and so forth). I turn now to what researchers have found regarding what infants might understand of the way objects move and what it might mean in terms of events in the physical environment. Do infants also display some ability to detect conditions in the environment that might set objects in motion, such as gravity, inertia, or collisions with other objects? The detection and understanding of such conditions, one of Kant's fundamental categories of reason, is an intrinsic part of how we make sense of the object world.

About forty years ago, the Belgian experimental psychologist Albert Michotte (1963) imagined clever ways to study the perceptual bases of our understanding of physical causality, in particular how we construe that the movement of an object may depend on the movement of another. He devised two-dimensional displays where a pair of geometric figures moved on a screen in a repeated sequence. For example, a red square moved linearly toward a blue square, came into contact with the blue square, and then the blue square started to move in a linear motion. In other events, the red square stopped when it contacted the blue one, which then started to move. Michotte presented these displays to adults and asked them to describe what they perceived. In multiple experiments, Michotte established that given the timing of movement and velocity of the two squares, adults perceived robust causal relations in these events. For example, they described the red square as "pushing" the blue square, or the blue square as "hauling" the red square—perceiving effort, inertia, and resistance in these abstract two-dimensional displays and enriching them with meanings, namely causal explanations.

Michotte demonstrated that these reliable impressions of physical causality are grounded in particular percepts about physical causality. This phenomenon shows how adults have the tendency to construe physical events in terms of causes and effects. An important feature of the adult mind is indeed the proclivity to detect causal relationships. This proclivity is at the origins of basic understandings, predictions, and theories about the object world, in particular how objects move and affect one another. Based on Michotte's observation and the fact that the perception of physical causality is in certain conditions so robust and obligatory, at least by adults, it might be that such proclivity is an intrinsic property of how the mind works from the outset of development.

Infancy researchers have addressed this question by testing young infants' capacity to discriminate between causal and noncausal physical events. For example, they familiarized infants with a red ball moving linearly behind a screen followed by a white ball coming out of the screen from the other side. The question was whether infants construe the movement of the white ball (the one coming out of the screen) as being caused by the movement (collision) of the red ball. In other words, do they make assumptions about what is happening behind the screen in terms of a causal event—the red ball hitting the white ball? The end of this experiment was an attempt to answer this question. Once familiarized with the partly occluded event, the screen was removed and infants' looking at two different test events was measured. For the noncausal test event, the red ball moved close to the white ball, but did not touch it. It stopped, and then after a delay the white ball started to move. For the causal test event, the red ball came into contact with the white ball, which then started to move. Infants as young as two months are reported to look reliably longer at the noncausal compared to the causal test event (Ball 1973; cited by Spelke 1985; 1991). Following the rationale of the violation of expectation paradigm, infants looked longer at the noncausal event because it is novel; it does not match the expected causal outcome, which they had construed in the partly occluded familiarization phase of the experiment.

Using a habituation paradigm, other researchers have reported with six-month-old infants similar evidence of an apprehension of causal relationships between objects (Leslie 1984). Infants were habituated either with a causal event (object A colliding with object B) or a noncausal event (objects A and B moving independently, with no physical contact). Once habituated, they were tested with the mirror opposite of either event. Those infants habituated to the causal event were shown to dishabituate (regain visual attention) to the mirror opposite test. In contrast, those who habituated to the noncausal event did not.

Following the logic of the experiment, these results indicate that six-month-olds perceived the mirror opposite of the causal event as more novel, because it reverses the causal relationship between the two objects. In other words, the reversal is meaningful only in relation to the causal event, if causality is detected. It is because infants detected physical causality in the causal event that they dishabituated to the reversal test event. Alternatively, because they did not detect any causality in the noncausal event, they did not dishabituate to its mirror reversal during posthabituation test trials.

Note that using the same basic procedure and design, some researchers have reported similar findings with ten-month-old but not six-month-old infants (Oakes and Cohen 1990). These researchers conclude that the detection of physical causality develops in the course of the first year, from the processing of independent object motions to the processing of the relationship—in particular any causal relationship—between the motions of objects. The debate remains open, and there is certainly much room for development to occur in the detection of physical causality during the first year of life and beyond, when it becomes part of children's explicit theories of what is happening in the object world. Infancy research, however, demonstrates that the proclivity to perceive causal events is an early fact of life. It might not be present from birth—infants are not necessarily born with a "causality detection module" as some might like to believe (Leslie 1994)—but the proclivity to detect causal relationships does emerge within the first two to eight months of life based on a process that remains to be elucidated.

Infancy research on the apprehension of physical causality points to the fact that infants are inclined, possibly from two months of age and definitely by ten months, to make sense of the object world in complex ways that move them beyond the immediacy of perceptual experience. This point is further supported by studies on the early ability to group objects together, compare collections, and infer quantity, all of which are highly abstract dimensions of the object world.

Early Sense of Numerosity

"Babies can count!" trumpeted a headline in my local paper several years ago. Journalists had picked up an article published in the prestigious British journal *Nature* by American infancy researcher Karen Wynn (1992). Using a violation of expectation paradigm, Wynn reported data suggesting that infants could detect the outcome of an addition and subtraction of one discrete object from a small collection of two or three objects. She interpreted this result as evidence of precocious *number concept* in young infants—that is, that they can recognize quantity and discriminate between the results of the two basic operations of adding or subtracting physical objects from a small collection. Four-month-old infants were shown to abstract numerosity from operations on concrete objects years before they could do so on symbolic objects (for example, digits) within the norms of a learned notational system. I will present these intriguing findings and discuss their interpretation. But first, it is important to define "abstracting numerosity" and distinguish the various degrees of cognitive processing it might involve.

In general, the sense of numerosity requires the abstraction of quantity from collections of discrete physical objects. It can imply different cognitive levels, from low, basic-level discrimination of small quantities to precise, complex inferences that are based on necessary and abstract principles. For example, I can have a global sense that there are more people watching the baseball game tonight compared to the last time I went to the ball game. I can be certain of it, even if I am unable to give a more precise estimate of the difference in attendance between these two games. My certitude is perceptually based, not based on counting, and does not imply any arithmetic ability or number concept in the strict sense I will define later. It is indeed possible to have a sense of numerosity at levels that we can assume imply different cognitive competencies such as perceptual or arithmetic.

Cognitive psychologists have documented this sense of numerosity that is based on some sort of direct perception. If presented with a collection of objects (such as a group of dots on a slide) for only a fraction of a second, not enough time to count them, we are able to tell accurately whether this collection has more or fewer items than another collection presented also for a short duration immediately afterward. This process of perceptual quantification without counting is referred to as "subitizing." Subitizing is shown to work with adults for small collections of objects not requiring explicit counting, up to approximately seven to nine items.

The ability to quantify objects, at least at a subitizing level, is not specifically human and does not have to be mediated by language. The animal literature is rich with demonstrations that avian and nonhuman mammalian species can discriminate among collections of objects based on some sort of quantification (Gallistel 1990). Here is an example involving a bird and its hunters, taken from Tobias Dantzig's classic book on number as the language of science:

> A squire was determined to shoot a crow which made its nest in the watch-tower of his estate. Repeatedly he had tried to surprise the bird, but in vain: at the approach of man the crow would leave its nest. From a distant tree it would watchfully wait until the man had left the tower and then return to its nest. One day the squire hit upon a ruse: two men entered the tower, one remained within, the other came out and went on. But the bird was not deceived: it kept away until the man within came out. The experiment was repeated on the succeeding days with two, three, then four men, yet without success. Finally, five men were sent: as before, all entered the tower, and one remained while the other four came out and went away. Here the crow lost count. Unable to distinguish four and five it promptly returned to its nest. (Dantzig [1930] 1954, p. 3)

For small numbers, the crow showed a remarkable sense of numerosity. The strategy on which it based its limited quantifying ability might have been a sort of tallying, or one-to-one correspondence between the entry and the exit of each man in the tower. As in the baseball example above, it does not imply necessarily counting or even simple arithmetic. Beyond four, the crow could not store the tally of events and finally was caught.

Another example of numerosity sense in nonhumans is the fact that rats can learn to associate a number of successive sounds to a matching number of actions on a lever, in anticipation of food. They do not seem to respond merely on the basis of rigid stimulus-response associations; instead, they have been shown to generalize such learning to other stimuli that engage a different sense modality (blinking lights, for example). Yet if crows, rats, and many other animals demonstrate a sense of numerosity, this sense is limited compared to the number concept developed by humans. The arithmetic and quantification abilities that human children eventually develop obviously surpass the limitations of animals' sense of number. It implies a number concept in the strict sense that is required to perform any arithmetic operations or precise inferences about quantities. Adding, subtracting, or dividing quantities to compare with absolute accuracy different collections of objects can only be based on number concept, not intuition of quantity, however reliable it might be. This concept rests on the combined mastery of two basic principles: cardinality and ordinality. Cardinality corresponds to the absolute quantity represented by a particular number: the "twoness" of two, the "twenty-oneness" of twenty-one, or the "hundredness" of one hundred. Ordinality, on the other hand, corresponds to the necessary relation of one particular number to the others: that two is necessarily greater than one but smaller than three and greater numbers. As already mentioned, the combined notions of cardinality and ordinality underlie any arithmetical deductions or counting operations that can be generalized to any collection, regardless of physical size: using these principles, even numbers that are too large to be fully comprehended, such as billions of stars in faraway galaxies, can be manipulated and related to other numbers.

What about human infants? If they show a sense of number, are they merely processing numbers at a low level like subitizing, or are they actually capable of counting—that is, do they display a precocious number concept, as the headline of my morning paper claimed?

To test whether young infants are capable of simple arithmetic, Karen Wynn devised the following simple and clever experiment using a looking-time procedure within the context of the violation-of-expectation paradigm discussed earlier. Five-month-old infants faced a puppet theater with a Mickey Mouse doll resting on the stage. After a few seconds, a screen rotated up occluding the doll, and the hand of an experimenter emerged from the side of the stage, adding another doll behind the screen. Following the action, the screen was rotated down revealing either one or two dolls. A possible outcome was classified as one where the result was consistent with the transformations that would have occurred if basic arithmetic principles applied (one object plus another object leaves two ob-

jects). An impossible outcome was also devised in which the result
was not arithmetically consistent (for example, one object plus one
object leaves one object).

Possible and impossible outcomes were alternated in successive
trials in which the infant's looking time was recorded. In one condition (subtraction), there were two dolls on the stage and a doll was
retrieved by the experimenter's hand from behind the screen. In another (addition), a doll was added. Results show that in both addition and subtraction conditions, infants looked significantly longer
at the impossible compared to the possible test outcomes. Similar
results are reported with a procedure involving three objects instead
of only two (that is, $3 - 1$ or $2 + 1$).

Wynn interprets these findings as a demonstration that young infants possess a true numerical concept—that is, that they combine
the principles of cardinality and ordinality at least for small numbers (up to three). Although her findings are based on observations
of five-month-olds, the author concludes that humans possess an
innate capacity to perform simple arithmetical computations. No
doubt journalists jumped on the news, spreading it to all the parents
keen on devising new cognitive drills for their children.

One alternative interpretation, however, is that rather than basing
their preferential looking on arithmetical competence and number
concept, infants reacted to the fact that the impossible arithmetical
outcome was in fact *physically* impossible. We have seen before that
infants, at least by five months, interpret the object world according
to core physical principles, including the fact that objects move continuously in space. In Wynn's experiment, infants might have based
their test reaction on the physical principle that objects cannot vanish or appear out of nowhere, rather than on calculations implying
number concept per se. To test the feasibility of such an alternative
interpretation, Tony Simon, Sue Hespos, and myself attempted to
replicate Karen Wynn's findings with same-age infants (four- to five-
month-olds), but adding a condition in which the outcome of the
transformation was physically impossible, yet arithmetically possible. In this extra condition, when for example the experimenter
added one puppet (*Sesame Street*'s "Ernie" in this case) to another

occluded Ernie, the test outcome was either two Ernies (arithmetically and physically possible) *or* one Ernie and one surreptitiously placed Elmo (a different *Sesame Street* character). The latter test is arithmetically possible (two things reappear), but physically impossible because it involves a new puppet coming out of nowhere (Simon, Hespos, and Rochat 1995).

The question was whether infants would react to the physically impossible outcome by looking at it longer, or on the contrary would override it and consider only the outcome from an arithmetic standpoint. The latter outcome would support further Wynn's provocative interpretation that young infants do show some concept of numbers for at least small collections of physical items. What we found supports Wynn's view. We replicated her original findings and found that infants did override the physical impossibility in our new condition.

It appears, then, that in addition to interpreting the object world according to core physical and causality principles, infants from at least four to five months of age also appear to abstract numerosity in simple physical events. This ability is obviously limited to very small collections of objects and is far from the arithmetical power that children eventually develop when they acquire language and are exposed to conventional numerical notations. But the evidence of early numerical abstraction and rudiments of number concept suggest that early in development there is more going on than mere perceptual subitizing and global numerical intuitions. By five months, infants do track objects in relation to one another as groups of physical entities, beyond their physical specificities (color, identity, size, and so on). They demonstrate a remarkable ability for *abstraction* from which they are inclined to infer and anticipate physical outcomes. The actual origin of the abstracting mind of the infant is still an open question. Ascribing innateness to such competence is not warranted considering that much develops and is experienced during the first year and beyond. As stated by Rochel Gelman, who has studied extensively the development of number understanding and who does not shy away from granting infants principled core knowledge and a capacity to represent cardinal numerosities:

To grant infants the ability to apply nonverbal counting and reasoning principles is not to say that they also know how to use the count words of their language as tags. This children surely have to learn. They have to find, commit to memory, and practice at using the count words correctly. Available principles can direct children's attention to inputs that have the potential to nurture the development in that domain. They also can serve as file drawers of memories and thereby keep together the kind of contents that, once understood, flesh out what were but skeletal structures at the start. But they cannot undo the need to learn in order to construct a full understanding. By limiting the innate knowledge base to *skeletal principles,* we make our position on this matter clear. (Gelman 1991, pp. 313, emphasis mine)

Finally, it is worth mentioning that some researchers, using computer modeling techniques, have been able to support new conceptualizations regarding the developmental origins of numerical competence—conceptions based on perceptual learning and discrimination rather than innate numerical competence. In particular, Tony Simon (1997) provides evidence that numerosity of the type expressed in infancy can be simulated by a machine that does not have a core representational knowledge consisting of both cardinal and ordinal concepts, but rather has simply been programmed to apply basic perceptual and attention principles.

Categorizing the Object World

Aside from quantification, which is a highly abstract way of categorizing the object world, research shows that very early on infants do perceive and memorize objects as a group or cluster of things: things that look alike, sound alike, or share similar attributes. Using the habituation/dishabituation paradigm, researchers have demonstrated, for example, that three-month-olds discriminate between animal categories such as horses and cats (Eimas and Quinn 1994).

In the experiment, infants were habituated with different exemplars of either category (for example, different kinds of horses or cats) and then tested with either a novel exemplar of the same category (for example, a new horse or new cat) or a novel exemplar

of another category (say, a giraffe or zebra). Recording of their looking time during slide presentation tests revealed that infants dishabituated or significantly regained visual attention for novel exemplars that crossed over a category boundary (for example, if the
image of a giraffe followed habituation to various horses). What this
shows is that by three months, infants are capable of picking up categorical attributes of objects, perceiving the invariant commonalities of things in the physical world. The research of Peter Eimas and
Paul Quinn suggests that young infants are already capable of forming basic-level categorical representations for animals. The exact nature of such representations, however, is still very much debated and
the topic of current research (see, for example, Mandler 1997). The
question is whether the categorical perception of young infants is already conceptual, in the sense that already by three months infants
would possess a *core understanding* of what, for example, dogs and
cats *mean* as contrasted classes of animals composed of varied exemplars. These early categories are probably more perceptual than
conceptual, arising from an ability to detect invariant physical attributes (small versus larger body size, nose configuration, presence
or absence of whiskers, and so on), rather than theories about how
things relate to each other. But this question is up for grabs and
there is no ready answer to the profound issue of how conceptual
categorization might relate in development to earlier, lower-level
perceptual categorization.

Whether perceptual or conceptual, evidence of precocious categorization demonstrates once again that from an early age infants
relate things to one another, and go beyond the immediacy of discrete perceptual experiences. Rather than experiencing each slide
projected to them as a discrete event, infants are shown to link and
actively organize their perception of the successive slides as a whole.

If young infants appear to categorize images of objects presented
to them in succession, they also appear to categorize the dynamic aspects of objects, namely the way they move around. In a sense, this is
a double cognitive feat because it requires both the ability to group
objects on the basis of how they look when stationary as bounded,
individual physical entities, as well as the ability to group them in re-

lation to their dynamic features, namely how they move together or in relation to one another. Some years ago, Swedish perception psychologist Gunnar Johansson (1973; 1977) filmed people in the dark with lighted electrical bulbs attached to their joints (elbows, hands, hips, and so forth). To the adult eye, when stationary, the person appeared on the film as a random, meaningless cluster of lights. But when moving, the lights were effortlessly perceived as a whole, specifying a person walking or performing meaningful actions (for example, dancing or lifting a heavy weight). Johansson's experiments demonstrated the remarkable ability of adults to perceive the point light displays as dynamic wholes, not merely a summation of the discrete movements of each light bulb.

It appears that the principles guiding adult perception of movement also hold for infants and the way they tend to form perceptual categories of dynamic events. Researchers have tested infants presented with point light displays like Johansson's and found an analogous propensity to discriminate and categorize these displays as dynamic wholes. Using a habituation paradigm, Bennett Bertenthal and his collaborators found that three- and five-month-old infants do discriminate between the point light displays of a moving person from a disorderly spatial and temporal patterning of the same person's point lights (Bertenthal, Proffitt, Kramer, and Spetner 1987; Bertenthal and Pinto 1993). In other words, infants regained visual attention ("dishabituated") to the presentation of disordered displays after being habituated to successive unperturbed point light displays of a moving person. More spectacular is the finding that if five-month-old infants did discriminate between the unperturbed and perturbed point light displays of a person moving, they did not do so in relation to a display specifying an unfamiliar creature, such as a spider (Bertenthal and Pinto 1993). A possible interpretation favored by the authors of the study is that by five months infants might already have a stored knowledge of the human form and the ways that people usually move. This finding about the unfamiliar creature further demonstrates that early on infant perception is categorical, not random or simply the result of an accumulation of sensory experiences with the environment.

Infants are actively engaged in grouping objects. Once again, research shows that there is an early proclivity among infants toward abstracting and grouping common attributes among things in the physical environment. The ability to categorize might be an intrinsic, low-level property of perceptual systems in all animals, and it is feasible that babies are born with such a propensity.

In a previous section, I presented evidence that newborns discriminate between their mother's voice and the voice of a female stranger. There are actually many studies demonstrating that prior to six months infants perceive the difference between similar speech sounds such as "ba" and "pa" or "ra" and "la" (Eimas et al. 1971; Jusczyck 1997).

As adults, we perceive the categorical contrast between "ba" (a "voiced" syllable) and "pa" (a "voiceless" syllable). These speech sounds are categorically defined in relation to when during the sound the vocal chords are activated and the lips are opened. The "voiced" syllable "ba" is produced by vibrating the vocal cords at or before the time the lips are opened. In contrast, the "voiceless" syllable "pa" is produced with the vocal cords vibrating only after the lips are opened (try it for yourself). Thus, both speech sounds are contrasted by their "voice onset time," or VOT. With the help of a synthesizer, it is interesting to vary the VOT slightly along a physical continuum, keeping constant all other aspects of the sound stimulation. In this experimental situation, adults perceive very distinctly only two types of sounds: either "ba" or "pa." Within one range of VOT, we perceive different expressions of one syllable, and suddenly, within another range, we perceive different expressions of the other syllable. This phenomenon corresponds to categorical speech perception. It is based on the categorical perception that allows us to understand, for example, spoken English regardless of the great variability in speech production and idiosyncrasies in style, pitch, accent, and command of English of all the individuals to whom we listen.

Using high-amplitude sucking techniques within a habituation paradigm (Jusczyck 1985), researchers have shown that young infants do categorically perceive speech in the same way that adults do, except that they are even more perceptive of differences in sound production prior to approximately six to nine months of age. It appears that by nine months after birth, infants have tuned their categorical perception of speech sounds to the contrasts that are relevant in the language to which they are most exposed. So for example, adult Japanese are known to have difficulty discriminating between the syllables "ra" and "la," because "ra" is not a relevant phoneme in the Japanese language. Prior to six months, however, Japanese infants are shown to perceive and discriminate between the two like Western infants and adults do. The Japanese infants progressively lose such categorical perception because it is not used in the language they are exposed to and that they eventually learn to speak (Kuhl 1993). What we see here is that categorical perception is an early fact of life progressively adapted to the particular cultural circumstances surrounding the infant (Jusczyck 1997).

A major take-home message that emerges from the recent research literature on infant perception and cognition of physical objects is the early propensity to process information beyond the immediacy of perceptual experience. Babies are inclined to relate their past, present, and future experiences with the object world. The way infants make sense of the object world is not radically different from the way adults do. But does that mean that from an early age infants behave like little scientists? What about their practical knowledge— as actors—of objects? How can we reconcile the fact that on the one hand infants discriminate, categorize, conceptualize and detect abstract features of objects, and on the other hand these competencies are not readily reflected in babies' actions on objects? For most of the first year, for example, babies make systematic errors in their search for hidden objects although they are capable of representing these objects. By the same token, it is only by the end of the first year that infants show that they can differentiate between means and ends by using objects as tools, although research shows that at a much earlier age they apprehend physical causality in their observation of dynamic displays. This apparent paradox calls for a distinction between two knowledge systems about the object world that develop in infancy, one of which develops in the context of systematic observations, and the other which develops in the context of self-generated actions on objects. In the next section and to conclude this chapter, I suggest that a major achievement in infant development is the integration of these two systems as distinct sources of knowledge about the object world, namely learning by looking and learning by doing.

"Knowing How" and "Knowing What"

As I alluded in a preceding section, Piaget's classic theory on infant development was flawed by his interpretation of infants' actions as the direct reflection of their cognitive competence. Recent infancy research demonstrates that infants know much more than meets the eye of an observer who focuses on babies' self-generated actions on objects. Babies are active explorers from birth, but relatively slow-developing, clumsy actors. They need to overcome many motoric and postural obstacles before they can perform unambiguously knowledgeable acts on objects such as reaching with anticipation and searching for hidden objects. It seems that these obstacles hinder the translation of their physical knowledge into action. As a matter of fact, in all experiments revealing precocious perception and knowledge, infants are provided with optimum postural support and observed in relation to motoric responses that are minimally taxing for the infant (for example, looking or sucking). Researchers provide such supportive conditions because the head of infants in the first months of life represents up to approximately one-third of their total body weight. Imagine carrying on your head a load weighing one-third of your body weight, having no balance whatsoever, and trying to do clever things with objects. If someone assessed you on the basis of your actions, you would certainly think the result was flawed and unfair.

Aside from postural and motoric constraints that prevent infants from readily acting out their physical knowledge, it might be that physical knowledge in general does not correspond to one system of knowledge, but two: knowledge gained by observing systematically objects in the environment, and knowledge gained from doing things with these objects. Both systems pertain to the same object world that babies learn about, but correspond to distinct types of knowledge: a practical "know how" versus a conceptual "know what" about objects, both of which seem to develop in parallel rather than in sequence as proposed by Piaget (Rochat 1999b).

Except for a few studies that explore early reaching behavior as an expression of object concept and perception in infancy, most research revealing precocious physical knowledge pertains to a "know what," or conceptual, system of knowledge. Infants reveal their knowledge as spectators, as opposed to actors, by attending visually to slides, puppets, and other props presented by the researchers within the context of preferential looking and habituation procedures. In this context, although they look actively, they do not perform any object-oriented actions that change the object world, such as pushing or grasping. They are contemplative rather than active.

Two researchers who take a different view are James J. Gibson and his wife, Eleanor Gibson. They have insisted that what is perceived and understood about the object world pertains first and foremost to what this world offers for action (the so-called affordances of objects). In J. J. Gibson's theory of affordances (J. J. Gibson 1979; E. J. Gibson 1988), what is perceived is what objects allow us to do: a surface provides a place on which to walk, a spoon helps us eat, and a pacifier gives infants something to suck on. In this theory, physical knowledge is primarily viewed as relative to a self-produced action such as eating, walking, or manipulating. So for example, the floor of a room as a physical feature of the environment will have a different affordance for infants who can or cannot yet locomote on their own. Empirical research shows that infants perceive differently the various slopes of an inclined walkway as they acquire new locomoting abilities (Adolph 1997). When starting to crawl or walk, they first tend to dash down the steep slope of the walkway as if oblivious of the danger of tumbling down. Eventually, they learn how to evaluate the steepness of a slope and adopt more cautious and safer strategies to negotiate such obstacles. Infants appear to repeat this process at each level of their locomoting development.

The theory of affordances takes into consideration that physical knowledge needs to be framed within functional constraints: what the perceiver can and cannot do as an actor in the environment. For the Gibsons, perception and action cannot be considered separately. In a sense, there is a resemblance between the theory of affordances and Piaget's view on early practical intelligence or "know-how" as it relates to infants younger than eighteen months and their ability to figure out the object world. But there are fundamental differences between the two theories. The Gibsons assume that affordances are directly perceived, without any conceptualization or representation involved. Piaget, on the contrary, suggested that developing "know-how" about objects leads to their eventual conceptualization. In contrast to the Gibsons, Piaget (1954) focused on the "know-how" of young infants to account for the origins of conceptualized physical knowledge, which he believed emerged only at the end of infancy, not before.

What the Gibsons and Piaget have in common, nonetheless, is their emphasis on action as central to infants' perception and cognition of the object world. This viewpoint is different from that taken in much of current research on infant physical knowledge. Gibson's theory of affordances certainly accounts for an important aspect of physical cognition. It deals with another facet of what infants, like any other perceiving organism, must learn in order to survive in the physical environment. Infants learn to detect the relevant perceptual information that specifies food, comfort, or danger: the nipple that feeds them, the distance at which something can be reached, or the drop of a step that could cause a fall. This detection is essentially direct, as suggested by Gibson; it does not require the thought process or representation that counting, apprehending physical causality, or conceptualizing hidden objects would entail.

If we try to reconcile what the theory of affordances is trying to account for and the evidence of an early conceptualization of the object, considering of course that they are both feasible and not mutually exclusive, then we have to assume that two different types of physical knowledge develop in infancy: one pertaining to the direct perception and control of practical things that can be done with objects (the "know-how" system), and the other pertaining to the indirect representation of what objects are, what is happening to them (the "know-what" system). But how feasible is the parallel development and dual existence of such systems of physical knowledge?

The notion that physical knowledge might be separable in its practical and conceptual components receives credence in light of intriguing pathological cases reported in the neuropsychological literature. These cases point to the fact that knowing about objects can be dissociated from performing particular actions with the same objects. For example, an adult patient suffering from brain damage (bilateral lesions of the occipital lobes) following carbonmonoxide poisoning is reported to be incapable of recognizing either the shape or the size of objects, but perfectly capable of acting on those objects in complex ways that entailed processing information regarding those physical properties. For instance, when asked to match the orientation of a held object to the orientation of a slot cut into another object, the patient performed poorly. In sharp contrast, when she was instructed to insert the card into the slot, hence instructed to *act* instead of simply compare, she was able to do so promptly and accurately (Goodale and Milner 1992; see also Gazzaniga, Ivry, and Mangun 1998).

Such observations in humans, as well as in nonhuman species with experimental brain lesions, have led neuroscientists to dissociate the brain system underlying the identification of objects (the "what" system) from the system underlying the performance of practical actions on objects (the "how" system). Both systems process analogous information regarding the object world but for different functional purposes: identification or practical action. By analogy, infants from birth probably develop both a "know-how" and a "know-what" about objects in the environment. How, then, do these knowledge systems relate to one another during development?

The experiences of learning to ride a bicycle or drive a car illustrate well how these systems might interact during development. When we learn to drive a car, we go through a first stage where each required action and sequence of actions—such as looking in the mirror, signaling with the blinker, pressing the clutch prior to shifting into gear, and so forth—are explicitly thought of and double-checked while monitoring our situation in the environment. Once learned and after a few hours of practice, the required actions for driving become second nature, transferable to almost any vehicle and performed without explicit thinking. Information appears to be perceived directly; the affordances of the road, the car, and the traffic implicitly detected. Actually, this sort of automatization of conscious learning can be jeopardized by the return of explicit awareness. If you start to think too much about your driving, you actually increase your chances of having an accident. People in sport competitions confirm that self-consciousness is one's worst enemy: tennis, golf, or billiard players commonly report that they lose their "touch" by thinking too much about their moves.

It appears that in learning new skills, the "know-what" system scouts the way and contributes to setting the stage for an eventual automatization of actions characterizing the "know-how" system. Typically, we reflect on the situation and probe the environment before acting. To guide the search for a lost object, for example, we try to figure out where we last saw the object and what might have happened to it. We explore weather situations and probe the thickness of the ice covering a lake prior to walking on it. If the action succeeded, then it is repeated with less or no explicit probing. In dealing with the object world, particularly in learning to perform actions on objects, there is a constant interchange between the "what" and "how" systems of physical knowledge. The same is probably true in infancy except that this interchange is developing (see Rochat 1999b for further discussion).

I will suggest in Chapter 5 that systematic probing of the environment and the corresponding "knowing what" system emerges by the second month after term birth, not before. At birth and during the first six weeks, infants manifest only practical knowledge or "know-how" via innate action systems such as sucking or visually tracking moving objects. Newborns detect and learn new affordances for actions, but this learning does not entail yet any interchange with a "knowing what" system as discussed here.

So far, I have discussed what infants perceive and know about themselves, and what they perceive and know about their physical environment. But what about their social environment? What do infants perceive, understand, and potentially learn from people? Obviously, this last question is central to any attempt to capture the nature of infant psychology. Infants depend on people who, in addition to providing basic care, reciprocate and support their development. From the outset, people are indeed privileged and special objects of knowledge.

4 | THE INFANT AND OTHERS

In the preceding chapter, I presented research suggesting that very early on infants behave as objective perceivers, expecting physical objects to behave according to core principles. These principles include the fact that objects are substantial, occupy space, and cannot be in two places at the same time. Because infants appear to apply these physical principles at an age when they cannot yet have much hands-on experience with objects, and because we should be wary of assuming that these principles are prewired in the neonate, it is likely that they are first acquired via active observation or contemplation of things behaving around them and independently of their own active intervention. But is this also the case for the development of what infants understand about others?

Intimate, one-to-one relationships are the cradle of social understanding. Although much can be learned from watching people at a distance and not being directly engaged in a social exchange, it cannot replace the learning opportunity provided by shared social experiences. This is particularly evident when considering the developmental origins of what infants perceive and understand about others. Infants do not develop a social understanding by merely engaging in social "voyeurism," observing and actively monitoring people around them. They learn by engaging in reciprocal exchanges with others.

Some fifty years ago, infant psychiatrist and psychoanalyst René Spitz made this point clear with tragic footage of infants from crowded orphanages. Deprived of one-to-one contact with caregivers, these infants rocked their heads back and forth as if negating any contact with the outside world (Spitz 1965). These infants fell back within themselves rather than opening up to the world of people. Unresponsive to social solicitations, they lost the little social learning opportunity left to them. Although not irreversible, this can delay and have dramatic effects on their development, in particular their social-cognitive development.

In general, social cognition can be construed as the process by which individuals develop the ability to monitor, control, and predict the behavior of others. This ability entails various degrees of understanding, from the perceptual discrimination of feature characteristics and emotional expressions, to the complex representation of intentions and beliefs as determinants of behavior (theories of mind).

Intersubjectivity and the Origins of Social Knowledge

Although people have bodies and physical knowledge can account for part of their behavior (for example, the fact that they can move on their own, hide or fall, are subject to the forces of gravity, and cannot be at two different locations at the same time), monitoring people and predicting what they are going to do next entails skills that go far beyond physical understanding. Social cognition entails the reading of affects, emotions, intentions, and subtle reciprocities: all the things that make people fundamentally different from objects. In other words, it entails the understanding of a private or dispositional world—that is, what people feel and what characterizes their individual inclinations. But how do we get access to such understanding?

To a large extent, people reveal themselves in the way they respond to us and how, via reciprocity, they convey a sense of shared experience. The same is true for animals and pets. Understanding an animal of a particular species observed in the wild or at a zoo, even for extended periods of time, is different from understanding the same animal raised as a pet. A sense of shared experience adds to social understanding and gives deeper access to the dispositional characteristics of individuals, whether they are human or not. The sense of shared experience that emerges from reciprocity is captured by the term intersubjectivity. To a large extent, the emerging sense of shared experience determines the development of social cognition in infancy.

Intersubjectivity entails a basic differentiation between the self and others, as well as a capacity to compare and project one's own private experience onto another (the "like me" stance). Pet owners obviously understand that their animals are not just like themselves, but the owners do project a feeling of shared experience (empathy) that bridges the difference between them. Such projective ability is at the core of social understanding and is instrumental to the understanding of others. Interestingly, subjective projection appears to be a recent development in primate evolution. The work of primatologist Frans de Waal (1996), for example, suggests that primate species with closer evolutionary links to humans display more frequent and varied empathic behavior toward individuals within and even outside their species. There is a possible link in phylogeny between the capacity for intersubjective projection and levels of social cognition. We will see that there is evidence that such a link exists in early ontogeny.

In comparison to the abundance of recent experimental research on the origins of physical knowledge, there have been few inquiries regarding the origins of social knowledge (but see for example Rochat 1999a). Clever experiments have helped us know much about the early onset of object permanence, counting ability, adaptive actions toward an object, and the early understanding of how things move in the world. We know far less regarding what infants understand about people at the origins of development: what makes people attractive, recognizable, and predictable for the infant. This is ironic considering the commonsensical view that infants develop social skills from an early age and that people are what babies seem to care about most from birth. Infants' attraction to people is obviously adaptive, given that their very survival depends on them.

Early behavior and the distribution of attention in newborns also reflect the fact that people provide richer perceptual encounters—are simply more interesting—than any other objects in the environment. We will see later that neonates seem particularly attracted to people, and in particular to the sounds, movements, and features of the human face. Social cognition is rooted in this early drawing together of infants and caregivers.

Subjective Experience and Reciprocity

The way to crack through the surface of people's dispositional world, and hence to access crucial information from which their behavior can be monitored, predicted, and controlled, is to reciprocate with them. Before discussing reciprocity as the mechanism by which infants map their own subjectivity onto the subjectivity of others, it is important to distinguish three basic categories of subjective experience: feelings, affects, and emotions. These categories are too often confounded, whether in the literature or in the common use of these terms. The definitions I propose below are meant to clarify these distinct aspects of subjective experience.

Feelings are the perception of specific private experiences such as pain, hunger, or frustration. In comparison to affects, this category of subjective experience generally lasts for a shorter time and ends following particular problem-solving actions such as feeding for hunger, comfort for pain, or fulfilling a goal for frustration.

Affects qualify the perception of a general mood or perceived private tone that exists as a background to both feelings and emotions. Affects are diffuse and protracted in comparison to feelings. They fluctuate along a continuum, from a low tone (depression) to a high tone (elation). To use a weather metaphor, affects are the perception of the global pressure system as it fluctuates from high to low pressure, and vice versa, over time.

Emotions are the observable (public) expressions of feelings and affects through movement, postures, and facial displays—as in the behavioral expressions of pain, joy, disgust, sadness, surprise, or anger. Emotions have specific, identifiable features

(Darwin [1872] 1965) that communicate the private experience of feelings and affects.

Feelings, affects, and emotions are three kinds of basic subjective experience that are part of infants' private sense of self, from birth and long before they can talk and theorize about them. Neonates clearly have feelings and affects that they express via specific emotional displays such as pain, hunger, or disgust. They cry in a certain way following the routine heel-prick procedure used by nurses in maternity hospitals to extract blood, and cry another way when hungry. Mothers typically recognize the basic needs of their new infants via remarkably subtle variations in their babies' behavior, which stands for feelings experienced privately by the infant (for example, pain, hunger, bliss, or comfort).

Intimate, one-on-one reciprocal exchanges between infants and their caregivers allow infants to develop an understanding of what they feel and experience from within. These private experiences are moderated from the outset by what appear to be long-lasting temperamental traits or affective baselines characterizing each individual infant (Kagan 1998a). For example, infants will react with more or less apparent inhibition in the face of novel situations, such as the encounter of a stranger or a mechanical toy suddenly moving closer. These basic temperaments along a "timidity-boldness" continuum are to some extent stable and part of an individual's idiosyncratic personality profile from birth through childhood (Kagan and Snidman 1991).

Regardless of the variety of stable temperaments expressed from birth, all infants develop a sense of shared feelings, affects, and emotions through the reciprocal, face-to-face exchanges that are so prominent during the first months. In these exchanges, affects, feelings, and emotions of the infant echo the affects, feelings, and emotions of the social partner, either by mirroring (Gergely and Watson 1996), contagion (Hatfield, Cacioppo, and Rapson 1994), or merely contingent reactions within a short time frame (Murray and Trevarthen 1985). We see these styles of exchange between mother and infant, for example, while they play games such as peek-a-boo or "I'm gonna get ya" (Fogel 1993; Kaye 1982).

From birth, parents and caretakers encourage the infant to match his or her own experience with theirs. Parents' initiations of face-to-face interactions with repetitive gestures, particular vocal intonation, and exaggerated facial expressions are the main course of the social regimen offered probably to all infants, at least all of the Western middle-class infants who are overwhelmingly represented in infancy research. These interactions are typically a running commentary by the parent of how the infant should feel.

Here is, for example, a casual observation I recorded while lounging by a swimming pool. It illustrates the kind of emotional support and assistance that young infants are typically given in one-on-one exchanges:

> A father in the swimming pool lowers his two-month-old daughter toward the waters surface. He holds her so that he can have a clear view of her face and so that she can see his entire face. While staring at her intensely, the father gently lets one of her bare feet touch the water and briskly removes it while commenting with a loud, high-pitched voice "Oootch, it's cold!" and displaying a greatly exaggerated expression of pain. This routine is repeated many times in a row, each time after a pause during which the infant regains her calm.

In this observation, the parent creates an emotionally charged context in anticipation of particular feelings in his infant (fear, pleasure, surprise, and so forth). He monitors the child to capture the expression of the anticipated feeling in order to echo her expression in an easily discernible (exaggerated) and contingent manner. It is as if the father was interviewing his daughter to discover her feelings and was creating a situation where he could show empathy and demonstrate his sheer pleasure to be with her. It is unlikely that the father wanted to give his daughter a swimming lesson or teach her about temperature, liquid, or the dangers of water. Note that this demonstration of empathy requires intimate, one-on-one contact. It mobilizes the full attention of the adult and requires a great sense of timing. Remarkably, the vast majority of parents have a natural talent for highly sophisticated interactional skills with their infant, a talent sometimes referred to as "intuitive parenting" (Papousek and Papousek 1987). The ability to express empathy by echoing affects and feelings is part of normal parenting across cultures and despite marked variations.

But what is gained from shared experience? Why would young infants bother trying to match their private feelings with those of other people? Feelings and affects are unquestionably major determinants of behavior and are crucial for monitoring, predicting, and controlling others' behavior toward us whether we please them or not, whether they are attentive to our actions or not. This can mean a lot for young infants, who depend on others to survive. Because of the prolonged immaturity characterizing human infancy (see Chapter 1), human infants need to relate to caregivers and stay near them. By developing intersubjectivity, infants can monitor and predict more accurately the behavior of those on whom they depend. Furthermore, the development of intersubjectivity is probably linked to the emergence of an understanding of intentions and beliefs underlying people's actions. Taking the perspective of others and predicting how another person would feel in a given situation is indeed a prerequisite to most theories of mind tasks or tasks implying inference of others' psychology ("folk psychology"), which children start to succeed in by the third year.

It is through the early development of intersubjectivity that infants can eventually consider the perspective of others in addition to, or in coordination with, their own. This ability to be "perspectival" (Tomasello 1999) is indexed by social cognitive skills such as joint attention and symbolic gestures, which emerge around the end of the first year. Symptoms of autism, in particular the social withdrawal characterizing autistic children, demonstrate the inseparability between the ability to share experiences with others and the ability to develop theories of mind. Autistic children are described as having the social-cognitive handicap of "mindblindness"—that is, they lack the ability to read others' minds (Baron-Cohen 1995). This deficit is not purely cognitive; it has devastating interpersonal consequences. The major challenge of parents and educators interacting with autistic children is to try to find common ground for communication and emotional exchange. Autism always includes either a lack of or hindered development of intersubjectivity (Hobson 1993).

The absence of intersubjectivity deprives individuals of the opportunity to develop prosocial behaviors, empathy, and moral judgments, which are obviously important byproducts of social cognition. But how do infants develop such abilities? When does intersubjectivity start to develop as the foundation of infants' monitoring, control, and prediction of other people's behavior? Researchers have started to address these questions by studying systematically infant behavior in the context of social exchanges, namely dyadic or face-to-face interactions.

The Importance of the Eyes and Face

Mothers and caregivers attempt to establish contact and communicate their affection to young infants in many ways—for example, by gentle stroking, rocking, talking, or singing. Most commonly, however, caregivers present their face conspicuously to the infant, at close range, parallel to the infant, and most importantly, with eye contact. This "en face" presentation allows them to monitor the result of their behavior on the infant. It is also an implicit attempt to make themselves as emotionally readable as possible for the infant.

This observation is banal: none of us turns our back to infants when dealing with them. Nevertheless, in light of what can be observed in other primate species, especially species that are more distant relatives, it appears that the dominance of face-to-face, eye-to-eye contacts might be unique to humans. Based on my own casual observations, eye-to-eye contacts between mother and infant in apes, and even more so in monkeys, are fleeting—although certain species such as Capuchin monkeys seem more inclined to have long contacts of this kind. In most species of apes and monkeys, protracted eye-to-eye contacts are typically confounded with signs of potential aggression. In humans, on the contrary, eye contacts are nurtured as signs of empathy and a willingness to share feelings—a predominant aspect of infant care.

At least in most Western cultures, children are taught to look in people's eyes. When there is a lack or avoidance of eye contact, we are quick to infer that the other is shy, embarrassed, or even deceptive. It is in the context of such mind reading that children are taught what is appropriate and what is not. Looking in people's eyes is usually a sign of overall social engagement and a readiness to deal with that person. In adults, however, it can indicate all possible motives, from love to envy, contempt to admiration, hate to compassion. For better or for worse, eye contact is most commonly a sign of social openness and an invitation to communicate. I am always struck when I observe lovers in public places staring endlessly into each other's eyes, oblivious of the commotion around them. This extreme eye-to-eye contact suggests a sharing of experience to the point of fusion. Love, including maternal love, has indeed something to do with fusional intersubjectivity and its accompanying blissful feeling of being as one. Once again, much of this phenomenon in humans is expressed via the presentation and reading of not only the eyes, but also the face.

If eyes are indeed windows to the psychological dispositions and subjective experience of others, the face as a whole, including the mouth, nose, and area around the eyes, stages the dynamic of such experience. Faces are the public theater of the mind. In the footsteps of Charles Darwin's classic study on the expression of emotions in animals and man, and the evolution of specific facial displays that accompany particular feelings, psychologists like Paul Ekman (1994) have documented further how reliable such displays are across cultures. Whether American, Japanese, or a member of hunter-gatherer tribes living in the remote forests of New Guinea, adults all use the same facial expressions to express feelings of sadness, joy, anger, or disgust. Humans have evolved universal ways of expressing emotions. Note, however, that cultural factors do influence when it is appropriate to display particular emotions. A political debate in Stockholm, Rome, or Dakar will most probably be animated in very different ways. Some cultures dictate more inhibition of emotions than others.

The universality and biological underpinning of emotional expression are evident when considering how newborns become public with their feelings: they cry and frown in specific ways in response to pain, smile and show great relaxation of facial muscles after feeding. As mentioned earlier, they tend to smile and display relaxed, positive affects in response to sweet smells. In contrast, they wrinkle their nose, blink, and purse their lips when they smell something sour. These facial expressions are basically similar to adults' and seem to show that these emotions are not learned but rather part of an innate, built-in affectivity. Emotional expression is not immune to development, however. What is present at birth is a set of basic (primary) emotions. Secondary emotions such as shame or guilt, with their own set of facial displays, start to emerge by the second year, as documented for example by children's reactions to their reflection in a mirror when they start to recognize themselves (Lewis and Brooks-Gunn 1979; Lewis 1992; Chapter 2).

The eyes and face are the primary features that infants monitor in others, and they particularly pay attention to the way these features show reciprocal feelings in the context of face-to-face exchanges. The predominance of face-to-face exchanges facilitated by caregivers certainly contributes to the development of early social cognition. But research also shows that infants are born with a particular attraction to faces and possibly also with a built-in ability to analyze and recognize facial features. Face-to-face interactions with caregivers might thus tap into infants' innate predisposition. But what evidence is there for such an early predisposition?

Some thirty years ago, when infancy researchers started to use novel experimental paradigms such as preferential looking to document visual scanning from birth, they discovered that visual exploration depended on what pattern was presented to the infant for exploration. In their seminal work (mentioned in Chapter 3), Robert Fantz and his colleagues found that even newborns demonstrate marked visual preferences when presented with two different patterns side by side (Fantz 1964; Fantz and Fagan 1975). Fantz and his colleagues discovered, for example, that newborns tend to prefer circular patterns such as the image of a bull's eye over a pattern composed of straight lines with a comparable amount of contrast (such as a checkerboard). The preference for circular patterns fits with the

idea of a basic predisposition to process facelike displays with circular outlines.

In relation to similar two-dimensional static displays, Marshall
Haith (1980) documented more precisely the actual oculomotor activity of newborns and young infants while they were engaged in
scanning such patterns. He found an overall tendency in infants
from birth to search for and align their pupils with the edges of the
outline figure (such as the apex of a triangle), after which they
would systematically scan these edges. This predictable fine-grained
visual activity suggests that visual exploration is determined by optimum stimulation, in particular the maximum firing of neurons in
the visual cortex. Maximum visual stimulation would correspond to
the scanning of regions offering the highest contrast. Haith's findings indicate that visual exploration in neonates seems to be determined by response to contrast and amount of stimulus energy.
Though probably an accurate account of how newborns explore
outlined geometric figures, this interpretation needs to be supple-
mented to account for slightly older infants' explorations of more
meaningful displays such as faces.

Between five and seven weeks, infants begin to devote dramatically more time to looking at faces—in one experiment, the increase
was from 22 to 87 percent of the time that an adult's face was shown
(Haith, Bergman, and Moore 1977). In general, until approximately
two months of age infants spend most of their exploration time
scanning the outside contour of a static face (Maurer and Salapatek
1976). This is part of the so-called externality effect found in infants
younger than two months, who are shown to be capable of processing external but not internal features of a pattern. If for example
they are visually habituated to a figure embedded in another (say a
small circle inside a larger square), they will dishabituate only to external changes (for example, a transformation of the larger square),
and not to changes internal to the figure (Bushnell 1979).

Interestingly, from approximately seven weeks of age, the externality effect seems to weaken when infants are presented with an animated face talking to them. In such circumstances and compared to
a silent, static face, seven-week-old and nine- to twenty-one-week-

old infants are more likely to explore the eyes of the face (Haith, Bergman, and Moore 1977; see Slater and Butterworth 1997 for further discussion). Here social context appears to override both the externality effect and a straightforward stimulus energy account of visual exploration. By the second month, infants show signs of becoming attuned to the eyes as a privileged communicative feature of an animated face, arguably the best index of feelings and affects.

In recent years, there have been some remarkable reports of newborns' ability to discriminate between the image of their mother's face and the image of a female stranger matched for overall features such as hair color and overall skin tone (brightness). Infants less than forty-eight hours old were found to look reliably more at the image of their mother compared to that of the other female stranger. In the context of an instrumental sucking paradigm, newborns aged between twelve and thirty-six hours were found to suck more on a dummy pacifier in order to see on a video screen their mother's face rather than a stranger's face (Walton, Bower, and Bower 1992). These findings suggest that immediately after birth infants not only process complex information about faces, but also appear to learn by picking up and storing patterns of features that correspond to familiar faces (see Bushnell 1998 for a review of research on the facial features determining early face recognition). If that is the case, then from birth infants process remarkably complex facelike patterns and are probably predisposed toward facial learning and discrimination.

Evidence of a predisposition to process facial displays is provided by experiments that recorded neonates' visual tracking of two-dimensional schematic facelike displays moving in front of them. Such experiments show that newborns tend to track significantly more of those facelike displays with eyes, eyebrows, nose, and mouth arranged in a natural way, compared to either a blank display or a display with scrambled (but symmetric) facial features (Morton and Johnson 1991).

So if infants have an innate predisposition to process faces, what do they use for it? We have seen that they probably use this ability to form templates of familiar faces such as their mother's. But what about others? When do infants start to use facial cues such as eye contact or emotional expressions to monitor their ongoing interaction with social partners? As adults, we attend to people's faces mainly to monitor and assess their disposition in the reciprocal context of communication. What are the developmental origins of such monitoring?

Simon Baron-Cohen (1995) recently proposed that healthy infants possess from birth two specialized mechanisms to monitor others and read their mental states. These mechanisms include an eye-direction detector (a specialized system to follow gaze in others) and an intentionality detector (a system to pick up information about others' planned action). These mechanisms are part of all healthy infants' evolutionary endowment at birth. According to Baron-Cohen, the "mindblindness" of autistic children would be accountable by deficiencies in, or even the absence of, such innate mechanisms. The intentionality detector is viewed as a built-in perceptual device that interprets motion stimuli, in particular self-propelled movements, in terms of goals or desires. So for example, if infants see an animal moving, the theory assumes that infants (from birth) are endowed with the ability to interpret this object in motion as "going somewhere."

As adults, we constantly and effortlessly interpret the movements of others as intentional. But so far, no clear empirical evidence supports Baron-Cohen's assumption that such interpretation is at work from birth. Later in this chapter, we will see that the interpretative power of intentionality probably does not emerge until about nine months of age.

There is more empirical evidence supporting the contention that very early on (at least by two to three months), infants are detecting eyes and where they are looking, manifesting the working of some kind of eye-direction detector as suggested by Baron-Cohen. Despite the "externality effect" displayed by young infants, two-month-olds look significantly longer at facelike drawings with eyes compared to those without any eyes (Maurer 1985). This suggests that from early on infants can detect the presence or absence of eyes on a face. More studies suggest that young infants also detect gaze direction. By six months, infants are reported to look two to three times longer at a face staring at them than at a face looking away (Papousek and Papousek 1974).

In a recent study, three- to six-month-old infants were systematically observed while interacting with an adult who either had her eyes fixated on them or averted her gaze 20 degrees off center (Hains and Muir 1996). Infants smiled significantly less in the averted gaze condition, even if the position of the adult's head remained the same. These results suggest that by three months infants are sensitive to eye direction in the context of face-to-face communicative exchanges.

In another recent study, Albert Caron and collaborators (Caron, Caron, Roberts, and Brooks 1997) report that between three and five months infants develop a greater sensitivity to eye contacts per se, independently of head orientation. Their research indicates that until the age of three months, the sensitivity to eye contacts depends on the social partner facing them. When the social partner turns her head to the side while maintaining eye contact (looking at the infant from the corner of her eyes), three-month-olds but not five-month-olds show a significant decline in smiling.

If early on infants are sensitive to gazing and eye contact when interacting with another person, they also seem to learn quickly that another person's line of gaze is referential, namely that it refers to things in the environment. For example, infants as young as three months are reported to orient their gaze and look in the same direction as in an adult face (D'Entremont, Hains, and Muir 1997). This face had only the eyes oriented either to the right or the left of the infant, and infants oriented their own gaze accordingly. This remarkable finding suggests that at least from three months of age, infants not only notice where others are looking, but tend to look there too (see also evidence by Hood, Willen, and Driver 1998; Symons, Hains, and Muir 1998). This ability is an early precursor of intersubjectivity and social competence, which emerge by the end of the first year when infants start to manifest explicit joint attention with another person in reference to an object.

It is worth noting that as adults, we are remarkably sensitive to eye contact and eye direction. It is hard to think of a more basic social "put off" than talking to someone who is avoiding your gaze or systematically looking at other parts of your body. Current infancy research strongly suggests that sensitivity to eyes and gaze direction is a foundational aspect of social cognition from which infants learn to monitor and understand others. Interestingly, it seems that our physical attributes as humans have evolved to help us notice where others are looking. The sharp contrast between the white sclera of the eyes and the colorful iris emerged relatively recently in primate evolution (Kobayashi and Kohshima 1997). The way human eyes are shaped also helps in this regard.

There is some evidence that gaze direction detection by four-month-old infants depends on whether the eyes are in an intact upright schematic face (Vecera and Johnson 1995). Infants appear less inclined to detect averted gaze in the context of a scrambled upright schematic face. Thus, early on, the perception of gaze direction is probably part of mechanisms responsible for the processing of faces as a whole. But what direct evidence do we have that infants interpret facial expressions as a whole in addition to where a person is looking? This is shown by research demonstrating that the face is a main stage of emotional experience.

Facial Expressions and Emotions

If feelings of pain, sadness, joy, or anger are expressed in specific ways from birth onward, with little variation across contrasted cultural contexts, how do infants perceive and make sense of such facial expressions in others? It is one thing to be innately inclined to produce emotional facial displays accompanying the perception (feeling) of a particular affective experience (affect). It is another thing to actually perceive and eventually comprehend what someone else is feeling from looking at his or her face. When and to what extent do infants perceive and understand emotions in others? This question is at the core of the early development of social cognition, in particular the understanding of others as having fluctuating dispositional qualities (for example, sometimes happy and sometimes blue).

By habituating infants to the picture of a face with a particular emotional expression (happy, sad, surprised, and so forth) and then testing them for dishabituation to novel expressions, researchers have demonstrated that young infants do discriminate among facial expressions. Infants between three and five months of age are reported to discriminate happy and sad faces from surprised faces; smiling faces from frowning faces; joyful expressions from angry or neutral expressions. At around the same age, infants are even reported to discriminate between different intensities of the same emotional expression (Nelson 1987).

Do infants, in discriminating among facial expressions, process more than surface characteristics of these expressions? Researchers have addressed this question empirically by habituating infants to different models of the same facial expression. For example, infants are habituated to a happy facial expression with a variety of toothy or toothless smiles, or eyebrows raised to different levels. Following habituation, infants were tested for dishabituation with a new model displaying either the same or a different facial expression. If infants dishabituate, it means that the infant is not just discriminating among superficial differences in facial expression; she is evaluating these expressions in terms of categories of emotions.

Research shows that by seven months, infants display some categorical perception, but it is still tentative—it depends on the facial expression that the infant has been habituated to. For example, categorical perception is evident when infants are habituated first to happy faces and then tested with faces displaying fear or surprise. But no evidence of this kind of perception is found when infants are habituated first to the fearful or surprised expression, then to a happy face (Nelson 1987).

What about infants younger than seven months? In one study by Caron, Caron, and Myers (1985), four-month-olds did not show any evidence of categorical discrimination when habituated with facial models displaying surprised or happy expressions, then tested with a novel model of either expression. In contrast, six-month-olds showed some generalized discrimination, but only when habituated with the happy expression first. Seven-month-olds in this study showed generalized discrimination whether habituated first to the happy or surprised expression.

As mentioned above, beyond perceptual discrimination of facial expressions, a central question regarding the origins of social cognition is how infants manage to know that a particular facial display stands for a particular class of feelings experienced by others. At least in our cultural context, caregivers stage face-to-face exchanges with exaggerated, typically cheerful affects accompanied by prolonged eye contacts and high-pitched voices—so it is reasonable to think that the meaning of emotions is taught via sharing in the context of such dyadic exchanges. These exchanges form the privileged context in which infants can learn to relate and eventually match their own feelings with those of others (taking the "like me" stance). Such an assumption appears particularly valid given that from birth infants show signs of imitation when interacting with others face-to-face.

Facial Imitation and Emotional Coregulation

Over the last twenty years, many studies have reported imitative responses in very young infants. These findings have forced researchers to reconsider the dominant view, in particular Piaget's, that the capacity for imitation starts only months after birth. In well-controlled laboratory conditions, neonates only a few hours old have been shown to reproduce a remarkably wide range of gestural acts modeled by an experimenter, such as tongue protrusion, lip pursing, and head and finger movements (Meltzoff and Moore 1977). But although such an early imitative ability has been replicated in various laboratories around the world, the interpretation of the phenomenon continues to cause much controversy. For some interpreters of neonatal imitation, it is essentially a fleeting phenomenon, limited to one gesture (such as tongue protrusion) and determined by low-level processes such as automatic release mechanisms (Anisfeld 1991) or rigidly triggered oral exploration (Jones 1996). Other theorists like Andrew Meltzoff and Keith Moore (1997) view neonatal imitation as the expression of a much richer ability, the expression of an active cross-modal matching between vision and proprioception. In particular, in the case of facial imitation, the infant sees the model and reproduces a corresponding gesture without any

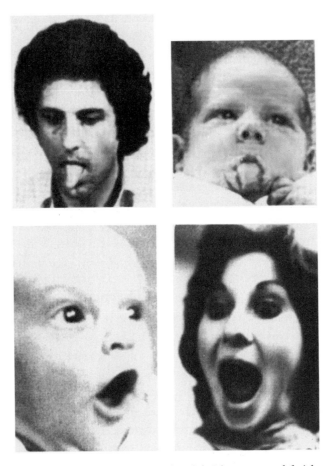

Figure 4.1 Infants at birth have reproduced facial gestures and facial expressions modeled by an experimenter—here a tongue protrusion (photo from Meltzoff and Moore 1977) and a surprise facial expression (photo from Field et al. 1982).

possibility of seeing how their own imitative response matches the model's example. Thus, if one accepts the view that infants are actually trying to match the specific behavior displayed by the adult, neonatal imitation does entail an active intermodal matching process. More importantly, it also means that infants from birth do not behave in a social vacuum, but rather are actively linking their own behavior to the behavior of others (Figure 4.1).

There is one particular study on neonatal imitation that suggests that young infants might be trying not merely to reproduce what another person does, but also to match the affect or mood of the social partner. Tiffany Field and her colleagues (Field, Woodson, Greenberg, and Cohen 1982) reported evidence that newborn infants tend to reproduce facial expressions of happiness, sadness, or surprise. In their study, newborns were observed while facing the experimenter, who displayed in succession these well-contrasted facial emotions. Newborns showed a significant widening of the lips when attending to the happy expression of the experimenter, an increased protrusion of the lower lip during the sad expression exposure, and an increased opening of the eyes and mouth when the experimenter looked surprised.

In infants' inclination and apparent capacity to reproduce these emotional expressions, there is an intriguing possibility that in addition to physically matching the expressions, infants might be experiencing vicariously the feelings of others. This is highly speculative, but it cannot be readily dismissed in light of some phenomena reported in the adult literature on emotions. There is some evidence that particular facial expressions are not only the consequences of specific feelings experienced by the person; they can also precede and *cause* particular feelings. Researchers have shown that adult participants instructed to move particular facial parts until they look, say, happy or sad, eventually do feel that way (Ekman, Levenson, and Friesen 1983; Meltzoff 1990). Via early imitation of facial expressions, infants might not only match the surface characteristics of others with their own, but also others' feelings (dispositional characteristics) in relation to their own. Early facial imitation could indeed play a crucial role in the establishment of intersubjectivity, which as we have seen is possibly an important means by which young infants learn to be affectively attuned to others.

The combination of adults' systematic encouragement and assistance during face-to-face exchanges and young infants' proclivity to imitate the facial expressions of others is an important aspect of the developmental origins of social cognition. If adults tend to initiate particular social responses in infants via exaggerated expressions that mirror what infants might feel from within, infants are not passive receivers of such initiatives. Evidence of early imitation suggests that these exchanges, even if first initiated by the adult, entail emotional coregulation by both social partners. By imitating each other, the infant-adult pair engages primarily in reciprocating affects and feelings. Such reciprocation is at the origin of intersubjectivity, which is itself a foundation of early social cognition. Via mutual imitation adults and infants can probe the degree to which they communicate with one another (are capturing each other's attention). Such monitoring is crucial in the formation of privileged relationships between infants and their primary caregivers.

By establishing privileged relationships and monitoring the reciprocation of affects and feelings, infants develop the rudiments of social understanding. They become discriminant of the motives and dispositions that drive people's behavior toward them. Recent research demonstrates that young infants do develop specific social expectations in face-to-face exchanges. By the second month, when starting to reciprocate by smiling and gazing for long periods toward others, infants become sensitive to timing in social interactions. With such timing comes communicative flow, and in particular a higher level of affective attunement by others toward the infant.

Detection of Social Contingency

From the time that infants start to reciprocate in face-to-face exchanges, they develop expectations regarding social partners and the way that they should respond in face-to-face interactions. Routine games, mirroring, and parental frames form a dynamic field of exploration for the infant from which invariants can be picked up and social anticipation can develop. In addition to and beyond their physical attributes, people can be identified in the way they relate to the infant: the timing of their interactions (both gesture and voice), the energy level of these interactions, and the overall mood expressed by their posture. These invariants specify the dispositional world of others in relation to the self.

An infant might start to expect to be picked up in a certain way when engaging in a joyful, playful interaction with a particular person. Mom might be in general gentler and softer in the way she plays with and handles her infant. Dad might be more forceful and vocal when interacting with the same infant. Infants appear to pick up these invariant characteristics that specify persons in the way they relate to them. Research suggests that at least by four to five months infants develop an attunement to their own mother's timing and relative contingency in interacting with them (for example, frequency of contingent, reciprocal smiles), and tend to generalize this attunement to stranger females whose behavior toward the infants matches their mother's. For example, a recent study (Bigelow 1998) shows that five-month-old infants raised by mothers who are highly responsive and prompt to respond to their infant in normal face-to-face exchanges prefer to interact (that is, respond more quickly with contingent smiling and vocalizing) with strangers who resemble the mother in this way. In contrast, infants raised by mothers who are significantly less contingent in face-to-face exchanges show more contingent responsiveness to strangers who, similarly, display less contingency. With this elegant study, Ann Bigelow demonstrates five-month-olds' sensitivity to the *familiar* level of contingency experienced with their mothers, independently of whether this level is high or low (Bigelow 1999). Within a few months, infants seem to adjust to the interactive style of their primary caregiver. This adjustment determines an early preference for social partners with a communicative style that is consonant with the style of their mother.

Researchers have reported that infants as young as two months, interacting with their mother via a closed-circuit video system, respond differently to her depending on whether she is interacting live or in a replay of previous interactions. Infants were reported to display a marked decrease in gazing and smiling as well as a significant increase in negative affects in the replay compared to the live condition (Murray and Trevarthen 1985; see also the recent work of Nadel, Carchon, Kervella, Marcelli, and Réserbat-Plantey 1999). This suggests that by two months of age, infants start to be sensitive to their mother's emotional attunement to them. In the replay condition, the mother was noncontingent: although she displayed positive feelings and affects, she violated the timing of response that specifies reciprocity and hence disrupted the sense of shared experience and intersubjectivity.

Note however that in a recent study (Rochat, Neisser, and Marian 1998), we failed to replicate these findings with same-age infants using the same experimental paradigm (closed-circuit video system). Such a phenomenon, if real, is fragile. Perhaps the closed-circuit video lacks ecological validity by removing important cues of reciprocity normally present in direct face-to-face exchanges. These cues include touching and distance regulation, which might be important for infants' ability to assess the communicative flow and affective attunement of others.

In order to capture what is detected by young infants in a more natural dyadic context than the closed-circuit video system, we recently explored the sensitivity of two- to six-month-old infants to interactions with an adult stranger (Rochat, Querido, and Striano 1999). The goal for this study was to capture how infants from two months on refine their ability both to detect regularities in ongoing social interactions and to develop specific expectations based on these regularities. We hypothesized that by two months of age infants, although they start to show signs of reciprocity, still have only a diffuse and undifferentiated sense of the other as a reciprocal partner. At this early age, the social skills and achievement of the infant might be due to the global monitoring of the presence or absence of an attentive social partner, not yet to the degree to which this partner is reciprocating. We hypothesized that infants progress from a global sense at birth of a social presence (in the sense of someone who offers intimate and animated eye-to-eye contact accompanied by engaging child-oriented speech, or "motherese") to, at about four months, having specific expectations of the social partner based on the *quality* of the interaction (for example, whether it is organized or disorganized, contingent or noncontingent, predictable or not). This development leads infants to differentiate among people in the subtle ways they relate to them.

In our study, we videotaped two-, four-, and six-month-old infants interacting with a female stranger in a face-to-face situation that did not include any touching. In two different experimental conditions, the experimenter introduced the infant to a peek-a-boo routine that was either structured or unstructured.

In the structured condition, the peek-a-boo routine was strictly organized into three phases (1) an approach phase in which the experimenter leaned toward the infant while saying "look, look, look" and maintaining eye contact, (2) an arousal phase in which once the experimenter was close to the infant she covered her face with her hands, then dropped her hands while saying "peek-a-boo!", and (3) a final release phase in which the experimenter leaned back to the original posture while saying a long, calming "yeaaah!" nodding the head, and smiling.

In the unstructured condition, the experimenter engaged in a scrambled or disorganized peek-a-boo game, with actions that were identical to the normal (structured) peek-a-boo game but did not coalesce to form the crescendo-decrescendo or tension-building and release script. For this condition, the experimenter was wearing an ear piece connected to a tape recorder that played instructions of random actions to be performed in front of the infant (hands up, say "peek-a-boo!" "look, look, look," lean forward, and so on). Note that the structured and unstructured peek-a-boo conditions were equal in duration and number of events (subroutines), varying only in their narrative power—that is, their ability to provide the infant with a simple script of tension building and release.

In scoring the infant's smiling and gazing at the experimenter, we observed an interesting developmental trend. Two-month-olds looked toward the experimenter and smiled equally in both the structured and unstructured conditions. They appeared equally attentive in both conditions and displayed no evidence of a differential response. In sharp contrast, both four- and six-month-olds demonstrated a significant increase in gazing during the unstructured compared to the structured condition. They also had longer periods of smiling during the structured condition.

Overall, the results of this study demonstrate that from four months of age, infants start to be attuned to the narrative envelope of routines provided by social partners. They detect regularities and patterns in the dyadic interaction and respond to them in synchrony. From this developing sensitivity to organized patterns of interaction infants develop more precise expectations about—and hence understanding of—who people are and how they will behave (Rochat, Querido, and Striano 1999).

Another recent study we performed in our laboratory (Rochat, Striano, and Blatt 2001) further captures the development of social expectations between two and six months. We studied infants' response to the sudden still face adopted by an experimenter in a face-to-face social exchange (Tronick et al. 1978; Muir and Hains 1999). In successive one-minute still-face conditions, interspersed with one minute of normal interaction, the experimenter adopted either a neutral still face (typical of studies using a still-face paradigm), a happy still face with mouth open and fixed smile, or a sad still face with wrinkled forehead, furrowed eyebrows, and frown. We scored the infant's relative smiling and gazing toward the experimenter in these various still-face conditions. In particular we compared the infant's response to the still face in comparison to the preceding normal, affectively positive interaction (still-face effect) and the infant's response to the still face in comparison to the following normal, affectively positive interaction (recovery effect).

In relation to gazing, we found an overall still-face effect (decrease in gazing duration toward the experimenter) in all conditions for the groups of four- and six-month-olds, but not for the two-month-olds. Two-month-olds did not avert their gaze during the happy still face. In relation to smiling, six-month-olds showed a markedly reduced recovery of smiling when the normal interaction resumed, independently of still-face conditions. In contrast to two- and four-month-olds, six-month-old infants appear to resist positive reengagement and reciprocity following any of the still-face episodes. This again suggests that they are building different expectations about the social partner based on the past unusual experience of the still-face episode.

In general, these observations indicate that by four to six months of age, infants are more sensitive to the dispositional cues displayed by people and these cues are the foundation for particular expectations regarding the way these people will behave. Depending on age, the still-face effect and the recovery from it appear more dependent on static emotional cues provided by the social partner during the still-face episode. It is as if between two and six months, infants develop an ability to consider the behavior of people beyond the here and now by relating current behavior to past interaction.

This development of social expectations finds its origins in a new conversational and contemplative stance that infants start to take in relation to others by the middle of the second month, as indexed by the emergence of socially elicited smiling, among other new behaviors (Wolff 1987). From this key developmental transition, which marks the end of the newborn phase and can be considered the psychological birth of a baby (see Chapter 5), infants develop a new understanding of people. Two-month-olds reciprocate in an undifferentiated way, sensitive mainly to the overall presence and positive solicitations of caretakers, whomever they are. At this early stage, others are differentiated from the self but not from each other. In their transactions with others, two-month-olds are mainly monitoring a presence, not assessing who this presence is, what her dispositions are, and what can be expected from her. In contrast, four- and six-month-old infants show signs of a growing sensitivity to subtle social cues such as the organization of a narrative offered by the adult in routine games, as well as the dispositional (emotional) cues expressed by the adult in these games. It appears that by six months infants can relate present face-to-face interactions with the quality and character of previous ones. This new "historical" perspective on people and the way they relate to them leads infants to develop rich social expectations based on increasingly subtle emotional and dispositional cues. This development accompanies the emergence of a new sense of shared experience in a dyadic context (primary intersubjectivity). It is from this development that infants prepare themselves for their next major developmental step in understanding others: the adoption of the intentional stance or the understanding of others as intentional agents.

Perceiving Intentions

Perceiving and understanding others as intentional are critical pre-requisites for the social cognitive development occurring beyond infancy. In particular, they are vital for the emergence of language, symbolic functioning, and theories of mind. Without an ability to detect others as intentional, it is hard to imagine how children could eventually learn to use conventional signs (language) to communicate and understand that something (a verbal sign) can stand for something else (be a referent). Language does indeed require the understanding that others are intentional or rational agents—that they do not randomly or automatically respond, but rather plan actions based on particular mental states, beliefs, and desires. Research suggests that although the discrimination of intentional action starts to be evident only by the end of the first year—or beginning of the second—young infants already appear to be sensitive to perceptual information that will help them to take an intentional stance, namely to start treating others as rational agents.

As adults, when we monitor our social surroundings and try to predict the behavior of others, we do not assume that people behave haphazardly. Rather, we fundamentally construe people as acting with goals in mind, as being intentional. If, for example, someone is staring at an open book, we assume that this person intends to gather information. Or if they point to an object, we assume that they want—intend—us to look at it. An important question is how infants develop such an assumption of intentionality by others, which is so fundamental to social cognition as well as to future theories of mind.

In adults, there is a robust, almost compulsive inclination to perceive meaningful physical and social causality. This inclination is so pervasive that we are eager to attribute intentions and even personalities to geometric figures based on the way they move on a screen. This was demonstrated over fifty years ago by the seminal works of Fritz Heider and Mark Simmel (1944), as well as Albert Michotte (1963), and has been confirmed by more recent studies (Basili 1976; Dittrich and Lea 1994). These studies documented that physical causality, dispositional qualities, and intentions were systematically perceived in the context of particular sequential movements of two or more geometric figures. Particular patterns of dynamic interactions between these abstract entities were associated with causal and social events: that one entity "caused" the other to move, by entrainment or by launching; that one is "chasing" the other with the intention of getting it (for example, that the red square "pushed" the blue circle, or the "nervous" yellow triangle is "trying to catch" the black circle who is "fleeing"). People tend to embellish their interpretations of how one entity moves in relation to the other with physical or social causality, and even to attribute intentions and dispositional qualities to these figures.

In one study (Rochat, Morgan, and Carpenter 1997), we attempted to capture the developmental origins of this phenomenon. We assumed that infants first develop a particular sensitivity and attunement to the kinds of dynamic perceptual information that adults believe specify social and intentional events. We tested three- to six-month-old infants (as well as a control group of adults) for their visual preference for two different dynamic displays showing abstract objects that adults perceive as interacting either intentionally or randomly. Both displays were presented to the infant simultaneously on two computer monitors placed side by side. Each display consisted of a pair of colored discs moving either independently (independent display) or in systematic interaction with one another (chase display). The discs never actually contacted one another.

The chase display was meant to specify an intentional, social event. In the chase display, one disc (the chaser) systematically approached the other (the chasee) at a constant velocity. When the chaser came close to the chasee, the latter accelerated away from it until it reached a relaxed distance, at which point it returned to normal speed. In the independent display, the movements of the discs were random. Except for the relative spatiotemporal dependence of the discs' movements, all dynamic parameters on the two displays were controlled and kept equal.

Adults, as well as six-month-old attentive infants (as opposed to infants that did not pay much attention to the displays), tended to look significantly longer at the independent display compared to the chase display. In contrast, the group of three-month-old attentive infants tended to look significantly more at the chase display. When ordering infants according to age in days and plotting the ratio of preference to the chase or the independent display as a function of age, there was a significant linear trend from chase to independent preference. Interestingly, post-test interviews of the adults indicated that they spent more time looking at the independent display, trying to pick up invariant dynamic patterns. They reported that the chase pattern in the other display was obvious and so required less attention. For commonsense reasons and because of an absence of direct evidence, we did not assume that the six-month-olds looked longer at the independent display for the same reason. But the results obtained with infants point to two facts: (1) from three months of age infants demonstrate a sensitivity to movement information that specifies social causality for adults (for example, chase versus random movements), and (2) this sensitivity is expressed differently and appears to develop between three and six months of age.

In order to test at what age infants might take an intentional stance in perceiving the chase display, we recently tested groups of three-, five-, seven- and nine-month-old infants (Rochat, Striano, and Morgan, submitted). Infants were habituated by looking at a red and a blue disc, identical in all ways but color, chasing one another on one computer display. For half of the infants of each age group, the blue disc was the chaser and the red disc was the chasee. For the other half it was the reverse. Once they reached a predetermined habituation criterion, infants were tested in successive posthabituation trials with either the same event or a role-reversal event. In the role-reversal event, the chaser became the chasee (and vice versa) by a color switch of the discs (for example, the blue chaser became the red, and the red chasee became the blue).

Results of this study yielded an interesting developmental trend. Infants younger than seven months did not show any signs of dishabituation (that is, a significant regain of visual attention) when the role-reversal event occurred. The group of seven-month-olds started to show signs of increased looking at the novel, role-reversal event, and by nine months, infants were definitely looking much longer at the role-reversal event. When we ordered all of the tested infants according to their age in days and plotted their dishabituation, we saw dishabituation starting at around seven months and increasing dramatically by nine months.

Considering that only the color labeled the role of each abstract protagonist on the computer display and that the protagonists were specified by the way they moved in relation to one another, we propose that the dishabituation starting to be expressed by seven-month-old infants and clearly expressed by nine-month-olds corresponds to the emergence of an intentional stance taken by the infant. This dishabituation is based, as in the previous experiment, on not only a discrimination of the pattern of relational movements of the two discs, but also a discrimination of a change in which disc is chasing and which is being chased. This means that infants start to construe social events as transactions between planning and motivated entities, a step beyond understanding that they are animated and move in different ways relative to one another.

Toward Secondary Intersubjectivity

The prototypical face-to-face, dyadic format of early social interaction changes in a marked way when infants start to engage in so-called triadic exchanges with others—that is, when they start to attend to the object world not merely in a self-absorbed way, but in conjunction with others. The term triadic stands for the three-way transaction taking place between the child, another person, and objects in the environment. The most widely studied triadic exchange is joint attention, when both the child and an adult attend simultaneously to the same object (Figure 4.2). The propensity of the child to look up toward the adult and then back to the object demonstrates that the child is checking the joint visual engagement of the other person and hence is aware of the relative "intentions" of others (that is, whether they are attending jointly to the same thing). This is a decisive, critical development occurring at around nine months of age (for more on the "nine-month revolution," see Chapter 5). It is decisive because it is the first clear indication that infants are starting

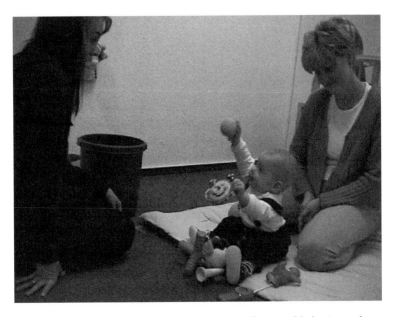

Figure 4.2 By nine months infants begin to manifest social behavior and can engage in triadic exchanges between themselves, objects, and people. As shown here, when playing with an object, they check if another person is simultaneously attending to the same thing, monitoring his or her line of gaze while offering the object. Immediately after this photo was taken, the infant returned to playing with and exploring the object. (Photo by T. Striano)

to understand that they and others can share views or perspectives (Adamson 1995; Tomasello 1995; 1999; Trevarthen and Hubley 1978). The infant's new ability to follow reliably an adult's line of gaze or to identify where an adult is pointing brings social exchanges and infant social cognition to radically new levels. Instead of learning about the dispositional world of others only through face-to-face exchanges, the infant develops a so-called secondary intersubjectivity or sense of shared experience with others in reference to a third party (an object, another person, or an event in the environment). How do infants make this developmental leap?

When an infant starts to follow a pointing gesture in reference to something happening in the environment, he or she begins to share attention to an event beyond the dyadic exchange. In general, by nine months infants appear capable of holding in mind and combining simultaneously multiple aspects of the social situation, in particular that (1) the social partner is engaged with them, (2) the social partner is intending to communicate something to them about something else, and (3) the social partner intends to relate to them in reference to this event or object. Primary intersubjectivity is linked exclusively to the first aspect of the social situation detected by the infant, whereas secondary subjectivity combines all three.

Interestingly, when infants start to show secondary intersubjectivity in a triadic context (that is, organized interaction between the infant, another person, and an object that they are jointly attending), they also start to try radically new behaviors in face-to-face, dyadic exchanges. In a recent study (Striano and Rochat 1999) we analyzed the reactions of seven- and ten-month-olds to the suddenly still face of a social partner. We found that most of these infants respond dramatically differently than younger infants do. Instead of being perturbed and stressed by the sudden dispositional change of the partner, they tried to reengage the partner with renewed positive behavior. This means that infants older than six months will initiate and shape social exchanges with others. In our particular study, infants tried to crack the experimenter's frozen expression via gaze-oriented vocalizing, touching, tapping, as well as coordinated gazing and clapping (Figure 4.3). More important, we established a significant positive correlation between the occurrence of such behavior and infants' propensity for gaze following, joint attention toward an object, or understanding of referential gestures such as pointing in a triadic contexts. In all, these observations suggest that around nine months of age, there emerges an understanding of others as intentional communicators, a radically new development that influences social exchanges at both the dyadic and triadic levels.

The transition from primary to secondary intersubjectivity is a giant step in social cognitive development. Infants graduate from highly ritualized and constrained face-to-face affective exchanges to communication and socially orchestrated exploration of the en-

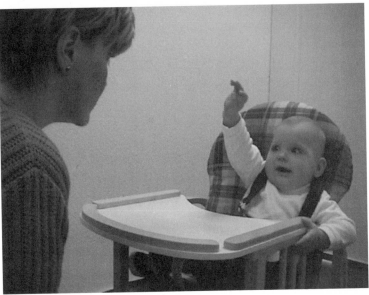

Figure 4.3 Accompanying the emergence by nine months of secondary intersubjectivity and triadic exchanges between the self, objects, and people, infants also begin to take more initiative in controlling exchanges with a social partner. These two seven-month-old infants try to reengage the adult experimenter, who has suddenly adopted an expressionless "still face," by simultaneously staring, vocalizing, and gesturing toward her (Striano and Rochat 1999; photos by T. Striano).

vironment at large. This development opens the door to cultural learning via teaching and imitation, a necessary progression that makes language development and symbolic functioning possible (Bruner 1983; Tomasello 1999). Without secondary intersubjectivity, infants could not learn from others the conventional signs (such as words) that refer to particular objects and events in the environment.

Although humans might be wired in particular ways to develop linguistic and symbolic abilities, it is by communicating with others in reference to objects and events in the environment that human infants develop the form and content of their linguistic and symbolic competencies. It is hard to imagine how infants totally deprived of social partners would develop either language or the ability to use one thing to represent another. The developmental transition from primary to secondary intersubjectivity is thus of great interest, particularly when considering that some researchers view it as being at the origins of what makes us human: the possession of creative linguistic abilities and the capacity to learn via the deliberate teaching by other, more experienced people. So, how can we account for this transition? The question remains wide open.

Accounting for the Emergence of Secondary Intersubjectivity

I would like to propose what I view as a likely developmental scenario based on what appears to be a reliable and marked change in the distribution of attention to people and physical objects during the first months of life. Although speculative and essentially descriptive, this developmental script helps us to think about the forces that might push the infant toward secondary intersubjectivity and triadic competencies.

We have seen that newborns are attuned to facial displays; they preferentially look at and track schematic representations of faces in comparison to nonfacial displays. So infants are born prepared to pay special attention to people. Caregivers obviously exploit and reinforce this early tendency in the ways that they interact with infants from birth: they systematically show infants their own faces, prop the baby to help maintain eye contact, and use exaggerated positive facial expressions. Hence dyadic face-to-face exchanges are the dominant form of early interaction between the infants and the environment. This form is specific to humans and is probably an important determinant of specifically human social cognition.

If face-to-face exchanges are dominant early in development, the nature of such exchanges changes markedly during the first year. As infants mature in their postural control and exploratory skills, they appear to pay increasing attention to physical objects, and consequently less to people. Interaction with people becomes increasingly a means to other ends, in particular access to physical objects such as food, toys, or other interesting physical entities in the environment. With the developing ability to manipulate and act on objects, infants expand their world to pay attention to objects, not just people in intimate one-on-one social relationships.

Analysis of early caregiver-infant interactions reveals that between two and six months of age infants spend significantly less time spontaneously maintaining eye contact or looking up toward others' faces, despite caretakers' continuing encouragement. In the multiple studies we performed in our laboratory on infants' reactions to the sudden still face of a social partner, we found that overall, infants between two and six months of age spend significantly less time looking at the other person, regardless of whether this person is engaged or still-faced (Rochat, Striano, and Blatt 2001). This developmental trend is part of general changes in the way that infants distribute their attention to capture more of what is happening in the environment.

From four months on, infants devote less and less time looking toward other people's faces. This decrease is linked to the fact that infants are becoming more skillful and faster at monitoring others' faces, which allows them to maintain minimum social contact while expanding their attention to events and objects elsewhere in the environment. So, typically, a four- to six-month-old infant will glance rapidly at and smile toward an engaging social partner, then quickly return to his involvement with objects. In general, research on infants' visual attention indicates that spontaneous looking time at displays—whether they are colored curved lines, flashing lights, or face-like—declines markedly between three and thirteen months of age (Ruff and Rothbart 1996). In trying to capture more of the world around them, long isolated staring episodes are replaced by multiple quick looks. From three months of age, infants show an increasing ability to shift, inhibit, and therefore distribute their visual attention to multiple aspects of the environment. From a person stage, which culminates with the emergence of smiling and primary intersubjectivity by the second month, succeeds an object stage in which infants start to demonstrate an increased interest in exploring physical entities in the environment.

Better control over posture and movement plays a central role in the privileged attention that infants start to devote to objects. Between four and six months, infants gain postural stability: they become capable of holding their heads straight and sitting without support. These advances in motor control free the upper limbs and dramatically increase the degrees of manual freedom used to explore midsize objects that are within reach (Rochat and Goubet 1995). The emergence of systematic eye-hand coordination by four months of age and the infants' compulsion to bring their hands in contact with objects to explore and manipulate them are certainly key factors in the transition from the person to the object stage. Successful reaching and deliberate attempts to manipulate objects expand babies' social universe. They become independent explorers of their environment, actively discovering what they can do with objects. But although infants become increasingly infatuated with objects, they do not become totally oblivious of people. They are still responsive and keep reciprocating with smiles and contingent vocalizing when facing an engaging social partner. Such instances are more fleeting, however, and infants appear increasingly distracted by objects and physical events.

As infants gain postural independence, develop systems to act on objects, and eventually by the end of the first year start to move and explore on their own, their attention to others becomes primarily oriented toward monitoring their relative proximity to people. The farther they venture away from their mothers, the more infants tend to look toward their faces (Sorce et al. 1985). This simple observation reveals the developmental dynamic underlying the transition from primary to secondary intersubjectivity. Social proximity and object exploration become increasingly incompatible when infants start to locomote independently. On the one hand, infants are pulled toward exploring objects and away from caregivers. On the other hand, they need their caregivers' presence and proximity.

The adapted way to solve this dilemma is for the infant to incorporate social partners into their exploration of the object world. Caregivers support these efforts and ease infants' exploration by pointing to and offering objects and by making the environment interesting and safe. Early object exploration is thus in many ways highly social. From a predominantly solitary infatuation with objects, which is aided by progress in postural and motor control, infants by nine months come back to people by engaging with them in relation to objects. This people/object stage is characterized by communication with others in reference to objects (gaze following, pointing, social referencing), as well as shared engagement (joint attention).

Interestingly, just prior to infants' entry into the people/object stage (nine to twelve months), they start manifesting a novel sense of exclusivity with their primary caretakers, reacting with marked anxiety when encountering or left alone with a stranger ("eighth-month" or "stranger anxiety"; see Spitz 1965). It is as if the development of a privileged, exclusive affective bond between parents and infants is a precursor of secondary intersubjectivity. It could be a necessary condition for the infant to integrate the object and people world via cooperation and shared engagement with objects (and hence for triadic competencies to develop). The growing attachment to a particular person certainly stimulates the tension between staying near that person and exploring objects, a tension that is resolved via joint engagement and triadic social skills. The separation anxiety starting to be manifested by eight-month-olds might indeed be an important correlate, if not determinant of, the developmental transition from primary to secondary intersubjectivity. More research is needed to support this claim. We do know, however, that the stranger anxiety that begins by around eight months is linked to the more general development of stable standards regarding caregivers, standards to which others become increasingly compared. Such comparisons entail active memory retrieval and representational abilities, general cognitive abilities that some researchers believe mature at around this age with the increase of frontal cortex involvement and its connection to other parts of the brain (Kagan 1984; 1998).

Implicit Theories of Mind in Infancy

A recent flow of research documents the developing understanding in children of other people's psychology, so-called theories of mind. By three to four years of age, children start construing others as having states of mind, beliefs, desires, and complex reasons for behaving one way or another. Such evidence is based on paradigms that place children in situations where they have the opportunity to infer the reasons for someone's behavior based on an understanding of that person's desires and knowledge. So for example, in the classic false belief task introduced first by Heinz Wimmer and Josef Perner (1983; see Hala 1997 for a review of the many follow-up studies), children witness with two protagonists (person A and person B) that a piece of candy is hidden under one of two cups. Person B leaves the room for a moment and while absent, the candy is moved under the other cup. Person B comes back and children are asked where they think Person B will look for the candy. The question is whether children understand that Person B, having not witnessed the unexpected transfer of the candy, holds the false belief that it is still under the original cup. Research demonstrates that it is only at around four years of age that children predict that Person B will look for the candy at the original location, hence construe that the person holds a false belief. In contrast, three-year-old children wrongly assume that Person B will look for the candy in the new location.

It appears that between three and four years of age, children start to show signs of explicit theories about what other people are thinking. False belief tasks, as the current litmus test of theories of mind, reveal that it is at around this age that children start recognizing that people behave as a function of beliefs that are either true or false.

If children at around four years of age begin to construe the mental life of others in terms of desires and beliefs, such theories of mind are typically revealed in the context of explicit verbal tasks. The results, however, are inseparable from the linguistic competence of the child because they are based on explicit verbal questions and responses. It is therefore possible that theories of mind might in fact be expressed first at the implicit level of children's spontaneous social behavior, long before their explicit (that is, linguistic) expression at three to four years of age. Furthermore, even if an important transition in the explicit understanding of others seems to occur between ages three and four, other developments certainly have led children toward this important step.

I would like to suggest that prior to the well-documented emergence of theories of mind in the verbal child, infants develop a sophisticated, although implicit (not yet verbalized) understanding of others as intentional—as having desires, feelings, and fluctuating affects. Such an implicit understanding would prepare and announce the development of explicit theories of mind. But what kind of evidence do we have of such early implicit understanding of people? What do we know about its nature? And to what extent can we assume that it is a necessary precursor of explicit theories of mind?

It is obvious that any construal of someone else's mental life requires some degree of relatedness between construer and construed. It is hard to imagine how someone might feel or think if we ourselves have not experienced the same thoughts or feelings. The comparison of self and others' perspectives on things, as well as the sense of shared affective experience (intersubjectivity) are foundational aspects of social cognition, and hence of theories of mind. In the false belief tasks, for example, the four-year-olds use some basic identification process to bridge their own subjective experiences with those of the protagonists whom they are monitoring and whose thoughts they are trying to discern. If children are told that someone is craving candy, their understanding of what this person's current motivational state is and what their next behavior will be (for example, lifting one of the cups to search for it) is based first on a sense of shared experience. The child must first remember what it feels like to crave something, then project this experience onto the other person. In other words, vicarious feelings are probably at the origins of an understanding of others' motivational states.

A basic prerequisite of the classic false belief task is that the child understand first that the person wants to look for it. The understanding of motivational states and intentions, or the "wants" that drive others' behavior, is a foundation for theories of mind. Only after children understand others as motivated and intentional can they eventually develop the explicit understanding of what beliefs these others might have.

Based on past experience, early on infants develop specific expectations about how people will communicate with them and interact face-to-face, and they measure the degree of communicative attunement of new social partners according to this reference. From about two months, infants are more responsive and display more positive affects to people whose interactive style is familiar and who meet the infant's expectation of a normal (familiar) communicative flow. Again, this is why they show distress to a sudden still face and attend differentially to disorganized play routines surreptitiously introduced by caregivers. In other words, early on infants demonstrate an implicit understanding of others as communicative agents in familiar face-to-face exchanges. From this understanding, infants can assess people's relative motivation to engage socially.

From the time that infants start to manifest primary intersubjectivity via smiling and eye-to-eye contacts with social partners, they learn about the dispositional qualities of people and how these qualities relate to their own. The early propensity of infants to imitate social partners as well as their strong reciprocal mirroring of caregivers are cases in point. Mutual imitation between infants and their caregivers, so prominent in early development, plays a central role in how infants develop intersubjectivity and shared motivational states. When communication is flowing via mutual imitation and protoconversation, infants and caretakers have the opportunity

which they construe and act in the world in specific ways. At each step, according to this view, behavior finds a temporary coherence, eventually crystallizing into a new coherent organization or structure.

The concept of stage is not new. The groundbreaking views of Jean-Jacques Rousseau on education (see Chapter 1) revolved around the idea of an orderly succession of distinct stages in child development. The concept of stage in development was further elaborated and continued to be taken as a central feature by those modern child psychologists accounting for perceptual, cognitive, motor, moral, gender and personality development (as Freud did in his stagelike account of psychosexual development). In all instances, developmental changes are portrayed as part of an overall scheme of behavior at particular points in developmental time. Of course, each theorist provides a different description of what the nature of these successive organizations might be, depending not only on the domain they investigate but also on the extent to which they view these successive behavioral schemes as permeating all domains of child development.

Piaget provides certainly the most elaborated domain-general, stage-based theory of child development. Cognitive development from birth is described by Piaget as a succession of breakthroughs in mental organization that guide action, perception, and eventually representational and abstract thinking. Accordingly, cognitive development is an orderly construction marked by phases of temporary behavioral coherence or general equilibrium between the environment and the child's action, whether this action is physical (for example, searching for a visible object) or mental (such as figuring out the whereabouts of an object that has disappeared). For the most part, Piaget focused his research effort on an account of the qualitative shifts marking the transition from one phase of child-environment equilibrium to the next. For example, he tried to demonstrate that when infants start to search systematically for hidden objects, they manifest a qualitatively different understanding of the world around them. From a conception of the world made up of unrelated, fleeting objects and events, the newly expressed search behavior of infants indicates that they now conceive the world as furnished by permanent objects moving in a coherent space (Piaget 1954).

According to Piaget, the emergence of object permanence in infancy is part of a general transformation of the infant mind that influences behavior in all domains: perception, motor control, imitation, and the conception of space, time, and causality. For example, object permanence and the way that infants start to search for hidden objects is an index of infants' general ability to represent things in their absence. In turn, the development of this general ability follows an orderly construction with discrete stages, or phases of equilibrium. Each stage corresponds to a particular lens through which children interpret and eventually understand the world around them. Borrowing from logic and mathematics, Piaget attempted to provide a formal description of the specific "optic" of each lens as a specific developmental stage. He described the structure of each one, how over developmental time one stage gets constructed as an extension and transformation of the preceding one.

Like the construction of a building, which proceeds from the foundation up, child development according to Piaget proceeds as a general succession of discriminable structures or organizations that have a logical order in their emergence, with each new organization incorporating the preceding one. These successive general organizations would be like the "babushka" dolls that fit inside each other, with each doll representing a particular structure characterizing the child at one point of his or her mental development. In a sense, child development would correspond to an expansion of the mind in successive, well-delimited as well as domain-general mental metamorphoses, or "revolutions"—as has been described in the history of sciences when scientists started to conceive of the universe in radically different ways. So, for example, a Copernican revolution occurred when scientists interested in cosmology started to conceive of the earth as part of the solar system and not at the center of the universe. Similarly, there would be a mental revolution in ontogeny when children start, for example, to conceive objects as continuing to exist even when they can no longer be perceived by them.

For many contemporary developmentalists, recent empirical evidence does not warrant such a "revolutionary" account. The argument against it rests primarily, but not exclusively, on two bodies of evidence that point respectively to the domain specificity of development and the apparent enrichment, rather than construction process, taking place in infant development.

A major problem encountered by Piaget and other general stage theorists of development is that in many instances, the child develops abilities that do not transfer to other domains of development. For example, there is now good evidence that language develops mostly independently from achievements in the sensorimotor domain. There is not a strict causal link between the competencies developed by the child for acting on objects and emerging linguistic competencies. Another case in point is the existence of children born with particular genetic defects (for example, Williams syndrome) who develop close to normal linguistic abilities but have markedly delayed sensorimotor skills and spatial cognition (Karmiloff-Smith 1992). Such facts support the idea of domain specificity in infant and child development. Rather than a succession of general stages, development would be best characterized as a collection of parallel developments within particular domains of competence (such as the linguistic, spatial, arithmetic, or perceptual). Contrary to general stage theories, these developments are conceived as being to a large extent compartmentalized and independent. Moreover, these developments are asynchronous, and their interaction is not straightforwardly predictable as in Piaget's idealized, grand, and coherent theoretical scheme.

Such an alternative account finds further validation in the fact that there are important differences in the way individual children develop. Some might be very active and develop swiftly in the realm of motor skills but be slower in the linguistic domain, and vice versa. Each infant has indeed a very different developmental trajectory, perhaps in part because each infant has a particular profile of asynchronous developments across domains. Some developmental theories, such as the dynamic systems approach to development (Thelen and Smith 1994) and the recent biologically inspired model of cognitive development proposed by Robert Siegler (1996), pay particular attention to individual trajectories in development as a way to uncover what should be the underpinning of any developmental inquiry, namely the process of change (see Chapter 6).

In studying children's developing ability to solve problems, such as math or practical physics problems, Siegler (1996) comes to the conclusion that rather than fitting a stagelike, "staircase" metaphor of cognitive development, children seem to develop in a less linear and more chaotic way. In this more complex developmental progression, each child generates numerous overlapping ways of thinking (that is, cognitive strategies, theories, and principles) that emerge and eventually disappear over developmental time. As Siegler puts it, his research led him to conceive cognitive development as a "gradual ebbing and flowing of the frequencies of alternative ways of thinking, with few approaches being added and old ones being eliminated as well" (1996, p. 86). Compared to a stagelike account, Siegler's view is more accommodating to the inescapable reality of interindividual differences and domain specificity in cognitive development.

Another source of major criticism regarding stagelike theories of development stems from recent progress in infancy research. If infants demonstrate much greater sophistication in their perception and understanding of self, objects, and people than was previously thought, in particular by Piaget and other stage or constructivist theorists, why wouldn't we assume that infants come to the world equipped with basic competencies that just need to expand and get enriched by experience? In contrast to a discontinuous, stagelike view of development, this "ready at birth" stance is sometimes taken as a much more parsimonious view of development, in particular infant development.

As suggested by Elizabeth Spelke (1991) and borrowing from Chomsky's innateness argument regarding the origins of language, infants must be born with some constraints as to how to proceed in developing knowledge. Suppose, like Piaget, that children construct knowledge about the world almost from scratch, experiencing first fleeting impressions of unrelated events from uncoordinated perceptual systems. Then how would they know that the chaos they currently experience is not the right approach and needs to be radically revised? Spelke eloquently makes the argument:

> If infants perceive a radically different world from adults, it is not clear how children ever develop mature physical conceptions . . . A child whose conceptions led him or her to experience a succession of changing appearances rather than a layout of enduring objects might learn more and more about such appearances: when two appearances coincide, when one appearance follows another, and the like. The child's perceptions would not lead him or her to believe, however, that the ephemeral character of experience is an illusion. (Spelke 1991, p. 135)

Spelke's argument calls for innate constraints and guidance in development. Following this rationale, her research does successfully demonstrate the existence of core constraints that guide object perception and physical reasoning at the origin of development.

Recent infancy research such as Spelke's calls for a revision of the notion of a rigid, progressive construction of basic notions in the child such as object permanence, causality, or number concept. The unveiling of unsuspected sophistication by young infants has further encouraged some researchers to conceive development as a progressive enrichment of capacities that are already in place at birth. The mechanisms that might cause such putative enrichment remain largely unstudied. A noticeable exception, however, is the work of Eleanor Gibson (1991), whose research in infancy is geared toward demonstrating that infants enrich their early perceptual sophistication by actively exploring and progressively differentiating things in the environment that can be acted on (see Chapters 3 and 6).

If infants are born more "pre-fabricated" and more constrained than was previously thought, and if Piaget's notion of stages needs to be seriously revised based on recent progress in infancy research, does this necessarily mean that infant development is a smooth and linear enrichment? Does this elude the possibility of qualitative shifts or key transitions marking significant and general changes in behavioral organization? I do not think so, but it all depends on your point of view.

Fine or Coarse Description: A Question of Scale

There are many possible stories to tell about what changes in infant development. To a large extent, these stories depend on the scale at which one observes infant behavior. This scale ranges from the microscopic and domain-specific approach of infant skill acquisition, such as manual reaching and grasping behavior, to the macroscopic and ecological scale of infants' developing adaptations to the environment, such as their growing affective attachment to certain individuals or their increasing attunement to particular communicative norms (for example, particular social expectations in face-to-face exchanges).

A close look at changes over short periods of time and an emphasis on the variety of individual expressions of such changes lead to a developmental account that is more complex and less orderly compared to an account of behavioral changes observed over a longer period of time with observations averaged over groups of same-age infants (Thelen and Smith 1994). For example, successful reaching toward and grasping of objects emerges at around four months of age. This is a reliable and well-documented behavioral landmark in the development of healthy infants that is reliably used to assess infant motor and cognitive development. As a part of overall development, the emergence of reaching behavior is orderly and predictable. Typically, it follows a period in which infants show a dominant propensity to bring objects to the mouth. It also precedes the ability of infants to sit independently (Bruner 1969; Rochat and Senders 1991). Such order and predictability can be found in all domains of development when the focus of observation is large. But the orderly picture becomes much more chaotic when the lens is changed to capture finer details.

In relation to the emergence of reaching behavior, individual infants observed weekly between, for example, two and five months show great variability. Esther Thelen and her collaborators (Thelen et al. 1993) conducted longitudinal observations using fine-grain movement analysis techniques on a small group of infants whom they followed individually in a standardized reaching task from the time they were nonreachers to the time they were proficient reachers. All of the infants eventually reached successfully for objects, and at around the predicted age of four months, but they appeared to develop this skill following remarkably different trajectories, the process of which seems to depend in part on their own body characteristics (for example, muscle-to-fat ratio) and overall temperament. Thelen and her collaborators demonstrated that infants develop along idiosyncratic paths to achieve the same motor goal, in this case to reach and grasp an attractive object. What is remarkable is that despite the great variability in developmental trajectories, all infants become eventually successful reachers at around the same time.

In general, you get very different images when you magnify things. Take the mark of a pencil on a piece of paper. At a reading distance it might form a smooth, solid curve as part of a meaningful letter. If now you look at a portion of it through a microscope, you will probably see a cloud of discrete black carbon dots on a fuzzy fiber background. If you magnify your letter further, you might eventually see a new order of smoothness and solidity. Each magnification entails a different description of what the letter is. This example applies to the description of infant development: at some levels there is noise and variability, at others there is on the contrary apparent order and predictability. It all depends on the scale of the observation.

The description that follows is only one way to characterize changes in infant development, and this way is deliberately coarse. The focus is on what appear to be major changes in infant psychological development, changes that are interpreted as key or revolutionary transitions. These transitions are revolutionary because they are interpreted as radical changes in the way infants attend and interact with the world. As in politics when governments are toppled, such revolutions entail a radical, pervasive change in what governs infant behavior.

Two such transitions are identified: one that occurs typically around the second month following full-term birth, and another by approximately nine months of age. Once again, this is only one way to portray developmental changes in infancy, but in my opinion, it captures cardinal points in the development of the infant mind. At each of these points, infants manifest a radical change in the way they attend, perceive, and understand themselves, objects, and people. This account should help to clarify these milestones despite the great variability of individual trajectories and domain specificity in development. It is also intended to focus on meaningful aspects of infant psychological growth, namely the development of radically different stances taken by infants in their interaction with the world.

The big picture of infant psychological development is a progression from behaviors at birth that are the expression of tightly linked, and to a large extent prearranged, perception-action couplings, to behavior that shows planning and representation (namely differentiation between means and ends and symbolic—referential—functioning). Interestingly, this ontogenetic progression may resemble in part the progression that might have happened at the scale of human evolution. A resemblance does not mean that the ontogeny of behavior strictly recapitulates cultural phylogeny. But there are intriguing analogies to be made, particularly if we consider some recent theories on the origins of the modern mind such as that by Merlin Donald (1991) on the evolution of human culture.

In his compelling account, Donald proposes that the symbolic and encultured mind of modern humans evolved from what he labeled the episodic mind of our primate ancestors, which was limited to dealing with time-bound (that is, immediate) concrete situations. In evolution, the episodic mind characterizes the level of cognition achieved by our closer primate relatives (such as great apes). Humans evolved a mind that goes beyond the immediacy of perception and action, a mind Donald calls mimetic: capable of producing conscious and representational acts that are intentional, and therefore add consciousness and planning to simply reflexive or instinctual acts. With language and the invention of conventional signs to signify the world, humans ultimately evolved what Donald labels a mythical mind: symbolic and encultured in nature. There is an inescapable analogy between Donald's account and coarse features of mental growth in early ontogeny: the transition from a mind operating in the here and now of perception and action, to a mind that becomes increasingly involved in planning and reflection, one capable of mentally simulating or representing to itself the state of things in the world—the way things are, but also the way things were, should be, and will be.

At two and nine months, key transitions mark the emergence of new principles governing the infant's mind. To parallel Donald's account, we will see that the key transition at two months is reminiscent of the emergence of a mimetic mind in early ontogeny. The key transition at nine months signals the first signs of a mythical mind, which brings infants to the threshold of the symbolic gate that typically marks the end of infancy. But first, let us consider the phase that precedes these remarkable transitions: the episodic mind at birth.

The Newborn Phase

Newborn behavior is not unpredictable, as it was once described (see Chapter 1). Neither is it a mere collection of rigid reflexes automatically triggered by specific stimuli like sneezing to a peppery smell, or jerking the leg in response to a tap on the knee. Instead of a collection of rigid stimulus-response linkages or automatic reflexes, infant behavior at birth is best described as expressing preadapted action systems that are adapted to tap into vital environmental resources.

The behavioral repertoire displayed by the infant at birth is complex and remarkably organized, although relatively simple compared to what it will become within weeks. Sucking, a hallmark of behavior in early infancy, is an excellent case in point. Well organized at birth, it consists of a remarkably flexible action system, open to learning and serving multiple functions, primarily the ingestion of food but also the perceptual function of exploring objects (see Chapters 2 and 3). Despite its predictable pattern of successive bursts and pauses, newborn sucking is not automatic. It does not occur on a fixed schedule, and it is not rigidly organized. On the contrary, it is now well documented that newborn sucking varies in subtle ways depending on behavioral states—whether the infant is in a sleep, awake, or hungry state. It also depends on the quality of the oral stimulation, such as its sweetness (Crook 1979), or the shape and texture of the pacifier (Rochat 1983). Like other behaviors displayed by newborns, such as rooting, orienting, kicking, tracking, and even imitating, sucking is a highly complex and open system geared toward environmental resources that are vital for the infant.

Even at birth, infants are attuned to resources such as faces and food. This does not mean, however, that they recognize these resources as objectified features of their environment, or that they are born with some conscious awareness of these features. This attunement simply means that infants are born preadapted to tap into vital aspects of their environment, namely to people, food, and perceptual novelty. The research reviewed in the preceding chapters points to propensities, preferences, and functional goals that guide and support infant behavior from birth. These propensities, preferences, and goals provide basic functional scaffolding to infant behavior early in life. They shape the ways that young infants act.

Like any other living creatures, infants are born equipped with basic anatomical as well as action systems that ensure their survival at birth and guide psychological development from the outset. These systems find their origin in millions of years of biological evolution, each individual does not have to assemble them from scratch through postnatal learning and experience.

The way babies are built as well as the way they behave immediately after birth reflects their preadapted orientation toward their environment. For example, the anatomical design of the mouth and the behavioral pattern of sucking that is ready to function at birth evolved in relation to specific objects that exist outside the womb: in particular, the mother's nipple. There is indeed an evolutionary codesign between the nipple that belongs to the environment of newborns and the preadapted sucking action that they are ready to perform.

In a similar way, there is an evolutionary codesign between particular facial expressions that signal specific emotions already in the newborn and the perceptual mechanisms that allow others to perceive and eventually relate to these facial expressions as shared subjective experiences. Just as sucking would be functionally meaningless without objects in the environment to suck on, facial expressions would be meaningless without an audience.

In short, infants are born with a high degree of readiness to behave resourcefully in the environment, both at the level of their physiological constitution and, more importantly for us, at the level of their behavioral functioning. They are born perceivers and actors in a meaningful environment, expressing innate organization, propensities, and goal orientations. It is obvious, however, that neonates have great behavioral limitations and leave much room for further development. But what are these limitations? What are the restraints on newborns and young infants' preparedness as perceivers and actors? What needs to develop in order to initiate and sustain their remarkable psychological growth?

The main limitation of newborn behavioral sophistication is that it is fundamentally stimulus-bound, and in a basic way purely opportunistic and nonvolitional: newborns do not yet show any signs of planning their actions or systematically probing their environment. If newborns pause before they act, it is not to contemplate what is going to happen next, but rather because their repertoire of responses is still sluggish and immature. With the possible exception of sucking and oral exploration, perception and action at birth reflect the immaturity of the central nervous system: behavior seems to unfold in slow motion compared to later periods.

The neonatal world is not a contemplative or conversational world, even if it might seem so to caregivers when they have prolonged eye contacts with newborns. In such instances, newborns often seem to look through you with a flat affect, and often end up closing their eyes and falling asleep. When smiling, usually it is with the eyes closed or semiclosed in the bliss of satiety that follows feeding. They express comfort and well being, but in essence, they do so involuntarily. In a world that oscillates between slow motion in a calm state and tense agitation in a crying state, newborns perceive and act directly, with no room for reflection and conscious simulation of what is going to happen next. This probably explains why infancy students have been too often inclined to describe newborn behavior as a collection of automatic responses or reflexes. Although we have seen that reflexes do not capture the adaptive and ecological nature of behavior displayed at birth, there is nonetheless an obligatory aspect in newborn behavior that is impossible to ignore—especially when considering the dramatic changes that occur by the second month, when infants start to show the unmistakable first signs of volitional perception and action.

The lack of apparent volition, however, does not mean that newborns or even fetuses are somehow stuck in a loop of preadapted action systems that organize their behavior. It does not prevent newborns and even fetuses from learning and developing new skills that transcend their basic behavioral repertoire.

We have seen in the preceding chapters that there is good evidence of habituation and learned perceptual discrimination in utero. For instance, immediately after birth, newborns prefer to hear their mother's voice over the voice of a female stranger (DeCasper and Fifer 1980). In all probability, this discrimination rests on prenatal learning and experience (DeCasper and Spence 1991).

Such remarkable evidence of pre- and perinatal learning also occurs in the olfactory and motor domains. This is demonstrated by recent evidence that newborns have a strong preference (preferred head turning) toward the smell of their own mother's amniotic fluid (Schaal, Marlier, and Soussignan 1998). Within hours after birth, infants also develop a preference for the smell of their own mother's milk compared to the milk of another mother who has just delivered (Marlier, Schaal, and Soussignan 1998). Early motor learning is evident in the learned propensity of newborns and even fetuses to bring systematically one of their thumbs to their mouth for sucking (Prechtl 1984; 1987). Clearly, this is a coordinated pattern that required some learning. As already pointed out by Piaget (1952) when describing the emergence of hand-mouth coordination that he erroneously interpreted as emerging by the end of the first month (see Chapter 2), thumb sucking is not an instinct; rather, it is a learned habit. In short, within the general context of preadapted action systems, there is much room for behavioral plasticity and development in the newborn.

Because the newborn behavioral repertoire is restricted compared to what it will become within weeks, it is also more predictable. As this repertoire expands, the possibilities for behavioral outcomes and behavioral complexity increase exponentially. For example, you can expect newborns to root toward the side of the mouth that is touched. Such expectations become much less certain with a two- or three-month-old whose range of possible responses has grown considerably: an infant of this age might root, but also might smile, turn away, show fear, or simply freeze. In addition to the growth of the behavioral repertoire, older infants also show more restraint and puzzlement in the face of novelty—that is, they start to show signs of action planning and deliberate probing of the environment.

Newborns have little control over what they experience around and within themselves. Their behavior is obligatory, an expression of tight couplings between perception and action within the context of preadapted action systems. The newborn phase ends when infants start to distance themselves from perceptual events and situations to achieve better control over them. In a sense, beyond the newborn phase, infants transcend the directness and immediacy of the preadapted action systems that they bring to the world. They become capable of bypassing the immediacy of perception to start reflecting on it. As we will see in the next section, within approximately six weeks neonates start to become unambiguously "meta": they deliberately plan actions with an apparent goal or directness in mind, not in immediate and direct response to randomly encountered situations in the environment. They start to develop intentionality.

This key transition by the second month corresponds to what can be considered as the second birth of the infant: their psychological birth, as opposed to their biological birth. I mentioned in Chapter 1 the major findings of recent research documenting fetal behavior. Through the use of high-tech ultrasonic devices, researchers have found strong evidence that behavior before and after biological birth is essentially identical in form and function.

Starting at approximately twenty weeks of gestation, fetuses' behavioral repertoire is not unlike that of neonates. They suck, grasp, move their eyes, swallow, and kick. They go through what appear to be comparable fluctuations in behavioral states, and as mentioned above, they learn and transfer this learning to auditory events that they experience outside the womb.

In general, then, research demonstrates the robust behavioral continuity between pre- and postnatal development (Prechtl 1984; 1987). The behavioral analogy between fetuses and newborns points to the fact that if birth is an important transition from a physiological and biological point of view, psychologically it might be an important transition mainly for the mother and others close to the infant. The behavior of infants does not index a key transition at birth. Even so, I do not mean to minimize the experience of pain that fetuses seem to experience during a difficult delivery as attested by their heart rate monitoring (which is intended to measure "fetal stress" during the process), as well as the unambiguous expression of pain (intense crying) that newborns normally manifest when taking their first breath.

But however painful the transition from the womb might be, all seems forgotten within minutes following birth. I am always struck to see in maternity wards the rows of bassinets with bundled newborns, usually sleeping away and by all appearances having already forgotten the painful journey they took minutes ago. Dressed with hats and gloves, they look as if nothing has happened.

In the face of the remarkable continuity between pre- and postnatal development, there is no good ground for confounding, as is commonly done, the psychological birth of infants with their biological birth. The origin of psychological development needs to be searched for either in the development of the fetus, or, as I shall suggest next, by the second month after biological birth, when healthy full-term infants start to reveal themselves as unambiguously volitional creatures.

The Two-Month Revolution

Paramount to the infant psychological development is the emergence of volitional or planned action, so-called intentionality. Intentionality is an elusive concept, its definition and meaning a classic philosophical conundrum. It captures the directness or "aboutness" of behavior: "that property of many mental states and events by which they are directed at or about or of objects and states of affairs in the world" (Searle 1983, p. 1).

In general, the concept of intentionality pertains to actions that are planned or thought of in advance. On the opposite end of the spectrum are actions that are in essence obligatory and accidental, or that occur haphazardly. Psychologically, the main feature of intentionality is the fact that it entails some mental distance between the actor and the environment. For example, the spill of a glass of wine by a dinner guest can be either accidental or intentional. I am sure that philosophers might argue against the "either or" statement because there might be some intermediary acts that entail a mixture of accidental and intentional features. For our purpose, however, we can say that it is accidental if while stretching the arm to pick up some bread, the loose sleeve of the guest hits the wine glass and causes it to spill. On the contrary, it is intentional if the guest, as part of the dinner conversation, wants to demonstrate a new trick to remove wine stains on a white tablecloth. In both cases, the event (wine spill) is identical and the morphology of the gesture possibly the same, particularly if the protagonist is intentionally faking a spill, but the psychology attached to it is radically different. One entails no anticipation and no planning, and the other does. In the intentional case, the individual acts in pondering and assessing the environment, anticipating effects on the audience (surprise) and consequences of his or her action (the eventual stain removal).

It is not until the second month that infants are unambiguously observed pondering and assessing the environment, expressing the first signs of mental distance and of becoming stimulus unbound. This represents a radical change in human infancy, what I tentatively label the two-month revolution.

At this juncture of development, infants grow from being direct perceivers and actors to active thinkers, evaluators, and planners. They reach new levels of cognitive functioning and interact with the environment on what appear to be radically different grounds. This is unmistakable to any observer of young infants, and particularly to parents. The diaries kept by some parents regarding the progress of their infant are typically very revealing of the two-month revolution, which can be also called "revolution with a smile."

As a parent and avid reader of baby diaries, my observations confirm that something very important happens in the second month. Infants open up to the world around them. Interestingly, this happening is reliably observed in relation to one particular, and very significant event: the emergence of the first socially elicited smile.

Parents observing for the first time their infant smiling while gazing at them or in response to their own smiles discover a person in their child: a person among other persons. It is invariably experienced by parents as a memorable first greeting of their child. It also indexes the fact that the infants have begun to perceive other persons as differentiated from themselves. In general, aside from being very gratifying to parents and caretakers, the emergence of social smiling is also, I suggest, among the first indices of the mental distance that differentiates intentional from automatic or random acts. After feeding and during sleep, newborns often smile, but this expression is fleeting and is not oriented toward others or situations in the environment. The socially elicited smiles that begin to be expressed in the second month are unambiguously correlated to events external to the infant, in particular the perception of other people's faces engaging in play games and other social exchanges. It becomes the mark of reciprocity with other people in the environment. In addition to smiling, other behaviors emerge at around six weeks of age that all confirm a new stance taken by the infant: a conversational and contemplative stance whereby infants start deliberately to reciprocate with others as well as to explore and think about the environment.

Infants at birth and during the first weeks of life spend most of their time sleeping. Rare and fleeting are periods of wakefulness in which they are not feeding, but simply attending to things that are happening around them. This is the main reason why the testing of neonates can be so tedious. It also explains why only a handful of courageous researchers venture into the study of newborns by using habituation or preferential looking methods, all of which require infants to be awake, alert, and calm—a rare behavioral state during the newborn phase.

We can assume that as infants become less stimulus-bound and start to adopt a conversational and contemplative stance, they should demonstrate a marked increase in the amount of time they spend alert and awake. Interestingly, at around the time that infants start to engage in social smiling, there is such an increase. By six weeks of age, the baby experiences the wakeful alert and active state for longer periods. This state is associated with infants looking and exploring, unlike other wakeful states in which the infant might be motorically active but not in relation to specific environmental events (Wolff 1987).

With the emergence of a conversational and contemplative stance by the second month of life, there arises a new range of action systems, namely intentional or planned action systems. These systems are not merely stimulus-bound but rather are based on the deliberate coordination of means and ends to achieve anticipated goals: reaching for a novel object, removing an occluder to see an object, finding new ways to contact an object (with the mouth, for example), or reproducing an interesting perceptual event (such as kicking a mobile to set it in motion). From the adoption of a contemplative stance, infants begin to plan and anticipate the effects of their own action. It allows them to discover new means to achieve the same goal (for example, reaching with a hand or leaning forward with the trunk to achieve oral contact with an object) or to discover that the same mean can achieve different goals (for example, kicking to either set a mobile in motion or produce an interesting noise). These discoveries form the core of intentional action development, arguably the main feature of cognitive development in infancy.

The Nine-Month Revolution

From the time that infants become deliberate and actively engaged in probing the environment (after the two-month "contemplative and anticipatory" revolution), they develop increasingly complex expectations and understandings about themselves, objects, and people. By nine months, however, another major breakthrough in infant development occurs. This key transition is the attainment by the infant of a novel understanding of how people relate to objects in the environment (that is, the emergence of triadic competencies; see Chapter 4).

Research shows that by nine months infants begin to treat and understand others as "intentional agents," somehow explicitly recognizing that like themselves, people plan and are deliberate in their actions. So, for example, infants will start sharing their attention toward objects with others, looking up toward them to check if they are equally engaged. They will start to refer to other people socially, and in particular to take into consideration the emotional expression of others while planning actions or trying to understand a novel situation in the environment. They will, for example, hesitate in crossing the deep side of a visual cliff if their mothers express fear (see Chapter 4). This understanding by infants that others make plans and are intentional brings infants' learning potentials to radically new levels because they can start to refer to others as models and in particular, as sources of novel perception, action, and understanding.

Prior to this transition, infants cannot be taught because they do not yet understand that others are trying to teach them. Reading a book to a child, for example, requires that both the child and the reader attend jointly to the story. The same is true for helping a child with a puzzle. If the caregiver is to be successful in telling a story or helping assemble a puzzle, the child must understand that the caregiver intends to help and is referring to the same object or task. This is what infants start to achieve by nine months; during this month there emerge the first signs of an ability to *cooperate* and learn by sharing with others (see, for example, the joint attention behavior depicted in Figure 4.2).

The nine-month transition is revolutionary because the infant's outlook on people is radically changing, from a focus on caregivers and attuned communicators to an awareness of others with whom one can also deliberately exchange information and feelings about things in the world. It is at this point in development that infants will start to use and understand declarative gestures, such as pointing or gaze following, and will attempt to control the attention of others and share an interest with them about objects and events in the environment.

The cardinal behavioral change is that infants are starting to engage others and be engaged by others in constructing shared topics of conversation about things that surround their relationship. It brings social exchanges beyond the intimacy of early face-to-face transactions. From developing a primary intersubjectivity or sense of shared interpersonal experience, infants are now opening up to the development of secondary intersubjectivity, or sense of shared experience in relation to objects and events in the world (see Chapter 4). This transition marks the first signs of infants' inclination to construct a shared world that can be referred to, discovered, enjoyed, learned, understood, and disambiguated in cooperation with others. This puts in place all major engines of cultural transmission, including teaching, cooperation in solving problems, and of course, language.

The emergence of secondary intersubjectivity and language are synchronous and correlated in development. It is well established that the development of triadic competencies such as joint attention or declarative gestures heralds the utterance of first conventional words (Tomasello and Farrar 1986). At a pragmatic level, language requires children to understand others as intentional listeners. It also requires them to understand that, with a potential listener, they can attend jointly to things in the world through arbitrary signs such as spoken words.

Words refer to things that are jointly understood. Because language is referential and serves a communicative function, its development depends first on the remarkable breakthrough in secondary intersubjectivity. It also announces the end of infancy, the preverbal period of child development. When infants start to walk and otherwise locomote on their own, they not only gain great physical independence, they also pass the threshold that will allow them to make a quantum leap in progress as toddlers and children: the "symbolic gateway."

The Symbolic Gateway

From the time infants start to contemplate rather than merely perceive and act on objects (after the two-month revolution), they become less literal in the cognitive processing of things happening inside and around themselves. Instead of just doing things and perceiving events, the contemplative stance allows them to start reflecting about these things and these events, to begin to raise questions about what they mean. By doing so, they learn that a certain behavior (say, a frown) stands for a certain state of mind (for example, pain), or that a particular physical event (perhaps a sudden occlusion of an object) stands for a particular outcome (its presence behind the occluder). This transition is the necessary precursor of symbolic functioning, itself a necessary condition for language to emerge.

What is language? It is the production and comprehension of arbitrary signs, whether gestured, uttered, or written, that convey meanings beyond their physicality. A certain hand configuration might mean "cow," and what you just read within quotation marks means a certain milk-producing mammal that moves in a certain way, moos, and so forth. These signs are arbitrary in the sense that they are learned as part of a system that has evolved over many generations and is one among many other coevolving systems, namely other existing languages as well as linguistic modalities (for example, spoken language, American Sign Language, Braille, pantomime, even cinema when editing conventions are considered).

What is remarkable with signs is that they allow us to convey and receive information about things in their absence. In the example of the cow, I can utter the word that refers to this creature and you know what I mean without my having to bring it physically to you. The word "cow" is what is called the signifier of the mooing, chewing animal, the so-called signified. More simply, the word "cow" refers to the actual animal, whether or not it is present or exists somewhere else.

Piaget (1962) viewed the child's ability to denote the signifier and signified as a major transition in development that marks the beginning of true representational thinking, when children start to use, understand, and manipulate signs standing for things in the world. Piaget refers to this new representational ability as the symbolic function, which he believed signals the transition from infancy to childhood and is necessary for language to emerge. Remember, however, that contemporary infancy researchers have proposed that already in the first months infants might be starting to conceptualize the world around them, and that such conceptualization implies some sophisticated representational abilities that Piaget denied occurred in young infants (Mandler 1992; see chap. 3 in particular).

The emergence of symbolic functioning is not sudden. Early signs appear at least by the second month when infants start to take a contemplative stance. Nevertheless, it is obvious that the expression of the symbolic function explodes by the beginning of the second year. Piaget was essentially alluding to this phenomenon in his account of what is at stake when infants and young children start to play symbolically, grab pencils to start scribbling, utter their first words, imitate people in their absence, reminisce about past events, and engage in pretend games. All of these activities rely on symbolic functioning and seem to coemerge between twelve and eighteen months, as infants make their way to toddlerhood. Their coemergence confirms that they all depend on the same general ability to function symbolically, but there is room for asynchrony in their development. For example, pretend play might possibly emerge prior or after graphic symbolism because of particular sensorimotor and expressive constraints in the individual child.

There are still many controversies about when infants and toddlers start to engage in "true" symbolic activities. For example, there is an obvious difference between an infant scribbling on a piece of paper and when the same child a few months later draws a kind of tadpole figure that he or she might label "Mommy" or "Daddy." The same is true for symbolic play. When do young children start to show clear signs of treating arbitrary objects as standing for real things? Is it when they start, for example, grabbing a banana to talk into it pretending it is a telephone? Or is it when they grab anything, a stone, a stick, a can—not only a banana—to be used as a phone? One could argue that bananas are not completely arbitrary because they have a curved form analogous to the part of a phone that is held, and hence that a banana invites the same phoning action. This is an example of an ongoing debate regarding what should be considered truly symbolic, or in this instance truly symbolic play (Harris 1991; Tomasello, Striano, and Rochat 1999; Striano, Tomasello, and Rochat 2001).

From the time they seem to engage in referential activities such as pointing, joint engagement, and all the triadic behaviors characterizing the nine-month revolution, infants develop an increasing ability to function symbolically. Before I give some examples of such development, be reminded once more that this progression extends back to the second month, when infants begin to adopt a conversational-contemplative stance and thus start to manifest less literal perception and more meaning-seeking behaviors. We have seen, for example, that by three months infants discriminate between a red and a blue dot moving independently on a computer screen and the same two dots seeming to chase each other (see Chapter 4). Beyond mere perceptual discrimination, by nine months infants appear to discriminate who is the chaser and who is the chasee when the roles are reversed. They begin to treat these dots on the flat screen as some creatures "intentionally" chasing each other, seemingly raising the question, "Who is doing what to whom?" From the literal perception of the dots moving in certain (related or unrelated) ways on the screen, infants begin to detect a socially meaningful causality signified by these moving dots. Between three and nine months, too, infants progress from literal to symbolic TV viewing.

A trademark of childhood is pretend and symbolic play. All children are great fantasizers, tending to reenact events they have seen or that they wish would or would not happen to them. They play with dolls, trucks, or airplanes, pretend to be doctors, teachers, and mail carriers. In the meantime, the adult culture as well as the huge toy and educational industries feed into this universal propensity by providing children all sorts of miniature replicas of real things, as well as stories that feed their fantasies. But how does all of that symbolic and pretend play develop? The answer is complex but one thing is certain: it does not emerge suddenly. It is the product of a long progression that starts in infancy.

To give a sense of this progression, I will briefly present some highlights of recent studies conducted to capture the emergence and development of symbolic play at the threshold of the symbolic gateway (Tomasello, Striano, and Rochat 1999; Striano, Tomasello, and Rochat 2001). One very nice aspect of children's propensity to engage in fantasy play is that it is relatively easy to obtain abundant information regarding their symbolic activities. My colleagues and I took advantage of this propensity by creating simple experimental situations that allowed a better understanding of what it takes for old infants and young children to engage in symbolic activities (Tomasello, Striano, and Rochat 1999). The goal was to harvest more information on the cognitive underpinnings of such activities and their development between eighteen and thirty-six months, when symbolic functioning appears to blossom. In a series of first experiments, we engaged children in a simple game in which we presented a group of four objects on a tray and asked each of them for one in various symbolic ways—for example, by showing them a replica of the object or by gesturing an action that could be done with the particular object. The child faced a large and colorful cardboard slide that ended on the experimenter's side. In successive requests (with gesture or by showing a replica), the experimenter asked children to put down the slide one of the four choice objects. We systematically recorded whether they picked and put down the slide the right object. This simple experiment allowed us to unveil some aspects of the development of symbolic comprehension.

We found that by eighteen months, children were significantly more successful at comprehending a request from the experimenter based on a symbolic gesture compared to a request that used a replica of the object. For example, these children were more successful at putting down the slide a real size plastic hammer when the experimenter pounded the floor with a closed fist (gesturing "hammering") than when a miniature hammer was shown. Looking closer at the behavior of these younger children, we found that when the miniature replica was used for the request, children were inclined to reach toward the replica held by the experimenter instead of the object it was supposed to stand for (that is, its referent). In other words, at this age children showed confusion between symbol and referent, probably because the symbol (replica) too closely resembled the object it was supposed to stand for. It is as if the symbolic link between the replica and the real object was somehow undetected by the child. A gesture, however, probably because it is physically more removed from the object it stands for, appears to be more readily understood as a symbol by eighteen-month-olds.

These observations are linked to a basic developmental hurdle that children have to overcome to function symbolically: the so-called dual representation problem (DeLoache 1995). Dual representation is when something (an object, a picture, a gesture) can be simultaneously that thing and the symbol of something else (a hammer, a car, a baby). For children to understand the symbolic nature of a photograph, for example, they need somehow to hold in mind that this piece of glossy paper is both a physical object with particular tangible characteristics (smell, weight, texture) and a representation standing for something else (Grandma, a beach, myself).

The hurdle of the dual representation problem corresponds to the difficulty of combining these aspects. In our research, when children reached for the replica instead of the object it was supposed to stand for, they confounded the physicality of the replica and its symbolic meaning: they did not yet overcome the dual representation problem. The fact that they did better with the gesture indicates that the development of symbolic functioning is progressive and dependent on circumstances and situational demands. For instance, twenty-four-month-olds do not manifest any apparent difficulty with the dual representation problem when the replica is simply a conventional miniature of the real object it is supposed to stand for (toy car for real car). Our research shows, however, that when the conventional use of an object is overturned so that it can be used as a symbol (for example, when a cup is used to stand for a hat, or a box to stand for a shoe with the appropriate gesture of either putting the cup on the head or putting the box on one foot), the performance of these children breaks down. By thirty-six months, a transgression of conventional use becomes less of a hurdle to children's symbolic comprehension (Tomasello, Striano, and Rochat 1999).

Once again, even when symbolic functioning appears to blossom in marked ways starting in the second year, a closer developmental look at it indicates an impressive progression toward increasingly abstract comprehension of symbols. Much research is still needed in this area to unveil further the nature of this development and how it is rooted in infancy.

It is interesting to note that in the realm of symbolic and pretend play, like in language development, comprehension is developed before production. In the same way that young children understand words before they can actually utter them in an appropriate way, they comprehend symbolic gestures and objects standing for other objects (see the experiment described earlier) before spontaneously producing such symbols on their own. In a recent experiment (Striano, Tomasello, and Rochat 2001), we found that it is only at around thirty-six months that infants clearly start to invent pretend games using objects to stand for something else (for example, a sock for a baby doll, a pen for an airplane, a box for a shoe). As we have seen, children start to comprehend what objects might stand for ten months earlier. This developmental gap between comprehension and production is pervasive across domains of symbolic functioning, indicating that the same general cognitive mechanisms and prerequisites underlie the symbolic gateway—perhaps something like the general process of differentiation between signifier and signified described by Piaget (1962). This process, however, appears to originate early in life and develop slowly beyond infancy, following general constraints that need to be further explained.

The general process underlying the emergence of the symbolic function is also evident when considering the comprehension and production of graphic symbols such as drawings. Children between two and three years of age, when asked to match a picture to the real object it represents, take a symbolic stance in such a comprehension task before they can produce a drawing that represents those objects (Callaghan 1999). In a series of controls, Tara Callaghan shows that this developmental gap between comprehension and production of graphic symbols cannot be explained by a mere lack of motoric skills required for drawing. None of the children had a particular problem holding a pen, and all were able to draw circles and lines that could have represented the object. Rather, it seems that this "decalage" is part of the general developmental pattern of symbolic functioning: it is found equally in the realm of language, symbolic play, and representational art.

When the symbolic gateway is opened at the end of infancy, a whole new universe of cognitive and learning opportunities opens up for what eventually becomes a talkative and increasingly independent young child. The child gains immensely: she can now, for example, contemplate the world, reenact past events, imagine virtual realities, and generate logical inferences about future outcomes. She can exchange abstract ideas with others within conventional symbolic systems using words, gestures, drawings, or mathematical formulas, or express love, hate, bliss, boredom, or blues via songs, poems, movies, symphonies, dance, books, drumming, or a simple eye exchange.

All these abstract and often obscure processes that make us human rest on the ability to function symbolically. Symbolic functioning makes for the uniqueness and power of human culture, for better and for worse. That is what makes us different from any other animal. That is also what infants prepare for and develop during the first months of life.

MECHANISMS OF INFANT
DEVELOPMENT

Whether infant development is continuous or discontinuous, made of successive stages, or marked by key transitions, an account of what changes as infants develop does not address the issue of the processes and mechanisms underlying and ultimately causing developmental changes. How can we go beyond the mere description of *what* changes in the rapidly developing world of infants to grapple with the more difficult questions of *how* and *why* infant development occurs?

Control and prediction are ultimate goals for researchers dealing with complex dynamic systems. There is always the drive, which is more or less explicit, to go beyond description and provide a causal account of such systems. Meteorologists focus on predicting the weather, tracking storms, and warning of future natural disasters. Economists devise all kinds of schemes to predict the future of the stock market or control inflation. Therapists try to control the health of their patients by predicting certain effects of their treatment. If control and prediction are common goals in most scientific endeavors, are they legitimate goals for infancy researchers, who deal with probably the most dynamic of all systems?

Dynamic systems range from relatively well-circumscribed artifacts such as airplanes or computers, to incomparably more intricate living systems like infants. What can be understood of them depends on the degree of their complexity. Trying to deal with the questions of what causes infants to develop the way they do, what drives them in their development, and what might boost or hinder their behavioral development is quite a different feat than trying to understand how machines or mechanical systems are assembled and what factors affect their operation.

Causes of behavioral transformations in infancy operate at multiple levels simultaneously, from the microscopic level of neurophysiological changes in the brain, to macroscopic changes in how the individual interacts with the physical and cultural environment. Given the complexity and number of interactions between these highly contrasted levels, it seems that any attempt to come up with definitive and simple causal accounts of infant development would be inadequate. Which level should we favor and limit ourselves to in our account? Brain mechanisms? Psychological mechanisms? Social and cultural mechanisms? How is it possible to integrate these various orders of phenomena, all necessary factors of infant development? Infancy researchers constantly struggle with these difficult, if not unanswerable, questions.

Regardless of the level at which one tries to account for changes in infant behavior, developmental processes and mechanisms need to be distinguished. These two basic aspects of development are too often confounded, although they have different meanings and lead to distinct developmental accounts.

Processes versus Mechanisms of Infant Development

Infants embody change, and it is hard to imagine investigating them outside of a developmental perspective. There are, however, radically different ways of approaching these changes: from the description of what happens as infants develop, to the account of how it happens and why. The what, how, and why questions form three basic categories of developmental questions, each leading to a different developmental account. The what question is descriptive and was addressed in Chapter 5 in the discussion of key transitions in infant development. The how question pertains to the way in which developmental changes occur and proceed. And the why question pertains to what causes developmental changes. This final question, which leads to an account of the agency or means by which a developmental change is produced, calls for mechanisms of development. These mechanisms, in principle, always have some predictive power over changes that might occur in the future. If processes correspond to how behavioral changes happen over developmental time, they do not imply that what happened will happen again in exactly the same way. Mechanisms of development, by contrast, are invariant means causing particular changes to occur in a predictable way.

Note, however, that both processes and mechanisms call for developmental accounts that go beyond the mere description of what happens as development proceeds. Both processes and mechanisms pertain specifically to the dynamic of changes: how they influence such processes, and how the initial triggering condition of such processes relates to mechanisms.

A concrete example will help make clear the distinction between processes and mechanisms. Suppose that you witness a car accident and you are called to testify about what you saw. You will be asked *how* you saw things happen: How fast were the cars going? How did they hit one another? These pieces of information regarding how things happened will help reconstruct the event, but not directly determine the potential causes of the accident. Instead these questions pertain to the dynamic of changes (the processes): what happened to the traffic when it was suddenly disrupted by the accident. *Why* this accident happened (the mechanism) is left to the decision of the jury and of the judge who will arbitrate any eventual punishment.

In any account of mechanisms or causal explanation, there is always a judgment call. In the scientific domain of infant development, this judgment pertains to the scale at which researchers observe infants, from the intricacies of brain mechanisms to the ecology of the whole organism in interaction with the environment. In reality, multiple levels of causal mechanisms interact with each other, from the physiological to the psychological and cultural. All of these levels are somehow connected, but they are difficult to treat in conjunction. This is where the aesthetic and subjective decisions of developmental scientists, from all walks of life, come in full view. Some decide to account for behavioral changes on the basis of brain growth and therefore will unveil principles of processes and find causes in the brain. Others will decide to account for behavioral changes at the level of perception and therefore will determine perceptual principles and causes. All of these principles and causal accounts are relevant. None is totally exclusive of the others: they all codetermine the development of infant behavior as part of one big, multilayered, and interactive system.

If infant development is the expression of such a complex interactive system, then is it still possible to talk about processes and mechanisms of infant development? Is it possible to isolate principles and causes that might account for developmental changes such as the transition toward independent sitting, manual reaching, or upright locomotion, as well as the expression of object permanence, eight-month-olds' sudden stranger anxiety, the adoption of an intentional stance, or the utterance of the first conventional word?

In terms of prediction, infancy researchers typically try to find developmental links or correlations between phenomena across levels and domains of functioning. So, for example, researchers test whether there is a link between the development of certain brain regions and a specific behavior in the infant. Recently, such research has led, for example, to the demonstration that there is a correlation between cortical frontal lobe development and the emergence of object permanence in infancy. In parallel and by the same researchers, this demonstration was also confirmed with monkeys, a group of which had a focal lesion of the prefrontal cortex and were tested in analogous object search tasks (Diamond 1990). Other researchers report a developmental link between particular ways of attending to visual stimuli in early infancy and later cognitive skills or patterns of intellectual functioning (Colombo 1993). Note that these researchers do not explore what mechanisms or causes underlie such a predictive correlation.

Alternatively, strict behaviorists like John B. Watson (1878–1958) or B. F. Skinner (1904–1990) tried to apply one kind of putative mechanism (conditioning) to as many domains of development as possible across the lifespan: from fear conditioning in babies, to verbal learning in children, to the origins of phobias in adults.

a necessary order of succession articulated around key transitions: the "two-month revolution," the "nine-month revolution," and the "symbolic gateway." But this is far removed from Watson's claims about individual infants' future personality and emotional development.

Is Infant Development Chaotic and Indeterminate?

Some developmental theories have emerged in recent years that are built around the indeterminacy of development: the idea that the essential nature of behavior and its development makes them unable to be strictly controlled or predicted. I allude here to current chaos and dynamic systems theory principles applied to psychology in general, and developmental psychology in particular (Abraham and Gilgen 1995; Thelen and Smith 1994).

In general, the dynamic systems approach applied to infants and their development posits that like any behavior, infant behavior is the result of the complex interaction of a great number of systems functioning simultaneously and distributed across many different levels: from the low level of brain, muscular, skeletal, or motivational functioning, to the high levels of perceptual, emotional, or cognitive functioning.

Chaos theory and dynamic systems thinking emerged as a new scientific tool in the domain of meteorology or the science dealing with atmospheric phenomena, in particular weather changes (Gleick 1987). Weather is a dynamic system par excellence: an observable and measurable phenomenon that is the product of multiple interacting variables. I will use it as a way to convey a sense of what it means to think in terms of dynamic systems.

Weather is the effect of constantly interacting air masses that evaporate and condense water, rush to places, and essentially exchange heat collected from the sun. Weather is fundamentally an ongoing process that has no prescribed goal or single cause. It is the result of an interaction among multiple variables that play an equal role. Causally speaking, it is an ultrademocratic system, where no one variable has more predictive power than any other. Because air masses around the planet are all connected and interacting, and because any atmospheric change at one location contributes to the perturbation of the atmosphere in general, one understands why predicting the weather beyond a few days becomes very tentative.

There is an indeterminacy attached to weather just as there is indeterminacy in infant behavior and development. It is only a posteriori, or after the fact, that one can trace the exact trajectory of a tornado that ploughed through a region of the Midwest or the exact destructive journey and changing force of a cyclone that rampaged through the Caribbean. It is also only a posteriori that one can reconstruct the exact developmental trajectory of individual infants—how they gained weight and grew tall, as well as the idiosyncratic ways they learned to walk, speak, or grew attached to particular individuals around them.

But even if it is impossible to achieve absolute long-term control and prediction of dynamic systems, weather or behavior alike, some reliable patterns of development do recur. This is the mesmerizing discovery that in chaos, there is actually order. Long-term recording of the movements of a metal pendulum set in motion by a stationary magnet, or the simultaneous audio recording of dripping faucets, reveal that such systems get into so-called momentarily stable attractor states. So, for example, the pendulum will go through periods of great agitation and then periods of calm. Similarly, the faucets will go through periods of synchronous rhythm in their dripping, followed by periods of cacophony. Such patterns can be anticipated but their exact timing cannot be predicted. In other words, if there are some orderly patterns in phenomena that are fundamentally chaotic, this order cannot be perfectly predicted. One can only reconstruct this order a posteriori. Even if all of the variables contributing to a dynamic phenomenon are known, the way they contribute to it is fundamentally random and hence cannot be reduced to a single initial cause.

The dynamic systems approach applied to infant development does not allow for much causal explanation. Rather, it invites infancy researchers to describe development in terms of fundamentally undetermined changes that are not prescribed by any particular mechanisms. To use the dynamic systems jargon, the development of infant behavior is fundamentally a soft assembly, the result of an interactive (fluid) process among multiple parallel and distributed systems at all levels of functioning. It is not based on "hard" prescriptions by modular structures, on any sort of "little man" or homunculus in the baby's head that dictates what develops next. These changes are primarily the expression of multiple control variables interacting chaotically at all times and at all levels of the functioning infant.

In the midst of apparent chaos and indeterminacy of infant behavior, researchers have looked for invariant developmental processes expressed at all ages and regardless of developmental domains. I present next two such processes, respectively the process of equilibration put forth by Piaget in his account of cognitive development, and the process of self-organization that is at the core of the more recent dynamic systems approach to infant development.

Equilibration

What infants share with all living organisms is the dynamic equilibrium between them and the environment. From the plant that absorbs the sunrays and synthesizes them, to microbes invading other organisms, to calves taking in nutrients through the mother cow's milk—all of these living phenomena have in common a transaction with the environment. And above all, what drives these transactions is the impulse to survive and proliferate.

In this process, organisms go through periods of relative balance, followed by periods of imbalance, which are in turn followed by actions that are more or less designed to restore balance. This is so-called homeostasis: the process by which, in response to environmental perturbations, a stable state is restored and maintained via more or less coordinated actions. One easily understood example of homeostasis is a thermostat that automatically maintains the climate in a building. Obviously, there is a major difference between thermostats and living organisms, particularly complex organisms like infants. But what is it?

Thermostats are closed-loop systems, functioning rigidly and generating fixed actions. They are set to respond to perturbations for a drop or increase of temperature in relation to a fixed amount, seventy degrees, for example. If the temperature bypasses this threshold, either on its way up or down, the thermostat will respond by triggering or stopping the cooler or heater. This is an "all or nothing," binary system that responds to a rigid set of constraints. It cannot learn and cannot evolve new sets of responses.

In contrast, infants are open-loop systems that continually reinvent themselves and evolve new ways to adjust to environmental disturbances. An open-loop system is a source of novelty and internal transformations. If thermostats, instead of performing rigidly in a binary fashion, generated new ways of sending messages to the climatization system, and maybe improve its communication to such system as a whole, then they would graduate to the class of open-loop systems.

The existence of living things rests fundamentally on the constant (fluctuating) exchange of energy with the environment. At a physiological level, this is how all organisms take in nutrients to generate the necessary energy that keeps them alive and allows them to proliferate. This fundamental process, metabolism, defines all living things.

A process analogous to metabolism takes place at the behavioral level when, for example, infants adjust their behavior to novel circumstances they encounter in their environment. Suppose that a blanket lands on a newborn's face, covering and obstructing the mouth and nose. The infant will become agitated and turn her head until the airways are freed and normal breathing has been restored. In this case, energy is metabolized and channeled into motoric actions (a head turn or movement of the arm and hands) that will eventually reestablish a stable state (regular breathing). Like the billions of microscopic cells that support it, infant behavior can be construed as an open-loop system that maintains a kind of stable state. This system is dynamic and developing in the sense that it is adaptable and can generate novel solutions to the problem of environmental changes.

I already alluded to Piaget's constructivist view of development with the central notion of successive and progressive stages (see Chapter 5). The model put forth by Piaget to account for the actual process underlying the transition from one stage to another is one that borrows from biology and evolutionary theories: the model of equilibration.

Piaget was a biologist by training, and although he elaborated the most influential theory of cognitive development, his Ph.D. dissertation was on the transmission of acquired characteristics in snails. In addition, parallel to his monumental contribution to the field of child development and genetic epistemology, he had a lifelong career of privately conducting botany experiments on similar evolutionary issues. Piaget's view is indeed quite unifying and encompassing, spanning various research domains typically picked singly by scientists. His view is encompassing because in his mind there was no fundamental difference between biological adaptation in species evolution (phylogeny) and the development taking place in the individual infant (ontogeny). For Piaget, analogous processes underlay both. In the same way that during biological evolution new organismic forms emerge as the result of transactions with environment, new behavioral and cognitive forms emerge in ontogeny from the interaction of the child with objects, people, and circumstances in the environment. Piaget's view is radically interactionist, with knowledge and behavior understood as the interface between children and environment. But what about equilibration?

Piaget postulated that infant development stems from two interacting forces: assimilation and accommodation. Assimilation is the human propensity to incorporate novel objects and situations encountered in the environment to what is already mastered, whether an action or a way of thinking about the world. Accommodation, by contrast, is simply the tendency to modify one's action in order to assimilate more objects and situations to what is already mastered or known. Piaget reduces the behavioral and cognitive novelty emerging in infant development to the combined operation of assimilation and accommodation.

As an illustration, neonates who are born with mastery over sucking will tend to repeat this action (functional assimilation), and assimilate all objects encountered with their mouth to this action, whether it is their mother's nipple, a bottle, or a toy lying in the crib. All objects contacting the mouth of the young infant will tend to be assimilated to sucking activities (generalizing assimilation). Likewise, some weeks later, the mere sight of a milk bottle will be assimilated to sucking (recognitory assimilation) and will cause babies, particularly if they are hungry, to become agitated and pull their tongues in and out in anticipation of food. The force of assimilation, whether functional, generalizing, or recognitory, is not sufficient in itself to cause novel forms of behavior in development.

Assimilation alone would make the infant a nondeveloping closed-loop system, imprisoned in endless repetition of the same rigid action schemes. Instead, behavioral novelty arises because of the force of accommodation that allows the assimilation tendency of infants to adjust to the variety of encounters in the environment. When looking closely at young infants' propensity to suck on everything they can put their mouth on, for example, one notices that their pattern of sucking is not stereotyped but rather variable. As mentioned in Chapter 3, newborns have different patterns of sucking for objects varying in shape, texture, or substance (Rochat 1983; 1987).

In Piaget's account, the forces of assimilation and accommodation are in constant coactivation, leading to novel behaviors—in particular novel organizations of action and cognition. In development, however, these forces reach some kind of general equilibrium, each corresponding to the Piagetian stages of infant development. At each stage, modifications of assimilatory schemes via accommodation occur within a range that does not transform the general order of the stage. We could call them micro changes compared to the macro changes of an actual developmental transition from one stage to another. Equilibration is the process of change in infant behavior as an open-looped system, the product of the adaptive interaction between organism and environment.

The model of equilibration is vast in its application, so vast that it can be easily criticized as being untestable and inherently circular. In Piaget's theoretical rationale, the dynamic of psychological changes in infancy is a special case of biological adaptation. It is part of the general process by which, at all levels of living, a balance is achieved between the forces by which an organism acts (assimilation) and the forces by which this organism adjusts its repertoire of action in the face of resistance from novel environmental circumstances (accommodation). This adjustment, within the context of an orderly succession of general stages, captures what developmental changes are about. Piaget's account of the developmental process has the merit of emphasizing the central role played by infants as actors in and constructors of their development.

The idea of infants as active participants in their development fits nicely with the current image of infants as explorers of the self, objects, and people in their environment, an image that emanates from most contemporary research in infancy (some of which I reviewed in this book). Finally, the general notion of equilibration as a central process of infant development is inseparable from the notion of behavioral organization, captured specifically by the Piagetian notion of stage. Whether or not we agree on the reality of stages in infant development, it is impossible to deny that there are structure and organization in behavior from birth (see Chapter 5).

As emphasized by Piaget's model of equilibration, an important aspect of infant development is indeed the passage from one level of organization to another. But other developmental accounts point to a less active or structuring role taken by infants themselves in this process. Rather, they emphasize self-organization: the spontaneous emergence of novel forms of behavioral organization from the parallel real-time functioning of multiple dynamic systems.

Self-Organization

In the process of equilibration put forth by Piaget, there is the underlying assumption that infants' activity structures their development. For example, we have seen in Chapter 3 that at around four months of age infants start to reach for objects they see. There is the possibility that sensorimotor systems such as hands and eyes come to be integrated not as the result of the infant's laborious structuring, as suggested by Piaget (1952), but rather because of peripheral causes such as the parallel, time-locked functioning of manual, visual, and postural systems. This idea is supported in part by research showing that patterns of eye-hand coordination in infancy emerge in interaction with other postural and action systems such as the development of independent sitting (Rochat 1992; Rochat and Goubet 1995; Rochat, Goubet, and Senders 1999) or crawling (Goldfield 1993). Like most natural phenomena, these developmental patterns are self-organizing—that is, they are probably not structured by some prescribing forces that are inherent in infants and guide their development. An increasing number of infancy researchers point to the process of emergent, self-organizing new forms of behavior as accounting for how infants develop (see, for example, Thelen and Smith 1994).

Nature is full of striking forms and organizations displayed in exquisitely balanced shape and symmetry: the snowflake, the leaves of a tree, the way our body is built, the "V" formation spontaneously adopted by flying geese. Such pleasing and pervasive order in nature is created by self-organizing principles arising from multiple discrete interactions among individual subsystems. At all levels of nature, when complex systems are simultaneously set in motion, they spontaneously reach stable states that emerge from their interaction itself. For example, the "V" formation adopted by a flying flock of geese is spontaneous and obviously not prescribed. Instead it emerges from the act of flying together: each individual goose follows the leader at the apex by lining up either to the right or the left of the goose ahead.

Probably the most striking evidence of how pervasive self-organizing phenomena are in nature is the fact that they are observable at all scales: from the way frozen molecules attached to each other form snowflakes, to the way complex systems such as flying geese reach a stable state in their interaction, to the way infants appear to reach stable behavioral states and organization in their development.

In addition to similar shapes, similar dynamic forms result from the process of self-organization. These forms correspond to regularities in the periodicity of events in nature. For example, life on this planet evolved in the context of a very precise cycle of light and dark, which is determined by the way the earth rotates on its axis and how it moves in relation to the sun. In turn, the behavior of all things on the planet resonates to the movement of the earth relative to the sun, from the freezing of water to the thawing of snow, the flowing of rivers to the geological erosion of vast landscapes, the opening and closing of flowers to our wake-sleep cycle. Biological clocks are an important aspect of all levels of our functioning, as demonstrated by how difficult it is to sleep after flying across different time zones. Such "clocks" and cycles express a self-organizing process in nature in which the mere interaction of multiple systems at various functioning scales creates a pattern.

Infant behavior, like any other natural phenomena, is recognizable by its regular shape and periodicity. Infants oscillate between well-delimited ranges of behavioral state variability (the crying, sleeping, fussy, and alert and active states). In dynamic systems theory, these identifiable ranges of behavioral variation are called attractor states. These are the same kind of periodic dynamic forms found everywhere in nature. But how do they help to account for the processes and mechanisms of infant development?

Some infancy researchers propose that early development, and in particular the early development of functional actions such as reaching, crawling, or walking, is a self-organized assembly originating from the spontaneous movements that the body, within its own constraints, affords for action. The own constraints of the body correspond to the way it is built and how it is capable of moving given gravity and changing environmental circumstances. So, for example, when young infants lay supine in their crib and move their legs, they do so in recognizable kicking patterns. Or a few weeks later, when they start to crawl, they do so in coordinated patterns of lower- and upper-limbs movement. These patterns might vary in velocity, amplitude, and trajectory, but they all have some invariant dynamic signature that make them recognizable as kicking or crawling. In these action patterns, the movements of the limbs do not occur independently, but rather are typically coordinated in invariant patterns of repeated alternance; for example, in the case of kicking, one leg flexes and the other extends (Thelen, Skala, and Kelso 1987). Is there a central control for the emergence of such dynamic forms of behavior? Probably not.

Researchers like Esther Thelen and her colleagues (for example, Thelen and Smith 1994) as well as Eugene Goldfield (1995) apply a dynamic systems approach to account for such development and provide a lot of convincing empirical evidence that patterns of sensorimotor actions could emerge in early development as self-organization. There are attractor states for infants' bodily movements, and these attractor states change as infants grow physically, achieve better postural control, or discover new possibilities for action with objects (that is, learn new affordances and develop new task goals). No one variable has priority in determining the development of an action pattern. Yet each contributing variable is changing over time, and each or only a few of them can be the control parameters of new forms of behavior.

To come back to my weather metaphor, theoretically either a butterfly wing flapping in Atlanta or a tropical storm in the Bay of Bengal could be the initial condition of a weather change in Beijing a few days later. Similarly, changes in the muscle-to-fat ratio of a growing infant could potentially determine a change in stepping pattern (Thelen and Fisher 1982), the emergence of new task goals such as kicking a mobile, or the developing ability to sit independently. They would all be the consequence of the temporal self-organizing assembly of parallel distributed dynamic systems (that is, postural strengthening, the development of perceptual systems, and so on).

In short, rather than being determined by a central command, new forms of behavior could also emerge from multiple systems developing side by side and in constant interaction. That is, new forms of behavior in infant development may correspond in part to organizational change "governed by a series of stabilizing and destabilizing attractors" (Goldfield 1995, p. 26). This change would be in part peripheral and distributed in its causation, rather than prescribed and centralized in the form of hidden cognitive or higher command structures (see the detailed exposition of this view in Smith and Thelen 1993; Thelen and Smith 1994).

As I mentioned earlier, many researchers have shown that the self-organizing process plays a role in determining infant behavior and development. But a lively debate exists regarding how much of infant development can be accounted for by this process. Most evidence comes from the developmental and adult motor control literature, along with some new efforts to apply the dynamic systems view to cognitive, in particular conceptual and language, development (Smith 1995). The problem is how to go beyond the powerful metaphor offered by the dynamic systems approach and get to the determination of what actually causes change to occur. Self-organizing principles refer to the how question of the developmental process, not the why question. As real as they might be, an account of self-organizing principles does not allow researchers to establish some hierarchy among the many interacting systems and subsystems that might trigger the initial steps in infant development. For example, what is the best predictor of developing locomotion in infancy? Changes in muscle-to-fat ratio? Progress in the perception of distal objects that are reachable only by moving the whole body? The development of visuo-vestibular balance?

As it stands, there is no convincing evidence that the dynamic systems approach to infant development allows us to answer such questions. As helpful and accurate as it might be, this approach remains essentially descriptive, accounting for the how question, not the why question, of infant development.

The model of equilibration discussed earlier and the principle of self-organization reviewed here provide powerful insights into some of the general principles by which infant development is guided. But it does not speak to what actually causes or drives development. I turn now, and for the remainder of this chapter, to theories and models that actually identify specific *mechanisms* that are both causes and vehicles of developmental changes in infancy.

Conditioning and Built-in Reward Systems

In this book, a recurrent theme has been infants' early propensity to learn. In relation to the self in infancy (Chapter 2), I conveyed the idea that from birth, infants learn to use their own bodies to produce, or reproduce an effect in the environment. Pavlovian classical and Skinnerian operant or instrumental conditioning, as well as circular reactions described by James Baldwin (1925) and particularly the object-oriented secondary circular reactions accounted for by Piaget (1952), all reflect behavioral plasticity and early learning experience. They cause novel forms of behavior and knowledge in infancy, and hence are genuine mechanisms contributing to infant development.

As we have seen in Chapter 5, the efficacy of early conditioning gave behavioral scientists the opportunity to try controlling and predicting development from the outset. Indeed some attempted to play the role of Nature itself by engineering infant behavior and development. Doing so is a bit like controlling the flow of a river by building dams. Scientists could guide and shape the development of infants by controlling their experience of the environment and their opportunity to learn the positive or negative consequences of events and self-produced actions. Like circus animals trained to behave in spectacular ways through a strict program and schedule of reinforcement (typically food immediately following the desired behavior), infants could be trained to speak, be potty trained, eat certain food, wave at people, and even feel in certain ways in relation to certain objects, events, or animals as in Watson's experiment of fear conditioning.

The recipe, in principle, could be simple and powerful. If parents and educators had total control over the environment of infants—namely the pleasant or unpleasant consequences of either perceived external events (Pavlovian classical conditioning) or self-produced action (Skinnerian operant conditioning)—then infants could be behaviorally shaped. Aside from ethical issues, however, there are many theoretical problems with such an idea. I will mention one that for me demonstrates that infant development cannot be merely reduced to a mechanism of conditioning. If conditioning is an important determinant of early behavioral changes, it is certainly not the only one.

If conditioning is a source of novel behavioral forms from birth, and if infants are indeed sensitive to the temporal relationship between temporally contiguous events, they are not sensitive to just any events. Infants learn what they can and want to learn. They might learn to suck in order to hear a particular voice, or to turn their heads in anticipation of a bottle when a light is turned on above their cribs, but they will not get reinforced by salty tastes; they will not reach, utter particular sounds, or wave their right hands at people with hats. They might do that in a few months of developmental time, but not in the newborn phase and probably not before the end of infancy. This simple observation is commonsensical but shows that learning by conditioning depends on other developmental changes: the development of infants' repertoire of action, their postural and motor control, their motives to communicate, and more importantly, their motives to learn. Infants will learn their first words when they are ready to function symbolically by the second year. In the same way, they will learn to walk independently only after they are ready to stand.

Yet conditioning clearly plays an important role in shaping our emotional life. It is the reason why certain smells, tastes, or specific situations trigger uncontrollable disgust, desire, or fear. In fact, I would argue that conditioning plays a central role in the most intense experiences of our lives.

Conditioning is certainly a powerful vehicle of behavioral change, learned responses, and habits, good or bad. At the origin of development, it is part of newborns' built-in survival kit. The most basic principle shaping behavior from birth is the fact that actions with pleasurable consequences tend to be repeated and events associated with pleasure tend to be searched for. By contrast, actions with painful consequences tend to be eliminated and events associated with pain avoided. This simple law of effect, first described by pioneer behaviorist Edward L. Thorndike (1874–1949), shapes and orients behavior at all ages and at all levels of biological evolution. It forms the basic orientation of behavior toward resourceful aspects of the environment, what is typically good for the organism and favors its survival such as nutritious and nonpoisonous food, or care and protection by providers like mothers.

At the level of motivation, pleasure is the foundation of the law of effect. Maximum pleasure and minimum pain is the motto for adults and infants alike. In general, behavior is always caught at some basic level into the pain-pleasure opposition, or what some learning theorists have construed as the opposite forces of approach and avoidance. From an evolutionary point of view, this dichotomy plays a crucial role in directing behavior toward resources in the environment that ultimately help in the process of survival and adaptation. Pain and pleasure need to be considered as the basic prescribed values guiding behavior at an "instinctive," automatic, nonreflective (unconscious) level.

There are good examples of how pleasure shapes behaviors in infants that are useful for their survival. In fact, these examples demonstrate that the brain of infants is built to dispense pleasure when infants do certain things and get in contact with certain objects in the environment that are instrumental to their survival. The human brain, like the brain of most brain-endowed species, has evolved its own reward system, manufacturing and dispensing its own pleasure inducing, highly addictive, and pain-killing chemicals. In other words, infants are born conditioned by preadapted pain-reducing and reward systems that guide them to learn certain behaviors and not others.

For example, it is now well established that the high concentration of sucrose in maternal collostrum, the mother's "first milk," is a source of intense pleasure for the newborn. Colostrum has great nutritive and immunizing values for newborns, and therefore contributes to their health and survival. It also gives infants a pleasurable sensation probably comparable to the "high" that heroin addicts experience. But how do we know that?

The ingestion of sucrose by rat pups or human newborns is shown to be associated with an activation of opioid pathways in the brain (Blass and Ciaramitaro 1994). When these pathways are activated, the brain produces its own versions of morphine, called endorphins. Chemical analyses reveal that endorphins duplicate the composition of the opiates processed from poppy flowers. What this means for newborns is that sucking the mother's nipple and feeding on the nutritive and immunizing breastmilk is a source of intense pleasure and therefore a very potent, built-in reward system.

I should mention that endorphins are not only part of a built-in reward system for certain behaviors but also help infants endure pain. The analgesic effect of sucrose (which once again, triggers opioid pathways in the brain), is evident in the finding that male newborns who receive water with sucrose just prior to unanesthetized circumcision cry significantly less than infants who do not receive such a concoction. In general, sucrose has remarkable calming effects on the newborn (Blass and Ciaramitaro 1994; Blass and Shah 1995).

When exercising a lot and cultivating brushes with physical exhaustion, we typically experience rushes of pleasure during and after what should be bouts with pain. This pleasure comes, at least in part, from endorphins, which are manufactured by the brain in response to exhaustion and the activation of pain centers. Actually, such rushes might account for the common psychological addiction to frequent physical exercise. It might also provide the psychobiological foundation of the paradoxical pleasure we often find in painful actions. In many human activities, such as sport and daring exploits, pain and pleasure are indeed confounded.

It is true, then, that conditioning is a mechanism of infant development: it can predict and control early behavioral changes. But conditioning cannot account for all aspects of behavioral development. Other mechanisms must account for what creates conditions for particular learning to occur. Indeed, even in the most controlled environment, infants cannot learn anything at any age. Finally, it appears that built-in reward systems orient infants selectively toward resources in their environment and help them cope with pain, and thus shape their behavior from the outset (see for example Blass 1999). External reward systems like those proposed by traditional behaviorists, although significant, can only account for a small part of infant behavioral development. One aspect left out is the active role played by infants themselves in setting up learning opportunities.

Habituation and Curiosity

Infants are not passive recipients of feedback from the environment. Rather, they are active explorers of their world, as noted by Piaget in his developmental account. In addition, reducing developmental changes to conditioning principles does not explain the orderly succession of phases or stages in development. So what other mechanism evident from birth actually captures infants' self-initiated, active propensity to learn and develop? I propose that the answer is a sort of built-in curiosity system, one analogous to the built-in reward system discussed earlier but without any precise psychobiological underpinning like opioid pathways.

At the very beginning of the book, I discussed habituation as a behavioral phenomenon that is pervasive in the animal kingdom. When presented with repeated exposures to a stimulation, the response typically associated with this stimulation tends to decrease. The habituation phenomenon has great adaptive value for any creatures, infants included: it allows organisms to take in and search for novel information, the basic ingredient of curiosity. In the wild, this process is crucial for survival. If a cow grazing in a field by a highway or a busy train track jumped and ran each time a car passed, the poor cow would be in motion twenty-four hours a day, unable to feed her young. Similarly, an antelope needs to discriminate between sounds associated with lions and the less threatening noises of the savanna. Habituation is the mechanism that allows such vital discrimination. It is also the mechanism that has allowed researchers to assess much of infants' competencies from birth (and even before) in perceiving the object world around them (see Chapter 3).

There are different possible interpretations of the behavioral plasticity that results from habituation in infancy. One "lean" interpretation would be that habituation observed in infants is the expression of a low-level mechanism such as neural fatigue (neurons in the brain shutting off when activated too frequently). But the neural fatigue model of habituation does not leave room for higher-order principles such as the quest for and anticipation of novel information, in which the organism as a whole tries to figure out and compare events in the environment.

There is convincing empirical support of this "fuller" interpretation. Suppose that an infant is lying on his back and presented with a rattling sound for few seconds either on his right or his left side. During the first presentations, the infant will systematically turn his head toward the stimulus. After a few presentations, the infant will suppress this response. If response suppression is due to neural fatigue, one would expect that the infant would behave increasingly as if he did not hear the stimulation anymore, like the cow who keeps on grazing in spite of the commotion on the nearby highway. Alternatively, if curiosity or a quest for novel information was at work, one would expect that rather than disappearing (extinction), the response would *change*—and this is exactly what happens. For example, some researchers have shown that instead of merely not turning toward a repeated sound, newborns habituate by tending to turn their head in the opposite direction (Weiss, Zelazo, and Swain 1988). It is as if they were searching for some new events in the location exactly opposite to the tiresome sound. Instead of mere neural fatigue and response extinction, newborns orient away from the known and closer to where novel events might occur. It is hard not to interpret this change of behavior as an expression of boredom and the quest for novel, more exciting stimulation. At least such an observation demonstrates that the habituation phenomenon in human newborns is not merely reducible to neural fatigue. Discovery is indeed what appears to be an inexhaustible source of pleasure in infancy and a central force driving infant development.

If infants from birth are attuned to novelty, it does imply that they discriminate between novel and known perceptual events. But what are the bases of such discrimination? In other words, what is novel and what is familiar for infants? I will suggest that the built-in exploratory and curiosity systems of infants are primarily oriented toward detecting invariant characteristics among perceptual events—that is, stable elements in the complex intricacies of perceptual experience.

The Search for Regularities

The drive to detect regularities in the flow of perception is actually at work all through the lifespan, and certainly across species. It is the basis of any learning from birth on and the foundation of cognitive changes in humans in language, memory, concept formation, formal thinking, and even motor skill development.

Regularity detection stands for what James J. Gibson (1966) and Eleanor Gibson (1969) discuss in the realm of perception and perceptual learning as the detection of invariant information. In his book *The Senses Considered as Perceptual Systems,* Gibson (1966) provides strong evidence that perceptual systems such as vision, audition, touch, and olfaction have evolved to pick up information readily available in the environment. This information corresponds to feature characteristics that remain constant in the midst of transformations.

To support the view that perceptual information is readily available in the environment, J. J. Gibson, in two other books (1950; 1979), describes the visual world as an intricate collection of surfaces on which light bounces and is finally captured by the eyes. The light bounces differently depending on the surface in the environment from which it is reflected: it will bounce toward the eyes one way when the surface is smooth like a mirror, and another if the surface is rough like a pebbled road. The bouncing of the light will also depend on how the surface is oriented in relation to the light source (such as the sun or a light bulb), and whether the perceiver is stationary or in motion. What Gibson shows is that the perceived environment is made of surfaces with different ratios of texture gradient or density change that are reflected directly in the light or optic array. This is the rationale for Gibson's famous (but often viewed as infamous) claim that visual information is in the light, not in the head of perceivers and actors. There is information in the invariant way that light bounces on surfaces in the layout prior to being captured by the eye. This information specifies these surfaces not only in terms of their relative orientation in three-dimensional space, but also, when moving, in terms of their relative rigidity and whether they are part of discrete, bounded objects in the environment. For Gibson, this information is ready to be harvested directly without having to be reconstructed mentally, as is often assumed by mainstream cognitive psychologists (Gibson 1979).

This brief account of Gibson's view on perception is important because it points to a far-reaching catalyst for development: the detection of regularities in the midst of varying experience. Eleanor J. Gibson, adding to her husband's theoretical views, proposed that the mechanism of invariant feature detection accounts for perceptual learning and development (E. J. Gibson 1969). Accordingly, from birth on infants would progressively pick up these invariant features by a process of differentiation, by sorting out what remains the same from what varies across successive perceptual experiences.

The detection and processing of invariant information is indeed an early fact of life. In learning, whether by conditioning or habituation, infants from birth detect regularities in the succession of perceptual events. In the case of habituation, they dishabituate when perceiving a stimulation as being different—that is, novel—because it does not match with a stimulation they had already been exposed to and grown familiar with. For example, an infant will stop turning her head toward a sound coming out of a stationary speaker, even if this sound varies in intensity depending on how her head is oriented toward the speaker. By expressing habituation and dishabituation, the infant forms some class or category of intensity variation, perceived as an exemplar of a category. Suppose now that a sound is presented to the infant with an intensity that is way above the range of variation of the other. The infant will quickly dishabituate, showing that she perceives the new sound as novel, as crossing a category boundary. The infant differentiates among *classes of stimulation*, each defined by ranges of variation within particular boundaries, so-called *category boundaries*.

Categorical perception is based on the detection of regularities among fluctuating perceptual events, and it is an early fact of life, evident even in neonates. In Chapter 3, I presented examples of research on early speech sound perception which provide examples of categorical perception by young infants. The mechanism of invariant feature detection is what underlies the early perception of speech sounds, the beginning of an understanding of gestures and sounds as referring to things in the world, the general propensity to sort things in certain ways. It is the mechanism by which entities in the environment are progressively related to each other, whether these entities pertain to the self, objects, or people.

The active search for regularities is thus a cornerstone of cognitive development in infancy and beyond. It is the mechanism by which progress in conceptualizing the world is made possible, the mechanism by which infants develop a sense of what is familiar and what is unfamiliar, known and unknown, novel and old, dangerous and safe, useful and not useful. It is based on this mechanism that infants will, for example, recognize their mother despite her continual change in appearance: the infant knows it is her even if she changes clothes, cuts her hair, puts on perfume, or modifies the intonation of her voice. It is based on this mechanism that infants will eventually learn to label with one single arbitrary speech sound a whole class of objects and events, learning for example that the sound "chair" stands for all the things that one can sit on, even if they vary in color, material, shape, or overall appearance. All chairs belong to the same "chair" class and are eventually encased into a rich hierarchical network of supra and superordinate categories such as stools, armchairs, lounge chairs, and overall furniture categories that contrast with other categories formed by other entities such as cars or trees. Infants' propensity at birth and beyond to search for what is common among successive perceptual experiences and to store knowledge about these commonalities for further conceptualization orients infants in their learning.

Social Mirroring, Imitation, and Repetition

Let us turn now to mechanisms that have a social origin. Infants' development is obviously determined by their social surrounding. But how exactly do social interactions influence infant development? In this section, I identify adult mirroring and infants' propensity to imitate as mechanisms that contribute significantly to infants' cognitive progress.

Imitation is generally understood as the process by which one behavior is mapped onto another. Mirroring is a perfect, absolute version of this process. Caregivers of infants have the compulsive tendency to do what mirrors do—and more. They do not just reflect back to infants what they detect as the infant's general mood and significant gestures, but exaggerate and amplify these moods and gestures. Furthermore, caregivers appear to use particular intonations and periods of silence when engaging in social mirroring with infants (Gergely and Watson 1999). These intonations and pauses correspond to invariant features in protoconversation, which, as discussed earlier, are probably detectable by infants from birth. In other words, the social partners of infants feed back to them an intelligible version of who they are, what they do, and how they are supposed to feel (see Chapter 4).

Not only do caretakers have the compulsion to reflect and exaggerate the behavior of infants; infants from birth also appear to imitate others. I have already reviewed some of the evidence from the infancy literature on neonatal imitation. Note however that the extent and reliability of neonatal imitation, as well as the mechanisms explaining it, remain controversial (see Anisfeld 1991; Bjorklund 1987; Jones 1996; Meltzoff and Moore 1997).

In their seminal work, Meltzoff and Moore (1977) report that infants only a few hours old reproduce the successive tongue protrusion, mouth opening, or hand clasping of an adult model. According to these authors (Meltzoff and Moore 1977; 1997), such observations demonstrate a built-in ability to map self-produced behavior onto the behavior of others, or "active intermodal matching" (AIM). If such mapping between perception and action exists at birth, it is most probably an important source of behavioral changes and learning about the self, objects, and people in infancy.

Infant imitation is geared toward not only the reproduction of behavior produced by others, but also the reproduction of self-produced behavior. Circular reactions manifested a few weeks after birth (Baldwin 1925; Piaget 1952), and the repetitive, rhythmic activities expressed from birth on and even prior to birth, can be construed as self-imitation. From birth, infants tend to engage in repetitive actions such as bringing their hands to their mouths, sucking by moving their tongues in and out of their mouths, waving their hands, or kicking their legs. In addition to a social, communicative function, there is also an ego function attached to imitation (Rochat 2001).

By reproducing their own action, or self-imitating, infants gain knowledge about themselves, their own capacity for action, and what specifies their own body as a unique, initiating entity in the environment. In Chapter 2 on the self in infancy, I explained that infants are actively engaged in exploring their own bodies. This exploration helps the infant detect invariant features that specify the body as situated, differentiated, and independently active in the environment (that is, those features that define the ecological self). The detection of such invariant perceptual features of the body is done primarily by repetition of an action or self-imitation. For example, repeated leg kicking in the crib, within a certain range and with a certain kind of force, might cause a certain auditory event (for example, the ringing of a bell attached to the crib's canopy). It is based primarily on such active reproduction of action that infants specify their own agency in relation to not only objects, but also people.

By imitating others infants also learn to use their social surrounding as a source of new knowledge about everything from tool use, to learning new words for things, to novel ways of doing things. Imitation has a social communicative function, as well as a cognitive or teaching function. It contributes to individuals' knowledge and is certainly a major instrument of cultural learning and cultural transmission (Tomasello, Kruger, and Ratner 1993; Tomasello 1999).

There is currently a very lively debate in the literature on primate cognition over whether imitation is a means of cultural transmission that is uniquely human (Whiten and Custance 1996). Some researchers argue that learning new behavior via modeling is very limited in nonhumans. Their research suggests that little intentional teaching via modeling and imitation is observed in primate species other than humans (Tomasello, Kruger, and Ratner 1993). Others argue that learning by imitation and deliberate teaching is not exclusively human: it is observed in the wild with chimpanzees, for example, which tend to teach newly acquired skills and affordances to their young. In one group of wild chimpanzees, the juveniles apparently learned from the adults how to crack the very hard shell of nuts using two stones, one as a hammer and the other as an anvil (Boesh 1993). Despite this controversy, it is clear that imitation and learning by watching others is much more prominent or at least more productive in humans than in any other species, primate or nonprimate. Imitation plays certainly a crucial role in human language development, determining the acquisition of new words and new grammatical forms. This language acquisition is primarily based on the mapping of one communicative intent onto another, which is achieved by modeling and reproducing the speech acts of more advanced others. In humans, it appears that imitation is an important determinant of development from birth and particularly when infants enter the symbolic gateway (see Chapter 5).

Piaget (1962) actually considers imitation as a means by which infants secure their entry into the symbolic gateway. At this time, infants start to model people, objects, or events in their absence as in pretend play (or "differed imitation"). Piaget views this type of true imitative activity as the opportunity for infants to develop their abilities. Note that Piaget distinguishes true imitation from "pseudo" imitation, which can be expressed early in the first year in the presence of the model (for example, reproduction of the tongue protrusion of a social partner). With "true" or differed imitation, infants learn to perform actions (signifiers) that stand for either the action of someone else or something else (signified). They therefore learn to behave symbolically. Piaget believed that infants start to engage in such symbolic exercises by approximately eighteen months, not earlier. More recent empirical evidence, however, suggests that differed imitation is a much earlier fact of life, manifested by infants as young as six weeks (Meltzoff and Moore 1992; 1997). It is therefore feasible that infants start acting on represented models and engage in symbolic exercises from a very early age. From this, we can conclude that there is a long and progressive journey toward the symbolic gateway. In this long journey, there is little doubt that imitation is an important vehicle of progress.

Imitation is also a way for the infant to socialize and communicate. By imitating, infants gain knowledge about people and maintain proximity with others (Uzgiris 1999). Considering the great dependence of infants on their social surrounding, this function is obviously crucial. But how can it be demonstrated?

I think that the most convincing evidence supporting the social-communicative function of early imitation is the simple fact that when infants imitate an action modeled by an adult, they do not reproduce the act once but many times. This repetition strongly suggests that infants imitate and reproduce the modeled act to maintain a communicative flow with the person who modeled the action. Imitation, in this case, serves to maintain a dialogue of sorts between the infant and the adult model (Killen and Uzgiris 1981).

Other evidence in the literature suggests that infants use imitation to learn who people are and how they relate to them. Imitation, at least starting at about nine months of age, becomes a means by which infants assess and eventually identify people. In an experiment by Andrew Meltzoff (1990), infants were tested when facing two adult experimenters sitting across a table from them. Each experimenter had an exact duplicate of a toy given to the infant to play with. In the test situation, one of the experimenters (the imitator) imitated as closely as possible and contingently all the movements performed by the infant on the object, (for example, when the infant banged the object, the imitator experimenter would simultaneously bang the object in an analogous way). Meanwhile, the other experimenter responded to all the movements performed by the infant on the object by simultaneously acting on the object, but not in an analogous way. So, for example, while the infant banged the object the contingent but not imitator experimenter would do something else to the object, like wave it.

Within this clever experimental arrangement, the infant could choose which of the two social partners to interact with. From nine months of age, infants look reliably more toward the experimenter who is imitating them. Even more interesting, by fourteen-months infants will try to trick the experimenter who is faithfully imitating them by performing swift, challenging actions that are difficult to reproduce (Meltzoff 1990). For example, the infant may slowly lean sideways while tracking the experimenter doing the same, and then, abruptly, change direction while looking and smiling at the experimenter. With this kind of behavior, infants show that they know they are being imitated. They seem to use this discovery to probe others in their communicative intents, in particular to see if they are engaging in a friendly, humorous game.

Social learning by imitation is evident even earlier in development. Infants as young as six weeks are reported as learning to associate particular gestures to particular people, and as using this association to discriminate among them. For example, if the mother models to the infant a tongue protrusion gesture and a stranger a mouth opening gesture, in subsequent tests infants reproduce each gesture significantly more in the presence of the original model (Meltzoff and Moore 1992). Such selective imitation indicates that early on infants' social responses depend on the identification of people—an identification that they have learned during previous face-to-face exchanges.

Trimming and Inhibition

One way to look at infant behavior and development is to consider the way that infants progressively gain control over their actions by getting rid of all superfluous noises and potential distractors to the achievement of functional goals such as reaching, attending, or communicating. The mechanism contributing to the achievement of such goals and ultimately to infant behavioral development is inhibition.

Inhibition is manifested at all levels of functioning, from the physiological level (which includes, for example, the movement of muscles) to the psychological level of motor control, attention, and higher-order cognition, including planning and anticipation. It is also the mechanism by which infants become eventually less impulsive and more in control of their fluctuating affective states.

The brain is an immensely complex network of billions of connected cells arranged into mind-boggling numbers of combinations and layered structures that interact with each other. Despite this immense complexity, the actual functioning of its constituting elements, the neurons or nerve cells, is disarmingly simple. Neurons are either activated or deactivated (that is, inhibited). The brain is therefore a gigantic web of discrete elements that play an all or nothing game, with each element boiling down to the binary functioning of + or − responses. At a coarser level of physiology, the biomechanics of the muscles attached to the skeleton and that make it move also boil down to the coupling of muscle groups that are either agonist (activating), or antagonist (counteracting or inhibiting of the tensions from agonist muscles). Movement control is indeed based on the exquisite balance between activating and inhibiting muscle groups. Such a binary balance is pervasive not only in the way the body works at the physiological level, but also probably in the way the mind works and develops at the psychological level.

When the mind focuses its attention on a task or the exploration of one particular aspect of the environment, it both activates what cognitive psychologists sometimes call "selective filters"—which bring particular information into attentional focus—and inhibits irrelevant information by blocking it out. In fact, the theories that currently dominate the study of attention in cognitive sciences consider that attention or the determination of mental focus is primarily due to mechanisms of inhibition or temporary trimming away of irrelevant, distracting information (Tipper 1995). We use inhibition as adults to ignore distractions so that we can concentrate on the task at hand, whether it is reading a book, solving a math problem, or searching for typos in a text. But how do mechanisms of inhibition influence infant development?

Inhibition might account for the transition from preadapted action systems (that is, reflexes), to a more voluntary control of action evident from about two months of age. It might also explain infants' progressive gains in mental composure and patience as they plan actions to solve problems, particularly starting at eight to nine months of age.

For a long time infancy researchers have noticed that the reflex responses recorded in healthy neonates—such as the Moro response (the spreading of arms following a sudden drop of the whole body), automatic stepping movements, or palmar grasp (flexion of the fingers following a palmar stimulation)—tend to weaken and disappear by the second month. The developmental account of this change continues to stir an important theoretical debate. For some researchers who apply the dynamic systems approach to infant development, the disappearance of reflex responses can be explained by changes in body configuration and the muscle-to-fat ratio (Thelen and Smith 1994). Accordingly, these responses would not vanish from the infant's repertoire, but rather would be occluded by peripheral factors. As a demonstration, Esther Thelen and collaborators showed that the stepping movements recorded immediately after birth and that disappear by two months actually reappear when the infant is immersed in water from the waist down. Thelen argues that the water helps the infant to counteract the force of gravity and compensate for the substantial weight he or she had gained (Thelen and Fisher 1983).

Other research, however, suggests that a major qualitative change does occur by the second month in terms of what part of the infant brain controls behavior. The recording of brain electrical activity (EEG) via multiple surface electrodes placed on young infants' scalps provides some evidence of significant changes in which regions of the brain control behavior between birth and three months. Important development in brain involvement and behavioral control occurs in the first weeks of life. Furthermore, aside from the apparent drop of archaic sensorimotor reflexes, by two months there are reliable changes in the way that infants attend to facial displays and discriminate faces: they graduate from observing only general external features to scrutinizing more detailed internal features of faces, in particular eyes and mouth (see Chapter 4). Such development is interpreted by current cognitive neuroscientists as the expression of a change from subcortically to cortically controlled visuomotor behavior (that is, behavior related to eye movements and overt visual attention) at around two months of life (Johnson 1993).

The idea of such brain-mediated change is not new and was put forth by Myrtle McGraw in the 1940s on the basis of her careful empirical work on the early development of motor activities, and in particular the fate of newborn archaic responses. She views the weakening and eventual disappearance of archaic reflexes in the three months following birth as the symptom of a transition from involuntary (subcortically mediated) to voluntary (cortically mediated) action. In this process, McGraw (1943) put forth the importance of inhibition as a developmental mechanism. Her idea is that in order for cortical structures to take control over motor activities, subcortical control needs to be inhibited. Accordingly, new, voluntary acts emerge in the infant repertoire at this age. Some authors propose even that such a transition temporally weakens infants' adaptive survival action repertoire and could account for the peak frequency of Sudden Infant Death Syndrome observed at around three months of age (Burns and Lipsitt 1991; Lipsitt 1979; Lipsitt et al. 1981).

Drops in performance and persistent errors are common features of infant development. Individual trajectories in the development of actions such as reaching demonstrate emerging, disappearing, and reappearing patterns of behavior. At a fine scale, development is not smooth but rather jagged, made up of alternating improvements and deterioration in performance, with overarching progress despite these developmental bumps. At times, although infants have information that they need to change their strategy in order to achieve a desired goal, they will blindly persist in reproducing the same failed attempts. For them to bypass these errors, they have to inhibit old patterns of action—which is not as easy as one might think.

The planning of action and the suspension (by inhibition) of old actions depend on the functioning of one cortical region: the frontal lobes. Monkeys subjected to a surgical lesion of the prefrontal cortex, for example, fail miserably in simple search tasks. If a pellet of food is placed in one of two covered wells several times and then, another time, placed in the other covered well, the animal will tend to either persevere in searching at the old location or search both locations randomly. They appear to have an impaired working memory and to have difficulty inhibiting old search patterns (Goldman-Rakic 1992).

The frontal region of the cortex is involved in the executive function of action and controls for the ability to break away from old habits to achieve new goals. In humans, one of the most pervasive symptoms in patients suffering from frontal region damage is inappropriately persevering (Gazzaniga, Ivry, and Mangun 1998). Immature brains also are subject to such errors. At around six to eight months of age, infants predictably persist in searching for an object at the last location they found it, despite a visible change in hiding place. Such ill-adapted persistence is linked by researchers to the immaturity of infants' prefrontal cortex (Diamond and Goldman-Rakic 1989; Diamond 1990). Once mature and functional, this structure is involved in inhibiting old successful behavioral patterns and tendencies, and thereby in helping the infant adjust to novel hiding circumstances.

In summary, there is little doubt that inhibition is an important mechanism of infant development, a mechanism by which established forms are cancelled or hindered to give way to novel, more adaptive ones. It is a general mechanism of suppression observable at all levels of infant development: from brain growth, to motor control, to cognition. In relation to brain growth in infancy, neural networks are shaped by the trimming of extra cells that are potentially functional at birth. The sculpting of neural networks that takes place in infancy is proceeded by a deactivation of those cells that will die (see Chapter 1). Neural development is not merely an additive process, it is also a subtractive one.

At the motor level, inhibition is the mechanism by which infants suppress superfluous and rigid responses to develop goal-oriented and flexible acts. Inhibition mechanisms could account for the apparent disappearance of reflex responses and certain behavioral propensities by newborns, such as the attention to faces. Inhibition at the motor level is analogous to the trimming or sculpting process observed in brain development. Both proceed in part by attrition, not merely by enhancing coordination.

In the realm of cognition, an important aspect of infant development is the ability to process information over noise. Inhibition at the cognitive level is the sorting and canceling out of irrelevant distractors, the elimination of false routes in solving problems, and the control of impulsivity. In these ways, inhibition contributes to the development of attentional composure and adaptive planning in infancy.

Explaining Infant Development with Machine Simulation and Connectionism

The infant world is a changing, evolving world. To make sense of it entails a developmental explanation. But what kind of developmental explanation? And what does it mean to explain infant development?

A simple way to solve this issue is to propose that explaining infant development means to predict and control the behavioral changes that ultimately shape development. According to this definition, infancy researchers would limit themselves to controlling environmental circumstances and playing on variations of reinforcement schedules in order to determine ways of modifying and shaping behavior (see the approach of strict behaviorists like Watson or Skinner). But is that an explanation?

Yes and no. Yes, because it does tell us what changes (behavior X at time 1 and behavior Y at time 2). It also tells us how it changes (via a conditioning mechanism) and why it changes (because of a particular schedule of reinforcement). But this account does not tell us what the developing mind of infants is made of, how it evolves as learning proceeds, or whether it develops using conditioning or other mechanisms. Behavioral engineering accounts are dismissive and noncommittal regarding most questions driving current infancy research.

As an alternative to behaviorism, some researchers have attempted to provide a developmental account of the infant world by simulating what might happen in the infant's mind: the processes of

from reproducing an analogous performance, actually represents the mental state (that is, belief system and intentionality) that is typically inseparable from the production of human action, speech acts, and other acts of meaning (see Bruner 1990 for a persuasive psychological account of this issue). In general, Searle's view questions psychologists' use of artificial intelligence (computers, robots, and other machines) as a tool to investigate mental life—it challenges the assumption that if a machine can be designed to reproduce a behavior, this behavior is explained.

Extending this question to connectionist modeling, which has been used to try to describe learning and development, one might ask whether the emergence of new behaviors simulated by a machine fully explains the emergence of analogous behavior in a child. Searle casts doubt on the issue by using his famous "Chinese Room Argument":

> The Chinese Room Argument shows that just carrying out the steps in a computer program is not by itself sufficient to guarantee cognition. Imagine that I, who do not know Chinese, am locked in a room with a computer program answering written questions, put to me in Chinese, by providing Chinese symbols as answers. If properly programmed I will provide answers indistinguishable from those of native Chinese speakers, but I still do not understand Chinese. And if I don't, neither does any other computer solely on the basis of carrying out the program. (Searle 1999, p. 36)

The Chinese Room Argument makes a strong case for the idea that simulating something is not the same as duplicating it. For example, engineering a robot that can learn to reach for three-dimensional objects in the environment or learn to walk does not duplicate what causes such development to occur in infants. In particular, it does not duplicate the motives of infants to learn to reach or walk. Nor does it tell us anything about the complex psychology behind the acquisition of these skills: how it happens as well as how it affects the infant's world as a whole. Like Searle locked in his Chinese Room, performing well but in a meaningless way, machine and formal models simulating infants and their development account for their performance, not what it means for them and their world.

The Equifinality Principle

The infant world is a dynamic, meaningful world. It is exquisitely rich and multiplicitous, and it deserves more than a simple explanation that reduces it to one or even only a few principles and mechanisms.

It is important to keep in mind that a fundamental principle guides all infants in their development: equifinality. That is, the same final state can be attained from different initial conditions and by following different trajectories. This principle applies to dynamic systems in general (von Bertalanffy 1968). It has profound significance and hopefully will become the major issue addressed by future researchers of the infant world eager to explore the ultimate open-looped, evolving dynamic system.

Some infants strive in environments that are dramatically impoverished. Other infants have difficulty coping in what seem to be very favorable surroundings. Some infants are very sociable, and others seem to discover things on their own. Some infants manifest early on an apparent good disposition, joyful and easily consolable. Others seem unhappy and cry for most of their first months of life. I remember doing research in an infant orphanage where numerous infants, although well-treated and loved, were literally parked waiting for adoption. Some of these infants appeared happy, striving despite their difficult departure in life. Others seemed frightened and obviously traumatized by the lack of the constant attention from a primary caretaker.

One way or another, the vast majority of these infants will grow up to become healthy toddlers; creative, independent, and striving children; and well-adjusted adults. How is that possible? How can such different initial circumstances, temperaments, and other personality traits lead to developmental outcomes that, on the whole, are comparable? The answer to this question is the holy grail of infancy research and developmental psychology in general.

In my opinion, the fact that equifinality is so evidently at work early in life reveals how vast the infant world actually is. There are multiple ways for infants to develop, many principles and mechanisms by which they become toddlers, children, and eventually adults. It is highly unlikely, if not presumptuous, to think that infant development boils down to a few mechanisms and processes simulated on computers or that lead to precise predictions. In reality, a cluster of processes and mechanisms operate simultaneously to cause the rapid and varied behavioral changes of infancy. Each individual infant represents a recognizable but also unique developmental outcome, a one-of-a-kind combination of multiple causes and circumstances. It is this combination of variability and stability that constitutes the essence of the infant world, an intriguing dynamic universe that we have barely begun to explore.

REFERENCES / INDEX

REFERENCES

Abraham, F. D., and A. R. Gilgen. 1995. *Chaos theory in psychology*. Westport, Conn.: Greenwood Press.

Abraham, K. 1927. The influence of oral eroticism on character formation. In *Selected papers of Karl Abraham*. New York: Basic Books.

Adamson, L. B. 1995. Joint attention, affect, and culture. In C. Moore and P. Dunham, eds., *Joint attention: Its origins and role in development*, pp. 205–221. Hillsdale, N.J.: Lawrence Erlbaum Associates.

Adolph, E. F. 1970. Physiological stages in the development of mammals. *Growth* 34: 113–124.

Adolph, K. E. 1997. Learning in the development of infant locomotion. *Monographs of the Society for Research in Child Development* 62(3): 1–140.

Ainsworth, M. D. 1969. Object relations, dependency, and attachment: A theoretical review of the infant-mother relationship. *Child Development* 40(4): 969–1025.

Anisfeld, M. 1991. Neonatal imitation. *Developmental Review* 11(1): 60–97.

Ariès, P. 1962. *Centuries of Childhood*. New York: Knopf, 1962.

Bahrick, L. E., L. Moss, and C. Fadil. 1996. Development of visual self-recognition in infancy. *Ecological Psychology* 8(3): 189–208.

Bahrick, L. E., and J. S. Watson. 1985. Detection of intermodal proprioceptive-visual contingency as a potential basis of self-perception in infancy. *Developmental Psychology* 21(6): 963–973.

Baillargeon, R. 1993. The object concept revisited: New direction in the investigation of infants' physical knowledge. In C. Granrud, ed., *Visual perception and cognition in infancy: Carnegie Mellon symposia on cognition*, pp. 265–315. Hillsdale, N.J.: Lawrence Erlbaum Associates.

Baillargeon, R., E. S. Spelke, and S. Wasserman. 1985. Object permanence in five-month-old infants. *Cognition* 20(3): 191–208.

Baldwin, J. M. [1884] 1925. *Mental development of the child and the race: Methods and processes.* London: Macmillan.

Ball, W. A. 1973. The perception of causality in the infant. Research report 37. Ann Arbor: University of Michigan Department of Psychology.

Banks, M. S., and J. L. Dannemiller. 1987. Infant visual psychophysics. In P. Salapatek and L. B. Cohen, eds., *Handbook of infant perception,* pp. 115–184. New York: Academic Press.

Banks, M. S., and E. Shannon. 1993. Spatial and chromatic visual efficiency in human neonates. In C. Granrud, ed., *Visual perception and cognition in infancy: Carnegie Mellon symposia on cognition,* pp. 1–46. Hillsdale, N.J.: Lawrence Erlbaum Associates.

Baron-Cohen, S. 1995. *Mindblindness: An essay on autism and theory of mind.* Cambridge, Mass.: MIT Press.

Basili, J. N. 1976. Temporal and spatial contingencies in the perception of social events. *Journal of Personality and Social Psychology* 33(6): 680–685.

Bertalanffy, L. von. 1968. *General system theory.* New York: George Braziller.

Bertenthal, B. I. 1993. Infants' perception of biomechanical motions: Intrinsic image and knowledge-based constraints. In C. Granrud, ed., *Visual perception and cognition in infancy: Carnegie Mellon symposia on cognition,* pp. 175–214. Hillsdale, N.J.: Lawrence Erlbaum Associates.

Bertenthal, B. I., T. Banton, and A. Bradbury. 1993. Directional bias in the perception of translating patterns. *Perception* 22(2): 193–207.

Bertenthal, B. I., and J. J. Campos. 1984. A reexamination of fear and its determinants on the visual cliff. *Psychophysiology* 21(4): 413–417.

———. 1990. A systems approach to the organizing effects of self-produced locomotion during infancy. *Advances in Infancy Research* 6(6): 1–60.

Bertenthal, B. I., and J. Pinto. 1993. Complementary processes in the perception and production of human movements. In L. B. Smith and E. Thelen, eds., *A dynamic systems approach to development: Applications,* pp. 209–239. Cambridge, Mass.: MIT Press, Bradford Books.

Bertenthal, B. I., D. R. Proffitt, and J. E. Cutting. 1984. Infant sensitivity to figural coherence in biomechanical motions. *Journal of Experimental Child Psychology* 37(2): 213–230.

Bertenthal, B. I., D. R. Proffitt, S. J. Kramer, and N. B. Spetner. 1987. Infants' encoding of kinetic displays varying in relative coherence. *Developmental Psychology* 23(2): 171–178.

Bigelow, A. E. 1998. Infants' sensitivity to familiar imperfect contingencies in social interaction. *Infant Behavior and Development* 21(1): 149–161.

———. 1999. Infants' sensitivity to imperfect contingency in social interaction. In P. Rochat, ed., *Early social cognition: Understanding others in the first months of life,* pp. 137–154. Mahwah, N.J.: Lawrence Erlbaum Associates.

Bjorklund, D. F. 1987. A note on neonatal imitation. *Developmental Review* 7(1): 86–92.

Blass, E. M. 1999. The ontogeny of human infant face recognition: Orogustatory, visual, and social influences. In P. Rochat, ed., *Early social cognition: Understanding others in the first months of life,* pp. 35–65. Mahwah, N.J.: Lawrence Erlbaum Associates.

Blass, E. M., and V. Ciaramitaro. 1994. A new look at some old mechanisms in human newborns: Taste and tactile determinants of state, affect, and action. *Monographs of the Society for Research in Child Development* 59(1): v–81.

Blass, E. M., T. J. Fillion, P. Rochat, L. B. Hoffmeyer, et al. 1989. Sensorimotor and motivational determinants of hand-mouth coordination in 1–3-day-old human infants. *Developmental Psychology* 25(6): 963–975.

Blass, E. M., and A. Shah. 1995. Pain-reducing properties of sucrose in human newborns. *Chemical Senses* 20(1): 29–35.

Boesch, C. 1993. Aspects of transmission of tool-use in wild chimpanzees. In K. R. Gibson, ed., *Tools, language and cognition in human evolution,* pp. 171–183. Cambridge: Cambridge University Press.

Bogartz, R. S., Shinskey, J. L., and C. J. Speaker. 1997. Interpreting infant looking: The event set–event set design. *Developmental Psychology* 33(3): 408–422.

Bower, T. G., and J. G. Wishart. 1972. The effects of motor skill on object permanence. *Cognition* 1(2–3): 165–172.

Bruner, J. S. 1969. Eye, hand and mind. In D. Elkind and J. H. Flavell, eds., *Studies in cognitive development: Essays in honor of Jean Piaget,* pp. 223–236. New York: Oxford University Press.

———. 1972. Nature and uses of immaturity. *American Psychologist* 27(8): 687–708.

———. 1983. *Child's Talk.* New York: Norton.

———. 1990. *Acts of meaning.* Cambridge, Mass.: Harvard University Press.

Burns, B., and L. P. Lipsitt. 1991. Behavioral factors in crib death: Toward an understanding of the sudden infant death syndrome. *Journal of Applied Developmental Psychology* 12(2): 159–184.

Bushnell, I. W. R. 1979. Modification of the externality effect in young infants. *Journal of Experimental Child Psychology* 28(2): 211–229.

———. 1998. The origins of face perception. In F. B. G. Simion, ed., *The development of sensory, motor and cognitive capacities in early infancy: From perception to cognition,* pp. 69–86. Hove, Eng.: Psychology Press/Erlbaum.

Callaghan, T. C. 1999. Early understanding and production of graphic symbols. *Child Development* 70(6): 1314–1324.

Caron, A. J., R. Caron, J. Roberts, and R. Brooks. 1997. Infant sensitivity to deviations in dynamic facial-vocal displays: The role of eye regard. *Developmental Psychology* 33(5): 802–813.

Caron, R. F., A. J. Caron, and R. S. Myers. 1985. Do infants see emotional expressions in static faces? *Child Development* 56(6): 1552–1560.

Carpenter, E. 1975. The tribal terror of self-awareness. In P. Hikins, ed., *Principles of Visual Anthropology*, pp. 56–78. The Hague: Mouton.

Clarkson, M. G., and R. K. Clifton. 1991. Acoustic determinants of newborn orienting. In M. J. S. Weiss and P. R. Zelazo, eds., *Newborn attention: Biological constraints and the influence of experience*, pp. 99–119. Norwood, N.J.: Ablex.

Clifton, R. K., B. A. Morrongiello, J. W. Kulig, and J. M. Dowd. 1981. Newborns' orientation toward sound: Possible implications for cortical development. *Child Development* 52(3): 833–838.

Clifton, R. K., D. W. Muir, D. H. Ashmead, and M. G. Clarkson. 1993. Is visually guided reaching in early infancy a myth? *Child Development* 64(4): 1099–1110.

Clifton, R. K., E. E. Perris, and A. Bullinger. 1991. Infants' perception of auditory space. *Developmental Psychology* 27(2): 187–197.

Clifton, R. K., P. Rochat, R. Y. Litovsky, and E. E. Perris. 1991. Object representation guides infants' reaching in the dark. *Journal of Experimental Psychology: Human Perception and Performance* 17(2): 323–329.

Colombo, J. 1993. *Infant cognition: Predicting later intellectual functioning.* Newbury Park, Calif.: Sage Publications.

Crook, C. K. 1979. The organization and control of infants' sucking. In L. P. Lipsitt and C. C. Spiker, eds., *Advances in Child Development and Behavior*, vol. 14. New York: Academic Press.

Dannemiller, J. L., and M. S. Banks. 1986. Testing models of early infant habituation: A reply to Slater and Morison. *Merrill-Palmer Quarterly* 32(1): 87–91.

Dantzig, T. [1930] 1954. *Number: The language of science.* New York: Free Press.

Darwin, C. B. [1872] 1965. *The expression of the emotions in man and animals.* Chicago: University of Chicago Press.

DeCasper, A. J., and W. P. Fifer. 1980. Of human bonding: Newborns prefer their mothers' voices. *Science* 208(4448): 1174–1176.

DeCasper, A. J., J.-P. Lecanuet, M.-C. Busnel, C. Granier-Deferre, et al. 1994. Fetal reactions to recurrent maternal speech. *Infant Behavior and Development* 17(2): 159–164.

DeCasper, A. J., and M. J. Spence. 1991. Auditorily mediated behavior during the perinatal period: A cognitive view. In M. J. S. Weiss and P. R. Zelazo, eds., *Newborn attention: Biological constraints and the influence of experience*, pp. 142–176. Norwood, N.J.: Ablex.

DeLoache, J. S. 1995. Early understanding and use of symbols: The model model. *Current Directions in Psychological Science* 4(4): 109–113.

D'Entremont, B., S. M. J. Hains, and D. W. Muir. 1997. A demonstration of gaze following in 3- to 6-month-olds. *Infant Behavior and Development* 20(4): 569–572.

de Vries, P. I. P., G. H. A. Visser, and H. F. R. Prechtl. 1984. Fetal motility in the first half of pregnancy, pp. 46–64. In H. F. R. Prechtl, ed., *Continuity of Neural Functions from Prenatal to Postnatal Life*.

Diamond, A. 1990. The development and neural bases of memory functions as indexed by the AB and delayed response tasks in human infants and infant monkeys. *Annals of the New York Academy of Sciences* 608: 267–317.

Diamond, A., and P. S. Goldman-Rakic. 1989. Comparison of human infants and rhesus monkeys on Piaget's A not B task: Evidence for dependence on dorsolateral prefrontal cortex. *Experimental Brain Research* 74: 271–294.

Dittrich, W. H., and S. E. G. Lea. 1994. Visual perception of intentional motion. *Perception* 23(3): 253–268.

Donald, M. 1991. *Origins of the modern mind: Three stages in the evolution of culture and cognition*. Cambridge, Mass.: Harvard University Press.

Eimas, P. D., and P. C. Quinn. 1994. Studies on the formation of perceptually based basic-level categories in young infants. *Child Development* 65(3): 903–917.

Eimas, P. D., E. R. Siqueland, P. Jusczyk, and J. Vigorito. 1971. Speech perception in infants. *Science* 171(3968): 303–306.

Ekman, P. 1994. Strong evidence for universals in facial expressions: A reply to Russell's mistaken critique. *Psychological Bulletin* 115(2): 268–287.

Ekman, P., R. W. Levenson, and W. V. Friesen. 1983. Autonomic nervous system activity distinguishes among emotions. *Science* 221(4616): 1208–1210.

Elman, J. L., E. A. Bates, M. H. Johnson, A. Karmiloff-Smith, et al. 1996. *Rethinking innateness: A connectionist perspective on development*. Cambridge, Mass.: MIT Press.

Fantz, R. L. 1964. Visual experience in infants: Decreased attention to familiar patterns relative to novel ones. *Science* 146(12): 668–670.

Fantz, R. L., and J. F. Fagan. 1975. Visual attention to size and number of pattern details by term and preterm infants during the first six months. *Child Development* 46(1): 3–18.

Fernald, A. 1989. Intonation and communicative intent in mothers' speech to infants: Is the melody the message? *Child Development* 60(6): 1497–1510.

Field, J. 1976. The adjustment of reaching behavior to object distance in early infancy. *Child Development* 47(1): 304–308.

Field, T. M., R. Woodson, R. Greenberg, and D. Cohen. 1982. Discrimination and imitation of facial expressions by neonates. *Science* 218(4568): 179–181.

Fogel, A. 1993. *Developing through relationships: Origins of communication, self, and culture.* Chicago: University of Chicago Press.

Freud, S. [1905] 1962. Three essays on the theory of sexuality. New York: Norton.

Frye, D. 1991. The origins of intention in infancy. In D. M. C. Frye, ed., *Children's theories of mind: Mental states and social understanding,* pp. 15–38. Hillsdale, N.J.: Lawrence Erlbaum Associates.

Gallistel, C. R. 1990. *The organization of learning.* Cambridge, Mass.: MIT Press.

Gallistel, C. R., and R. Gelman. 1990. The what and how of counting. *Cognition* 34(2): 197–199.

———. 1991. Subitizing: The preverbal counting process. In W. O. A. Kessen, ed., *Memories, thoughts, and emotions: Essays in honor of George Mandler,* pp. 65–81. Hillsdale, N.J.: Lawrence Erlbaum Associates.

Gallup, G. G. 1971. It's done with mirrors: Chimps and self-concept. *Psychology Today* 4(10): 58–61.

Gazzaniga, M. S., R. B. Ivry, and G. R. Mangun. 1998. *Cognitive neuroscience: The biology of mind.* New York: Norton.

Gelman, R. 1991. Epigenetic foundations of knowledge structures: Initial and transcendent constructions. In S. G. R. Carey, ed., *The epigenesis of mind: Essays on biology and cognition,* pp. 293–322. Hillsdale, N.J.: Lawrence Erlbaum Associates.

Gergely, G., and J. S. Watson. 1996. The social biofeedback theory of parental affect-mirroring: The development of emotional self-awareness and self-control in infancy. *International Journal of Psycho-Analysis* 77(6): 1181–1212.

———. 1999. Early socio-emotional development: Contingency perception and the social-biofeedback model. In P. Rochat, ed., *Early social cognition: Understanding others in the first months of life,* pp. 101–136. Mahwah, N.J.: Lawrence Erlbaum Associates.

Gibson, E. J. 1969. *Principles of perceptual learning and development.* New York: Appleton-Century-Crofts.

———. 1988. Exploratory behavior in the development of perceiving, acting, and the acquiring of knowledge. *Annual Review of Psychology* 39: 1–41.

———. 1991. *An odyssey in learning and perception.* Cambridge, Mass.: MIT Press.

Gibson, E. J., and A. S. Walker. 1984. Development of knowledge of visual-tactual affordances of substance. *Child Development* 55(2): 453–460.

Gibson, J. J. 1950. *The perception of the visual world.* Boston: Houghton Mifflin.

———. 1966. *The senses considered as perceptual systems.* Boston: Houghton Mifflin.

———. 1979. *The ecological approach to visual perception.* Boston: Houghton Mifflin.

Gleick, J. 1987. *Chaos: The making of a science.* New York: Viking.

Goldfield, E. C. 1993. Dynamic systems in development: Action systems. In L. B. T. E. Smith, ed., *A dynamic systems approach to development: Applications,* pp. 51–70. Cambridge, Mass.: MIT Press, Bradford Books.

———. 1995. *Emergent forms: Origins and early development of human action and perception.* New York: Oxford University Press.

Goldman-Rakic, P. S. 1992. Working memory and the mind. *Scientific American* 267(17): 111–117.

Goodale, M. A., and A. D. Milner. 1992. Separate visual pathways for perception and action. *Trends in Neurosciences* 15(1): 20–25.

Goodale, M. A., A. D. Milner, L. S. Jakobson, and D. P. Carey. 1991. A neurological dissociation between perceiving objects and grasping them. *Nature* 349(6305): 154–156.

Gottlieb, G. 1971. Ontogenesis of sensory functions in birds and mammals. In E. Tobach, L. R. Aronson, and E. Shaw, eds., *The biopsychology of development,* pp. 67–128. New York: Academic Press.

Gould, S. J. 1977. *Ontogeny and phylogeny.* Cambridge, Mass.: Harvard University Press.

Gustafson, G. E. 1984. Effects of the ability to locomote on infants' social and exploratory behaviors: An experimental study. *Developmental Psychology* 20(3): 397–405.

Hains, S. M. J., and D. W. Muir. 1996a. Effects of stimulus contingency in infant-adult interactions. *Infant Behavior and Development* 19(1): 49–61.

———. 1996b. Infant sensitivity to adult eye direction. *Child Development* 67(5): 1940–1951.

Haith, M. M. 1980. *Rules that babies look by.* Hillsdale, N.J.: Lawrence Erlbaum Associates.

———. 1998. Who put the cog in infant cognition? Is rich interpretation too costly? *Infant Behavior and Development* 21(2): 167–179.

Haith, M. M., T. Bergman, and M. J. Moore. 1977. Eye contact and face scanning in early infancy. *Science* 198(4319): 853–855.

Hala, S., ed. 1997. *The development of social cognition*. Hove, Eng.: Psychology Press/Erlbaum/Taylor and Francis.

Hamburger, F. 1975. Cell death in the development of the lateral motor column of the chick embryo. *Journal of Comparative Neurology* 160: 535–546.

Harris, P. 1991. The work of the imagination. In A. Whiten, ed., *Natural Theories of Mind*, pp. 283–304. Oxford: Blackwell.

Hatfield, E., J. T. Cacioppo, and R. L. Rapson. 1994. *Emotional contagion*. New York and Paris: Cambridge University Press and Editions de la Maison des Sciences de l'Homme.

Heider, F., and S. Simmel. 1944. An experimental study of apparent behavior. *American Journal of Psychology* 57: 243–259.

Hespos, S. J., and P. Rochat. 1997. Dynamic mental representation in infancy. *Cognition* 64(2): 153–188.

Hobson, R. P. 1993. *Autism and the development of mind*. Hove, Eng.: Lawrence Erlbaum Associates.

Hood, B. M., J. D. Willen, and J. Driver. 1998. Adult's eyes trigger shifts of visual attention in human infants. *Psychological Science* 9(2): 131–134.

Johansson, G. 1973. Visual perception of biological motion and a model for its analysis. *Perception and Psychophysics* 14(2): 201–211.

———. 1977. Studies on visual perception of locomotion. *Perception* 6(4): 365–376.

Johnson, M. H., ed. 1993. *Brain development and cognition: A reader*. Oxford, Eng.: Blackwell.

Jones, S. S. 1996. Imitation or exploration? Young infants' matching of adults' oral gestures. *Child Development* 67(5): 1952–1969.

Jusczyk, P. W. 1985. The high-amplitude sucking technique as a methodological tool in speech perception research. In G. K. N. A. Gottlieb, ed., *Measurement of audition and vision in the first year of postnatal life: A methodological overview*, pp. 195–222. Norwood, N.J.: Ablex.

———. 1997. *The discovery of spoken language*. Cambridge, Mass.: MIT Press.

Kagan, J. 1984. *The nature of the child*. New York: Basic Books.

———. 1991. Continuity and discontinuity in development. In S. E. H. W. S. Brauth, ed., *Plasticity of development*, pp. 11–26. Cambridge, Mass.: MIT Press.

———. 1998a. Is there a self in infancy? In M. D. S. R. J. Ferrari, ed., *Self-awareness: Its nature and development*, pp. 137–147. New York: Guilford Press.

————. 1998b. *Three seductive ideas*. Cambridge, Mass.: Harvard University Press.

Kagan, J., and N. Snidman. 1991. Temperamental factors in human development. *American Psychologist* 46(8): 856–862.

Kagan, J., N. Snidman, D. Arcus, and J. S. Reznick. 1994. *Galen's prophecy: Temperament in human nature*. New York: Basic Books.

Kalnins, I. V., and J. S. Bruner. 1973. The coordination of visual observation and instrumental behavior in early infancy. *Perception* 2(3): 307–314.

Karmiloff-Smith, A. 1992. *Beyond modularity: A developmental perspective on cognitive science*. Cambridge, Mass.: MIT Press.

Kaye, K. 1982. *The mental and social life of babies*. Chicago: University of Chicago Press.

Kermoian, R., and J. J. Campos. 1988. Locomotor experience: A facilitator of spatial cognitive development. *Child Development* 59(4): 908–917.

Kessen, W. 1965. *The Child*. New York: Wiley.

Killen, M., and I. C. Uzgiris. 1981. Imitation of actions with objects: The role of social meaning. *Journal of Genetic Psychology* 138(2): 219–229.

Kobayashi, H., and S. Kohshima. 1997. Unique morphology of the human eye. *Nature* 387(6635): 767–768.

Kuhl, P. K. 1993. Innate predispositions and the effects of experience in speech perception: The Native Language Magnet theory. In B. de Boysson-Bardieu, ed., *Developmental neurocognition: Speech and face processing in the first year of life. NATO ASI series D: Behavioural and social sciences*, vol. 69, pp. 259–274. Dordrecht, Netherlands: Kluwer Academic Publishers.

Legerstee, M., D. Anderson, and A. Schaffer. 1998. Five- and eight-month-old infants recognize their faces and voices as familiar and social stimuli. *Child Development* 69(1): 37–50.

Leslie, A. M. 1984. Spatiotemporal continuity and the perception of causality in infants. *Perception* 13(3): 287–305.

————. 1994. ToMM, ToBy, and Agency: Core architecture and domain specificity. In L. A. G. S. A. Hirschfeld, ed., *Mapping the mind: Domain specificity in cognition and culture*, pp. 119–148. New York: Cambridge University Press.

Lewis, M. 1992. *Shame: The exposed self*. New York: Free Press.

Lewis, M., and J. Brooks-Gunn. 1979. *Social cognition and the acquisition of self*. New York: Plenum Press.

Lewis, M., M. W. Sullivan, and J. Brooks-Gunn. 1985. Emotional behaviour during the learning of a contingency in early infancy. *British Journal of Developmental Psychology* 3(3): 307–316.

Lipsitt, L. P. 1979a. Critical conditions in infancy: A psychological perspective. *American Psychologist* 34(10): 973–980.

————. 1979b. The pleasure and annoyances of infants: Approach and avoidance behavior. In E. B. Thoman, *Origins of the infant's social responsiveness*, pp. 125–153. Hillsdale, N.J.: Lawrence Erlbaum Associates.

Lipsitt, L. P., et al. 1981. Perinatal indicators of Sudden Infant Death Syndrome: A study of thirty-four Rhode Island cases. *Journal of Applied Developmental Psychology* 2(1): 79–88.

Locke, John. 1692. *Some thoughts concerning education*. Printed for A. and J. Churchill.

Mahler, M. S., F. Pine, and A. Bergman. 1975. *The psychological birth of the human infant: Symbiosis and individuation*. New York: Basic Books.

Mandler, J. M. 1992. How to build a baby: II. Conceptual primitives. *Psychological Review* 99(4): 587–604.

————. 1997. Development of categorisation: Perceptual and conceptual categories. In G. S. A. Bremner, ed., *Infant development: Recent advances*, pp. 163–189. Hove, Eng.: Psychology Press/Erlbaum/Taylor and Francis.

Marlier, L., B. Schaal, and R. Soussignan. 1998. Neonatal responsiveness to the odor of amniotic and lacteal fluids: A test of perinatal chemosensory continuity. *Child Development* 69(3): 611–623.

Maurer, D. 1985. Infants' perception of faceness. In T. N. Field and N. Fox, eds., *Social Perception in Infants*, pp. 37–66. Hillsdale, N.J.: Lawrence Erlbaum Associates.

Maurer, D., and P. Salapatek. 1976. Developmental changes in the scanning of faces by young infants. *Child Development* 47(2): 523–527.

McGraw, M. B. 1942. *The neuromuscular maturation of the human infant*. New York: Columbia University Press.

Mead, G. H. 1934. *Mind, self and society*. Chicago: University of Chicago Press.

Meltzoff, A. N. 1990a. Foundations for developing a concept of self: The role of imitation in relating self to other and the value of social mirroring, social modeling, and self practice in infancy. In D. B. M. Cicchetti, ed., *The self in transition: Infancy to childhood*, pp. 139–164. Chicago: University of Chicago Press.

————. 1990b. Infant imitation and memory: Nine-month-olds in immediate and deferred tests. In S. H. M. E. Chess, ed., *Annual progress in child psychiatry and child development, 1989*, pp. 3–17. New York: Brunner/Mazel.

————. 1995. Understanding the intentions of others: Re-enactment of intended acts by eighteen-month-old children. *Developmental Psychology* 31(5): 838–850.

Meltzoff, A. N., and R. W. Borton. 1979. Intermodal matching by human neonates. *Nature* 282(5737): 403–404.

Meltzoff, A. N., and M. K. Moore. 1977. Imitation of facial and manual gestures by human neonates. *Science* 198(4312): 75–78.

———. 1992. Early imitation within a functional framework: The importance of person identity, movement, and development. *Infant Behavior and Development* 15(4): 479–505.

———. 1997. Explaining facial imitation: A theoretical model. *Early Development and Parenting* 6(3–4): 179–192.

Michotte, A. 1963. *The perception of causality.* London: Methuen.

Montagu, A. 1961. Neonatal and infant immaturity in man. *Journal of the American Medical Association* 178(23): 56–57.

———. 1964. *Life before Birth.* New York: The New American Library.

Morgan, R., and P. Rochat. 1997. Intermodal calibration of the body in early infancy. *Ecological Psychology* 9(1): 1–23.

Morton, J., and M. H. Johnson. 1991. CONSPEC and CONLERN: A two-process theory of infant face recognition. *Psychological Review* 98(2): 164–181.

Muir, D., and S. Hains. 1999. Young infants' perception of adult intentionality: Adult contingency and eye direction. In P. Rochat, ed., *Early social cognition: Understanding others in the first months of life,* pp. 155–187. Mahwah, N.J.: Lawrence Erlbaum Associates.

Murray, L., and C. Trevarthen. 1985. Emotional regulation of interactions between two-month-olds and their mothers. In T. M. Field and N. A. Fox, eds., *Social perception in infants,* pp. 177–197. Norwood, N.J.: Ablex.

Nadel, J., I. Carchon, C. Kervella, D. Marcelli, and D. Réserbat-Plantey. 1999. Expectancies for social contingency in two-month-olds. *Developmental Science* 2(2): 164–174.

Neisser, U. 1991. Two perceptually given aspects of the self and their development. *Developmental Review* 11(3): 197–209.

———. 1995. Criteria for an ecological self. In P. Rochat, ed., *The self in infancy: Theory and research,* pp. 17–34. Amsterdam: North-Holland/Elsevier.

Nelson, C. A. 1987. The recognition of facial expressions in the first two years of life: Mechanisms of development. *Child Development* 58(4): 889–909.

Oakes, L. M., and L. B. Cohen, 1990. Infant perception of a causal event. *Cognitive Development* 5(2): 193–207.

Papousek, H. 1992. Experimental studies of appetitional behavior in human newborns and infants. *Advances in Infancy Research* 7: xix–liii.

Papousek, H., and M. Papousek. 1974. Mirror image and self-recognition in young human infants, vol. 1: A new method of experimental analysis. *Developmental Psychobiology* 7(2): 149–157.

———. 1987. Intuitive parenting: A dialectic counterpart to the infant's integrative competence. In J. D. Osofsky, ed., *Handbook of infant development*, 2d ed., pp. 669–720. New York: John Wiley and Sons.

Piaget, J. 1952. *The origins of intelligence in children.* New York: International Universities Press.

———. 1954. *The construction of reality in the child.* New York: Basic Books.

———. 1962. *Play, dreams and imitation in childhood.* New York: Norton.

Povinelli, D. J. 1995. The unduplicated self. In P. Rochat, ed., *The self in infancy: Theory and research,* pp. 161–192. Amsterdam: North-Holland/Elsevier.

Prechtl, H. F. R. 1984. *Continuity of neural functions: From prenatal to postnatal life.* Oxford: Blackwell Scientific Publications.

———. 1987. Prenatal development of postnatal behavior. In H. S. H.-C. Rauh, ed., *Psychobiology and early development,* pp. 231–238. Amsterdam: North-Holland.

Rochat, P. 1983. Oral touch in young infants: Response to variations of nipple characteristics in the first months of life. *International Journal of Behavioral Development* 6(2): 123–133.

———. 1987. Mouthing and grasping in neonates: Evidence for the early detection of what hard or soft substances afford for action. *Infant Behavior and Development* 10(4): 435–449.

———. 1989. Object manipulation and exploration in two- to five-month-old infants. *Developmental Psychology* 25(6): 871–884.

———. 1992. Self-sitting and reaching in five- to eight-month-old infants: The impact of posture and its development on early eye-hand coordination. *Journal of Motor Behavior* 24(2): 210–220.

———. 1993. Hand-mouth coordination in the newborn: Morphology, determinants, and early development of a basic act. In G. J. P. Savelsbergh, ed., *The development of coordination in infancy,* pp. 265–288. Amsterdam: North-Holland/Elsevier.

———. 1997. Early development of the ecological self. In C. Z.-G. P. Dent-Read, ed., *Evolving explanations of development: Ecological approaches to organism-environment systems,* pp. 91–121. Washington, D.C.: American Psychological Association.

———. 1998. Self-perception and action in infancy. *Experimental Brain Research* 123: 102–109.

———, ed. 1999a. *Early social cognition: Understanding others in the first months of life.*

————. 1999b. Direct perception and representation in infancy. In R. Fivush, G. Winograd, and W. Hirst, eds., *Ecological approach to Cognition: Essays in Honor of Ulric Neisser*. Hillsdale, N.J.: Lawrence Erlbaum Associates.

————. 2001a. The ego function of early imitation. In A. N. Meltzoff and W. Prinz, eds., *The Imitative Mind*. Cambridge University Press.

————. 2001b. Origins of self-concept. In G. Bremner and A. Fogel, *Blackwell Handbook of Infancy Research*. Oxford: Blackwell Publishers.

Rochat, P., E. M. Blass, and L. B. Hoffmeyer. 1988. Oropharyngeal control of hand-mouth coordination in newborn infants. *Developmental Psychology* 24(4): 459–463.

Rochat, P., and N. Goubet. 1995. Development of sitting and reaching in five- to six-month-old infants. *Infant Behavior and Development* 18(1): 53–68.

Rochat, P., N. Goubet, and S. J. Senders. 1999. To reach or not to reach? Perception of body effectivities by young infants. *Infant and Child Development* 8(3): 129–148.

Rochat, P., and S. J. Hespos. 1996. Tracking and anticipation of invisible spatial transformation by four- to eight-month-old infants. *Cognitive Development* 11(1): 3–17.

————. 1997. Differential rooting response by neonates: Evidence for an early sense of self. *Early Development and Parenting* 6(3–4): 105–112.

Rochat, P., and R. Morgan. 1995. Spatial determinants in the perception of self-produced leg movements in three- to five-month-old infants. *Developmental Psychology* 31(4): 626–636.

Rochat, P., R. Morgan, and M. Carpenter. 1997. Young infants' sensitivity to movement information specifying social causality. *Cognitive Development* 12(4): 441–465.

Rochat, P., U. Neisser, and V. Marian. 1998. Are young infants sensitive to interpersonal contingency? *Infant Behavior and Development* 21(2): 355–366.

Rochat, P., J. G. Querido, and T. Striano. 1999. Emerging sensitivity to the timing and structure of protoconversation in early infancy. *Developmental Psychology* 35(4): 950–957.

Rochat, P., and S. J. Senders. 1991. Active touch in infancy: Action systems in development. In M. J. S. Weiss and P. R. Zelazo, eds., *Newborn attention: Biological constraints and the influence of experience*, pp. 412–442. Norwood, N.J.: Ablex.

Rochat, P., and T. Striano. 1999a. Social-cognitive development in the first year. In P. Rochat, ed., *Early social cognition: Understanding others in the first months of life*, pp. 3–34. Mahwah, N.J.: Lawrence Erlbaum Associates.

————. 1999b. Emerging self-exploration by two-month-old infants. *Developmental Science* 2:206–218.

Rochat, P., T. Striano, and L. Blatt. 2001. Differential effects of happy, neutral, and sad still-faces on two-, four-, and six-month-old infants. *Infant and Child Development.*

Rochat, P., T. Striano, and R. Morgan. Submitted. Who is doing what to whom? Young infants' sense of social causality in animated displays.

Rogoff, B. 1990. *Apprenticeship in thinking: Cognitive development in social context.* New York: Oxford University Press.

Rovee-Collier, C. 1987. Learning and memory in infancy. In J. D. Osofsky, ed., *Handbook of infant development,* 2d ed., pp. 98–148. New York: John Wiley and Sons.

Ruff, H. A., and M. K. Rothbart. 1996. *Attention in early development: Themes and variations.* New York: Oxford University Press.

Schaal, B., L. Marlier, and R. Soussignan. 1998. Olfactory function in the human fetus: Evidence from selective neonatal responsiveness to the odor of amniotic fluid. *Behavioral Neuroscience* 112(6): 1438–1449.

Searle, J. R. 1980. Minds, brains, and programs. *Behavioral and Brain Sciences* 3(3): 417–457.

————. 1983. Intentionality: An essay in the philosophy of mind. Cambridge: Cambridge University Press.

————. 1990. Minds, brains, and programs. In M. A. Boden, ed., *The philosophy of artificial intelligence,* pp. 67–88. Oxford: Oxford University Press.

————. 1999. Can computers make us immortal? *New York Review of Books* 46, no. 6 (April): 34–38.

Siegler, R. S. 1996. *Emerging minds: The process of change in children's thinking.* New York: Oxford University Press.

Simon, T. J. 1997. Reconceptualizing the origins of number knowledge: A "non-numerical" account. *Cognitive Development* 12(3): 349–372.

Simon, T. J., S. J. Hespos, and P. Rochat. 1995. Do infants understand simple arithmetic? A replication of Wynn (1992). *Cognitive Development* 10(2): 253–269.

Siqueland, E. R., and C. A. DeLucia. 1969. Visual reinforcement of nonnutritive sucking in human infants. *Science* 165(3898): 1144–1146.

Slater, A. 1997. Visual perception and its organisation in early infancy. In G. S. A. Bremner, ed., *Infant development: Recent advances,* pp. 31–53. Hove, Eng.: Psychology Press/Erlbaum/Taylor and Francis.

Slater, A., and G. Butterworth. 1997. Perception of social stimuli: Face perception and imitation. In G. S. A. Bremner, ed., *Infant development: Recent advances,* pp. 223–245. Hove, Eng.: Psychology Press/Erlbaum/ Taylor and Francis.

Slater, A., D. Rose, and V. Morison. 1984. Newborn infants' perception of similarities and differences between two- and three-dimensional stimuli. *British Journal of Developmental Psychology* 2(4): 287–294.

Smith, L. B. 1995. Self-organizing process in learning to use words: Development is not induction. *Minnesota symposium on child psychology,* vol. 28. Mahwah, N.J.: Lawrence Erlbaum Associates.

Smith, L. B., and E. Thelen, eds. 1993. *A dynamic systems approach to development: Applications.* Cambridge, Mass.: MIT Press.

Sorce, J. F., R. N. Emde, J. J. Campos, and M. D. Klinnert. 1985. Maternal emotional signaling: Its effect on the visual cliff behavior of one-year-olds. *Developmental Psychology* 21(1): 195–200.

Soussignan, R., B. Schaal, L. Marlier, and T. Jiang. 1997. Facial and autonomic responses to biological and artificial olfactory stimuli in human neonates: Re-examining early hedonic discrimination of odors. *Physiology and Behavior* 62(4): 745–758.

Spelke, E. S. 1985. Preferential-looking methods as tools for the study of cognition in infancy. In G. K. N. A. Gottlieb, ed., *Measurement of audition and vision in the first year of postnatal life: A methodological overview,* pp. 323–363. Norwood, N.J.: Ablex.

———. 1991. Physical knowledge in infancy: Reflections on Piaget's theory. In S. G. R. Carey, ed., *The epigenesis of mind: Essays on biology and cognition,* pp. 133–169. Hillsdale, N.J.: Lawrence Erlbaum Associates.

———. 1998. Nativism, empiricism, and the origins of knowledge. *Infant Behavior and Development* 21(2): 181–200.

Spelke, E. S., K. Breinlinger, J. Macomber, and K. Jacobson. 1992. Origins of knowledge. *Psychological Review* 99(4): 605–632.

Spitz, R. A. 1965. *The first year of life: A psychoanalytic study of normal and deviant development of object relations.* New York: Basic Books.

Stern, D. 1985. *The interpersonal world of the infant.* New York: Basic Books.

Striano, T., and P. Rochat. 1999. Developmental link between dyadic and triadic social competence in infancy. *British Journal of Developmental Psychology* 17(4): 551–562.

Striano, T., M. Tomasello, and P. Rochat. 2001. Social and object support for early symbolic play. *Developmental Science.*

Symons, L. A., S. M. J. Hains, and D. W. Muir. 1998. Look at me: Five-month-old infants' sensitivity to very small deviations in eye-gaze during social interactions. *Infant Behavior and Development* 21(3): 531–536.

Teller, D. Y., and M. H. Bornstein. 1987. Infant color vision and color perception. In P. Salapatek and L. Cohen, eds., *Handbook of infant perception: From sensation to perception,* pp. 185–236. New York: Academic Press.

Thelen, E., D. Corbetta, K. Kamm, J. P. Spencer, et al. 1993. The transition to reaching: Mapping intention and intrinsic dynamics. *Child Development* 64(4): 1058–1098.

Thelen, E., and D. M. Fisher. 1982. Newborn stepping: An explanation for a "disappearing" reflex. *Developmental Psychology* 18(5): 760–775.

———. 1983. The organization of spontaneous leg movements in newborn infants. *Journal of Motor Behavior* 15(4): 353–382.

Thelen, E., K. D. Skala, and J. S. Kelso. 1987. The dynamic nature of early coordination: Evidence from bilateral leg movements in young infants. *Developmental Psychology* 23(2): 179–186.

Thelen, E., and L. B. Smith. 1994. *A dynamic systems approach to the development of cognition and action.* Cambridge, Mass.: MIT Press.

Tipper, S. P. 1992. Selection of action: The role of inhibitory mechanisms. *Current Directions in Psychological Science* 1: 105–109.

Tomasello, M. 1995. Joint attention as social cognition. In C. J. Moore and P. Dunham, eds., *Joint attention: Its origins and role in development,* pp. 103–130. Hillsdale, N.J.: Lawrence Erlbaum Associates.

———. 1999. *The cultural origins of human cognition.* Cambridge, Mass.: Harvard University Press.

Tomasello, M., and J. Call. 1997. *Primate cognition.* New York: Oxford University Press.

Tomasello, M., and M. J. Farrar. 1986. Joint attention and early language. *Child Development* 57(6): 1454–1463.

Tomasello, M., A. C. Kruger, and H. H. Ratner. 1993. Cultural learning. *Behavioral and Brain Sciences* 16(3): 495–552.

Tomasello, M., T. Striano, and P. Rochat. 1999. Do young children use objects as symbols? *British Journal of Developmental Psychology* 17(4): 563–584.

Trevarthen, C., and P. Hubley. 1978. Secondary intersubjectivity: Confidence, confiding and acts of meaning in the first year. In A. Lock, ed., *Action, gesture and symbol,* pp. 183–239. New York: Academic Press.

Trevathan, W. R. 1987. *Human birth: An evolutionary perspective.* Hawthorne, N.Y.: Aldine de Gruyter.

Tronick, E. Z., H. Als, L. Adamson, S. Wise, and T. B. Brazelton. 1978. The infant's response to entrapment between contradictory message in face-to-face interaction. *Journal of the American Academy of Child Psychiatry* 17: 1–13.

Uzgiris, I. C. 1999. Imitation as activity: Developmental aspects. In J. B. G. Nadel, ed., *Imitation in infancy: Cambridge studies in cognitive perceptual development,* pp. 186–206. New York: Cambridge University Press.

Van Wulfften Palthe, T. W., and B. Hopkins. 1993. Development of the infant's social competence during early face-to-face interaction: A longitudinal study. *Journal of Child Psychology and Psychiatry and Allied Disciplines* 34: 1031–1041.

Vauclair, J., and K. Bard. 1983. Development of manipulations with objects in ape and human infants. *Journal of Human Evolution* 12: 631–645.

Vecera, S. P., and M. H. Johnson. 1995. Gaze detection and the cortical processing of faces: Evidence from infants and adults. *Visual Cognition* 2: 59–87.

von Hofsten, C., 1982. Eye-hand coordination in newborns. *Developmental Psychology* 18: 450–461.

von Hofsten, C., and S. Fazel-Zandy. 1984. Development of visually guided hand orientation in reaching. *Journal of Experimental Child Psychology* 38: 208–219.

von Hofsten, C., and K. Lindhagen. 1979. Observations on the development of reaching for moving objects. *Journal of Experimental Child Psychology* 28: 158–173.

von Hofsten, C., and L. Rönnqvist. 1988. Preparation for grasping an object: A developmental study. *Journal of Experimental Psychology: Human Perception and Performance* 14: 610–621.

Vygotsky, L. 1978. *Mind in society: The development of higher psychological processes*, ed. M. Cole. Cambridge, Mass.: Harvard University Press.

de Waal, F. 1996. *Good natured: The origins of right and wrong in humans and other animals*. Cambridge, Mass.: Harvard University Press.

Walton, G. E., N. J. Bower, and T. G. Bower. 1992. Recognition of familiar faces by newborns. *Infant Behavior and Development* 15(2): 265–269.

Watson, J. B. [1924] 1970. *Behaviorism*. New York: W. W. Norton.

———. 1928. *Psychological care of infant and child*. New York: Norton.

Watson, J. S. 1972. Smiling, cooing, and "The Game." *Merill-Palmer Quarterly* 18(4): 323–340.

———. 1995. Self-orientation in early infancy: The general role of contingency and the specific case of reaching to the mouth. In P. Rochat, ed., *The self in infancy: Theory and research*, pp. 375–393. Amsterdam: North-Holland/Elsevier.

Weiss, M. J., P. R. Zelazo, and I. U. Swain. 1988. Newborn response to auditory stimulus discrepancy. *Child Development* 59(6): 1530–1541.

Whiten, A., and D. Custance. 1996. Studies of imitation in chimpanzees and children. In C. M. G. B. G. Heyes, Jr., ed., *Social learning in animals: The roots of culture*, pp. 291–318. San Diego: Academic Press.

Wiesel, T. N., and D. H. Hubel. 1965. Comparison of the effects of unilateral and bilateral eye closure on cortical unit responses in kittens. *Journal of Neurophysiology* 28: 1029–1040.

Wimmer, H., and J. Perner. 1983. Beliefs about beliefs: Representation and constraining function of wrong beliefs in young children's understanding of deception. *Cognition* 13(1): 103–128.

Wolff, P. H. 1987. *The development of behavioral states and the expression of emotions in early infancy: New proposals for investigation.* Chicago: University of Chicago Press.

———. 1993. Behavioral and emotional states in infancy: A dynamic perspective. In L. B. T. E. Smith, ed., *A dynamic systems approach to development: Applications,* pp. 189–208. Cambridge, Mass.: MIT Press, Bradford Books.

Wynn, K. 1992. Addition and subtraction by human infants. *Nature* 358(6389): 749–750.

Yonas, A., M. E. Arterberry, and C. E. Granrud. 1987. Four-month-old infants' sensitivity to binocular and kinetic information for three-dimensional-object shape. *Child Development* 58(4): 910–917.

Yonas, A., and C. A. Granrud. 1985. Reaching as a measure of infants' spatial perception. In G. K. N. A. Gottlieb, ed., *Measurement of audition and vision in the first year of postnatal life: A methodological overview,* pp. 301–322. Norwood, N.J.: Ablex.